ANCIENT TREES
LIVING LANDSCAPES

ANCIENT TREES
LIVING LANDSCAPES

RICHARD MUIR

TEMPUS

Once a forest, but now scarce a grove,
For the few still standing straight and unbending as the gathering
Winds hound tattered standards through the thorns and thickets

First published 2005

Tempus Publishing Limited
The Mill, Brimscombe Port,
Stroud, Gloucestershire, GL5 2QG
www.tempus-publishing.com

British Library Cataloguing in Publication Data.
A catalogue record for this book is available from the British Library.

ISBN 0 7524 3443 8

Typesetting and origination by Tempus Publishing Limited
Printed in Great Britain

Contents

Introduction

This is a book about trees as important elements in the historical landscape. It is not intended to be a guide to the aesthetic appreciation of landscape, though there can never be a sharp divide between the normative and the objective – between an *emotional* involvement in scenery and the *clinical* explanation of landscape. Those long-forgotten country people who planted hedges, managed woods and told tales about trees were far from being immune to the immeasurable and nameless sensations that we experience in the presence of trees. The importance of the influence of perception in our comprehension of the settings that we inhabit is recognised in the final chapter.

Along with facets like roads and trackways, fields, settlements, places of worship and so on, trees and woods constitute a major class of landscape features. As such, they are worthy of investigation as important components of scenery in their own right. They are also of very considerable interest because of their contribution to the total landscape, with most kinds of landscape in Britain deriving much of their personality from the presence of trees. Within any landscape, trees interact with and condition other features of the setting, and they are also affected by such features. Therefore, they can provide vital clues about the other facets of the landscape. Trees in a landscape park may be derived from the hedgerows of an older, working, countryside; rows of pollards might mark the former limits of a wood, while ancient free-standing trees could have been boundary landmarks for centuries.

The sources of information that underpin this book are mainly derived from fieldwork. I have made very little use of palynological data, partly because I have no expertise and partly because its conclusions are rather too coarse for the purposes concerned. When pollen can be derived from a bog or pond it offers a loose guide to what trees were around in particular periods, but problems of inequality between different trees in terms of pollen production and differences in its dispersion rob us of precision. It is rather like knowing that there were cavalrymen, infantry and artillery present in an army without knowing how many of each or how they were disposed on the field of battle. Of more value, in this context, are earthworks, which may show us the positions of old hedgebanks, ridged ploughland, hedge-girt routeways, dwellings, wood banks, and so on. Old maps which plot particular trees and record place names that may have arboreal associations are extremely valuable, The 1st edition Ordnance Survey 6" to 1 mile map is a treasury of information – not least because it reveals the spectacular decline in hedgerow trees since the mid-nineteenth century.

I have used common rather than Latin names for trees and animals. One very good reason for doing so is that to use the latter form of naming would create an illusion of precision. Medieval chroniclers generally did not record which sub-species they were describing – indeed there is something of a debate about whether their references to maple might concern field maple or the sycamore, which traditionally was not regarded as being present then.

One theme that I have always stressed is that any one country, region or locality of Atlantic Britain is as important as any other. Lewis is no less worthy of our attention than Lewisham; Co Kerry and Kent are equally fascinating, as are Pembrokeshire and Cambridgeshire. The published work on trees and woodland is strongly slanted towards the south-eastern quadrant of England. There are very practical reasons for this: this is where the specialists live and are employed. I have drawn most of my recent research from Northern England, with forays into Scotland, and it would have been foolish to travel to the other side of the country when I can find fascinating challenges on my doorstep where the opportunities for original work are far greater. Fortunately, this part of the realm is under-studied in terms of trees and many other things, so the work presented here may go some little way to redressing the balance.

As to my inspiration, I was very fortunate to grow up in countrysides in the Yorkshire Dales which were extremely 'well treed' if not exceptionally well wooded. As I travelled in the school bus as it chugged and struggled up the 'banks' or valley sides, I went past Elton Spring Wood, through pastures studded with pollards, along Hampsthwaite Hollins and down Lund Lane, unwittingly encountering a Norseman's wood or 'Lund'; the Hollins where the bondsmen of medieval Hampsthwaite grew holly as winter fodder, and the former 'spring' or coppice wood. Like much else at the time, my tree-climbing skills were of the 'could do better' type, but there was a stag-headed oak pollard with a helpfully sloping trunk that was made even more climbable by a lightning strike that had removed both bark and roundness. Much time was spent up there. Each time that I have returned to it over almost the last half century I have been amazed that it has changed in no way that I can discern. It has brought home the fact that trees and humans respond differently to time.

With regard to the realisation that trees *as landscape features* can be studied in an organised manner, recognition should be made of Dr Oliver Rackham and his 1976 book *Trees and Woodlands in the British Landscape*. My serious involvement with trees as subjects for research began about a decade ago with a study of the landscape history of pollards in Nidderdale. Later, I was delighted to show Ted Green, who has done so much to promote our understanding of ancient trees, over my favourite sites. Ted has the power of original thought combined with an uncomplicated enthusiasm that burns like a beacon in this colourless world of quangos and their apparatchiki. It was also very instructive and enlightening (for me!) to supervise Ian Dormor as he researched woodlands in the Yorkshire Dales for his Leeds University doctorate. Most recently, I have been involved with deer parks within woodland research and in case study work for the Nidderdale AONB. Driving to give a workshop, I pass all those woods and those trees that survive from my childhood. Now, I can explain all about them – but whether, with a head full of learning, I *know* them in as meaningful a way as a child *knows* a special tree or magic wood, I doubt. Around 1997, my son, Kieran, claims to have seen Eeyore very clearly in Nidderdale's Low Winsley wood. He maintained this claim for several years and who can prove he is wrong?

I hope that this book will encourage some people to look at trees and woodland in the landscape in a different way. If I can influence serious amateur enthusiasts to put worthwhile projects in place, I shall be delighted. When I was young, the only people with any professional interests in woods were foresters, and their efforts were generally more concerned with the coniferisation of old deciduous woods and the afforestation of open fells. Today, however, an abundance of people associated with heritage industries are involved in woods in some way or other. Old trees and woods create plenty of employment. Surprisingly, the number of people who are bravely prepared to make personal stands on conservation issues does not seem to have risen proportionately with the employment. One large issue concerns the removal of trees and woods for purposes of road widening, house building or whatever. The second issue, hardly less important, is illuminated by landscape research and concerns traditional systems of management. In most places, the pollarding of hedgerow trees has been neglected for around two centuries. The remaining pollards are mainly quite old, and each one that dies and is not replaced takes us closer to the day when hedgerow pollards will disappear from our countrysides. It is not sufficient just to replant. It must be done using appropriate, indigenous stock and, once planted, the tree should then be maintained in a traditional manner. Such work provides plenty of opportunities for enthusiasts.

If amateur enthusiasts can combine together to discover and explain old trees as features of the historic landscape, the case of protecting them will be made far more powerful. In many rural areas the perspectives that dominate are those of the parks and gardens department in the adjacent borough authority. To the landscape gardeners there, a 50-year-old monkey puzzle tree in a municipal park is likely to be deemed more important than an 800-year-old landmark oak out in a rural setting. To my, unfashionable, way of thinking, understanding is not achieved by being towed along in a party on some expensive community archaeology project. It is about looking as sections of countryside with as much penetration as one can muster, going home and pondering, coming back to look at things in a different light, checking the maps in a local archive and persisting until, like Sherlock Holmes, one is left with the only answer that fits the facts.

In illustrating this book I have largely employed my own photographs and maps that I have produced in digital form myself. This work has involved considerable expense and I am extremely grateful to the *Leeds Philosophical and Literary Society* for a generous donation towards the illustration costs.

REFERENCES

Muir, R., 2000, 'Pollards in Nidderdale, a landscape history', *Rural History* 11.1, pp.95-111.
Rackham, O., 1976, *Trees and Woodlands in the British Landscape*, Dent, London.

1

Landscapes with trees

Most British landscapes are landscapes in which trees play a significant or a dominant role. This situation is not really reflected upon the shelves of our libraries. There, trees tend to be treated from a botanical and taxonomic perspective and to be described in terms of their physiology and relationships to other plants. In any substantial library, there is likely to be a section on commercial forestry, where one can discover information about the cultivation and disposal of economically significant species. There will also be a well-stocked section that considers trees from the plantsman's perspective, where the horticultural and landscape architectural merits of trees are described. However, the section, if there is one, that concerns trees as components of the cultural landscape, that treats them as important sources of evidence in landscape archaeology and as windows upon past rural communities and lifestyles cannot occupy much shelf space.

Here, I look at trees, mainly but not exclusively, from a perspective that I sometimes refer to as 'landscape detection'. The trees, woods and hedges are seen, in association with other landscape features, as clues that can contribute to a better understanding of the way that a countryside and its communities have evolved. This is not a timeless approach. In the unlikely event that humans survive for another four centuries or so, all the trees that germinated in the medieval period will probably have gone. Time after time in researching this book I have referred to maps compiled by the surveyors who produced the 1st edition of the Ordnance Survey maps at a scale of 6" to 1 mile. Though they were plotted just a century and a half ago, in many places they mark around eight hedgerow trees for every one that survives today. It is also true that when out for a ramble we do not see the evidence of ancient tree management practices as seen by the old practitioners. Rather, we see neglect: contorted relics that caricature these practices. Today, coppices are not composed of fronds carried upon thickets of wands or poles, but as clusters of stems, each stem thick as a strong man's thigh. The long-neglected coppice looks like a place in which giant squid have been buried, with clusters of their huge tentacles reaching vainly to the sky. Similarly, the pollard is seldom seen as the lollipop with its stem crowned in a leafy fuzz that masks the slender poles within. Rather, we see the old pollards with their massive, hollow trunks supporting a few gigantic, twisting boughs that threaten to break off under their own weight.

The material here is arranged in a thematic manner and this chapter is concerned with providing information on some essential features and concepts. It is an arrangement based on convenience, allowing this chapter to be used as a reference guide and freeing the subsequent chapters of basic explanations. Significant headings are as follows:

The wildwood/parkland debate

The old textbooks, quite wrongly, maintained that prehistoric people in Britain were dwarfed by the almost limitless expanses of natural woodland that covered most of the islands. The following interpretation provided by Windle in 1897 had little changed as the conventional wisdom 50 years later:

> The immense forests, with which the lands was covered, condensed the rain, fallen timber choked up the streams, and caused them to spread their waters into wide marshes, so that only the highest grounds lifted themselves from the morasses and woods…. It is a little difficult to realise how great a portion of the surface of this island was covered in forest at the time [of the Roman occupation] and even down to a much later period (p.119).

It was generally thought that, whilst the Romans, and later the Anglo-Saxons, may have undertaken some clearance, large areas of wildwood persisted to be removed in the course of the Middle Ages. Gradually, the evidence of air photography and the discovery of artefacts by field-walking showed that prehistoric communities were often living on the clay lands that had been thought to have been cloaked in forest. The last expression of these flawed beliefs was associated with the myth of the 'Caledonian Forest', described in the final chapter. Actually, human intervention and the manipulation and transformation of woodland began as soon as trees recolonised the post-glacial landscapes and brought with them the woodland Mesolithic cultures. Only the very first people to move into an area would see truly virgin forest.

But what did this wildwood look like? In an excellent and widely read book, Rackham wrote: 'For most of the post-glacial period the predominant vegetation of Britain has been continuous forest of various kinds' (1976, p.40). He qualified this by saying that the more detailed nature of such forest was uncertain. It is probably true that all the experts, including the palynologists, envisaged a near-interminable closed-canopy forest mitigated only by altitude or water-logging.

New ideas claim that the ancient landscapes of Europe may not have been blanketed in 'wildwood' but may have had a 'parklike' character with clearings grazed by herbivores, rather like this modern scene from the New Forest

More recently, the work of the Dutch civil servant, F.W.M. Vera, has led many people to change their ideas about the closed forest system of climax vegetation. He presents a different view which sees ecological evolution being governed in large measure by the large herbivores, whose feeding habits produced a quite different and more diverse landscape of open grassland, tree clumps, groves and solitary trees within a pattern of more continuously wooded country (2000). Ted Green has emphasised the importance of complex biological processes in landscape formation:

> These natural glades would have originally been created primarily by the direct action of plant pathogens, such as fungi, bacteria and viruses, assisted by insect defoliators and other insect pests, and occasionally by wind-blow and, very rarely, by fire. Once the glades had been created in this manner, they would have been maintained primarily by either wild or domestic browsing animals' (pp. 101-2).

The implications of these ideas are very considerable. If correct, they show that wood pasture is not solely the product of a large-scale transformation of landscapes by farming communities, and they suggest that the widespread liking for parkland countryside might go much deeper than issues of aesthetic taste.

We can encounter the ancient woodlands in the Mesolithic 'bog oaks' that are hauled from the peat beds of the Fens *(left)* and the stumps of long-lost forests preserved in the peats on the otherwise virtually treeless island of Lewis *(above)*

The Neolithic assault on the ancient woods of Europe was made possible by the development of effective axes of polished flint and stone. This beautiful Welsh example, buff speckled with brown like a waterhen's egg, will certainly have been a prestige ceremonial item

Wildwood survival

The extent of the survival of even semi-natural woodland and the time of its eventual disappearance are uncertain. Rackham (1976, p.65) considers that 71 massive oaks taken from the Forest of Dean in 1241-65 for the Dominican friary at Gloucester might have represented the last of the wildwood. However, the English kingdom as it existed at the time of Domesday Book was not heavily wooded. The best evidence comes from Derbyshire, Lincolnshire and Yorkshire where the records provide the areas of woods rather than numbers of swine supported or payments for pannage rights.

> The Domesday Survey of Yorkshire shows almost at a glance how fitfully the great county was wooded; the vast number of manors of the East Riding, and not a few in the other two divisions, were practically destitute of timber. On the other hand, considerable stretches of woodland were recorded in a number of manors in the very places where, from subsequent history, timber might be expected (V.C.H. Yorkshire p.501).

The agistment of livestock in rented woodland grazings will have made scenes such as this extremely common in medieval and earlier times

From deeply back in prehistoric times, most British woods were subjected to powerful cultural controls and to understand woods and their relics we must explore these controls. Evidence of intense and diverse human usage comes from every wood with surviving documentation. For example, the warden's accounts for woods in the 'Forest' of Skipton ('chase' would be more apt) for 1322–3 reveals nine vaccaries or cattle farms in woodland territory; the 'agistment' of various teams of plough oxen in rented woodland grazings; the removal of dead wood; the lopping of boughs from ash trees in woods and parks, doubtless as browse for deer and cattle, while 'cablish' or uprooted trees were also put to good use. Accounts for the same territory for 1302–3 record payments of 'cheminage' for taking minerals through the woods; payments for nuts and payments for honey and beeswax as well as the proceeds from agistment, vaccaries and cablish. Other accounts for the Barden sector of the Clifford's estates note the proceeds from pannage, the acorns devoured by foraging swine, from husset or holly fodder and from bark-loppings, which must have been destined for a tannery. The wood could also yield rents, fines or taxes and the 1326–7 accounts show the agistment of sheep in elm woods and the fining of the Prior of Bolton 2s (10p) because his animals had escaped into the Clifford's woods (*op. cit.* pp. 510–1).

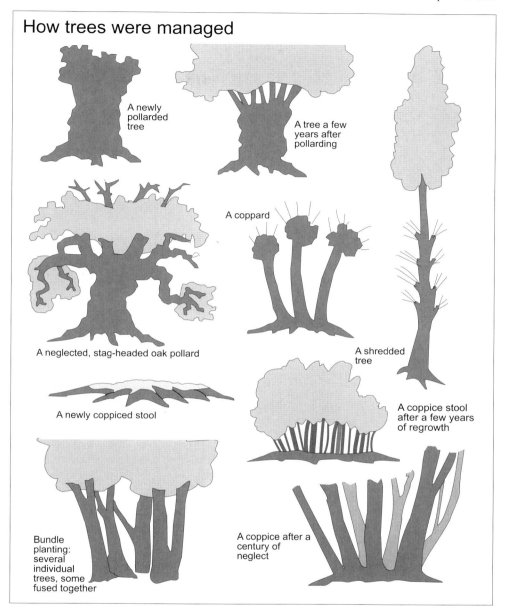

How trees were managed

A newly pollarded tree

A tree a few years after pollarding

A coppard

A neglected, stag-headed oak pollard

A shredded tree

A newly coppiced stool

A coppice stool after a few years of regrowth

Bundle planting: several individual trees, some fused together

A coppice after a century of neglect

Wood pasture

Wood pasture is an association between grazing and timber/browse production. It was apparently widespread in England at the time of Domesday Book (1086) and presumably during much earlier times as well. In Domesday Book, wood pasture is recorded as *silva pastilis* and its greatest proportional extent appears to have been in Derbyshire, where it covered almost a quarter of the county. There is an excellent account of medieval wood pasture in Rackham, 1976, (p.119 *et seq*). The juxtaposition of pollards and pasture involved an ecologically sensitive coexistence and the attractions of leaf fodder required that the trees concerned should be pollarded to produce their harvest above the reach of the animals. The significance of these trees as producers of lopped fronds for deer and cattle has probably been undervalued. It is generally accepted that, in the course of the Middle Ages, wood pasture was replaced by coppiced woodland, which could not incorporate grazing but which produced a greater output of timber for fuel and light timber. In the north of England, the removal of gnarled wood pasture pollards seems to have taken place in the seventeenth and eighteenth centuries. The author devoted some time to discovering a small, surviving, upland wood pasture of stunted oak pollards in the mid-1990s. Visiting it just a few days before writing this section, it was a delight to see a mixed herd of Friesian and shorthorn cattle in residence. With dappled shade, trunks to rub against and the possibility of some leaf browse, the cattle looked far more 'at home' than they might in any field.

Coppice/coppice and standards

Evidence of coppiced timber has been discovered in archaeological contexts ranging from the Neolithic wetland trackways of Somerset through to modern times. Readers may have noticed that when deciduous trees are felled – a phenomenon that has sadly accelerated in the urban parks and avenues with the rise of the litigation culture – the tree does not die. Unless the stump is poisoned, it will soon sprout a mass of shoots. In former times, such a stump, cut almost level with the ground, would become a coppice stool. Within a dozen or a dozen-and-a-half years, its shoots had become rods and poles, which might be converted into faggots, wattle, hafts, shafts, be stripped of bark for the tanning industry or employed for many other purposes. There may well be coppice stools alive, though probably neglected, that were alive and yielding poles at the time of Domesday Book, for as with pollarding, coppicing rejuvenates and envigorates the tree. As the medieval period progressed, coppices expanded and the production of timber from them became highly organised. Numerous place names have derived from coppices, including words for woods managed in this way, with 'Spring' being very common in northern England and 'Fall', which can be a clearing, less so. The link with words like 'Copse' and 'Copy' is more obvious. There are various names associated with the divisions of spring woods 'Hag' is probably the commonest and 'Pannal' is sometimes found. These divisions would be cut in rotation, helping to produce a regular stream of light timber from the wood of which they were parts.

A tiny fragment of surviving wood pasture discovered by the author on the watershed between Nidderdale and Wensleydale. The land was once owned by Fountains Abbey and local legend claims that a monk of Fountains is buried under each tree

The management of coppice woods was relatively labour-intensive and it was essential that domestic livestock and deer should be kept out of the hags, for, once inside, the leafy shoots springing from the stools would soon be browsed away. In the case of the springs controlled by Fountains Abbey, after the abbot and convent had created a coppice, the monastery accepted responsibilitry for fencing it on the first occasion, but thereafter, the tenants, under the supervision of the cellarer, were responsible for maintaining the fence. When Richard Atkinson was appointed to the sergeantship of the abbey's grange of Haddokstanes, the detailed agreement required him to prevent the agistment of cattle from outside and: '… to keep all the woods and "sprynges" belonging to the grange without making or allowing any waste, and … to present or cause to be presented all trespassers or trespasses made in the woods and "sprynges" at the court of Morker' (Michelmore, lease 227). A period of seven years was apparently regarded as being the duration for which such protection was necessary (Michelmore, 1981, Nos 202, 279).

The transport revolution, that made other sources of fuel available, and the importation of cheap softwood timber led to the neglect of coppiced woods during the nineteenth century, and the value of many coppiced stools was seen in terms of shelter for pheasants. The old system was well down the road to extinction by 1915, when Raymond told how the cutter of pea and bean sticks had walked away and abandoned bundles of sticks in the woods and the hurdle maker had left his 'sails' or sections of wattle panelling to blow in the wind.

A coppice stool in Hayley Wood, Cambridgeshire

Only the charcoal burners were still at work, as a countryman explained: 'There's nothen proper busy now but the charcoal burners. They be to work over here in the forest. Can't burn enough o'it. Light to haul - hot vire, not noo smoke - that's what they do make use o'-over there [in the trenches]' (p.454). This demand for charcoal revived some coppices, and the Board of Agriculture and Fisheries brought out a Special Leaflet to explain the processes of production for charcoal, which was both a component of explosives and a source of fuel for the braziers warming the troops.

The typical medieval wood was one of coppice with standards, in which the underwood was coppiced, while timber trees, most frequently oaks, stood above the coppiced stools as maidens or standards and were felled according to a different, much longer rotation. These trees were probably not deliberately planted and would result when selected seedlings were exempted from the coppice cycle. They would produce heavier timber that could be used for structural purposes, like house building or boat building. Even so, they were generally felled before they were a century old and still of quite modest girth. Timber from coppice standards and from older woodland trees was normally prefabricated at or near the felling site, reducing the demands on a usually inadequate transport system. The coppice with standards system is virtually extinct, though I saw it in operation in Wolves Wood, Suffolk, where the underwood was coppiced to give shelter to encourage bird life.

Coppice with standards
– the typical later medieval
form of woodland at
Wolves Wood in Suffolk,
where the old practice
was renewed for bird
conservation

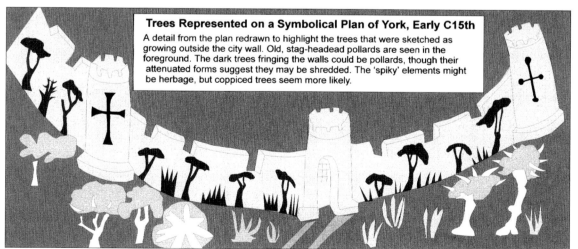

Trees Represented on a Symbolical Plan of York, Early C15th

A detail from the plan redrawn to highlight the trees that were sketched as
growing outside the city wall. Old, stag-headead pollards are seen in the
foreground. The dark trees fringing the walls could be pollards, though their
attenuated forms suggest they may be shredded. The 'spiky' elements might
be herbage, but coppiced trees seem more likely.

Medieval woodland boundaries and partitions were marked and guarded by the earthworks of woodbanks which were often crowned by alignments of pollards, as seen here in the Black Down Hills

Bundle planting

One of the characteristic sights of a woodland ramble is that of contorted and long-neglected coppice stools bearing thick stems that rear upwards like the feathers on a battered shuttlecock. This appearance is deceptively replicated where bundle planting has been practised. A hedge or boundary, a tree clump in a park or some other setting could be created or restored by planting not a single seedling or sapling, but a fistful of them, all in the same hole. The expectation was probably that one could be expected to prosper, but sometimes several would become trees and as their girths swelled, individuals might grow together and unite. The young trees in a bundle could be of different species.

Pollards

Ancient, distorted pollards are characteristics of many countrysides in all the countries of mainland Britain. Much space will be devoted to the topic and so the treatment here is brief. Most typically, the countryside pollard is a tree of considerable age, and because pollarding has normally been neglected for a couple of centuries or more, the trunk is supporting massive branches that threaten to

The three groups of trees in this photograph could all result from bundle planting.

break under their own weight. Trees were pollarded for both leafy browse and poles, and by 'beheading' the tree above the reach of the larger animals, the soft young growth was protected from the browsing that would soon have destroyed a coppice. In effect, pollarding raised the coppice stool to a height of around 8ft (2.4m) above the ground. As well as the conventional lollipop-shaped pollard, there were other forms that could be produced by different systems of management. A secondary pollarding a few feet along the branches spreading from the boll or bolling produced a form with club-like main branches, used in both urban garden boundary plantings and in some countryside trees pollarded for browse. Multiple bollings were produced when a tree was clipped frequently in many places for browse. Seen but infrequently in most regions are 'coppards', a hybrid form of management, and coppard coppice trees are coppiced and then pollarded at around the conventional height. They are locally frequent, as in Epping Forest (Green, p.103). The bundle planted trees could later be pollarded to produce close-set multiple pollards. The Shepherd's tree is one in which the main branches survived but a small portion of the subsidiary branches were lopped for browse.

Shredded trees are not pollards and are infrequently seen today. The system involved the removal of side branches, presumably for browse, producing a vertical, attenuated form. An inspection of rural scenes depicted in paintings of the seventeenth and eighteenth centuries suggests that the shredding of trees

A magnificent beech pollard in the New Forest

Hornbeam pollards and coppards in Epping Forest

may not have been uncommon in some regions. An ancient pollard that was seemingly close to death could be rejuvenated and send forth a new branch or stem which might in turn be pollarded. Arthur Rackham incorporated tortured tree forms in his illustrations in a neo-Gothic style and close to my desk I have his faithful representation of just this type of tree. Large trees, like the oak, ash, horse chestnut or lime, are most frequently associated with pollarding, though the technique could be applied to less obvious subjects, such as alder, more usually coppiced, or even common hawthorn or birch.

Hollins

Hollins were holly groves or stands of holly within larger woods and they were exploited as a source of winter fodder. Holly in hedgerows makes a good barrier for the thorny leaves that are unpalatable. Above the reach of browsers, however, the tree does not 'anticipate' attack and so its evergreen leaves are not armoured with sharp thorns. In former times, men would shin up the trees in a hollins and lop off branches which could then be stored in a laithe (barn) or a smaller helm and fed to animals that were becoming ravenous with the onset of winter. In the northern dales, hollins were immensely important within the

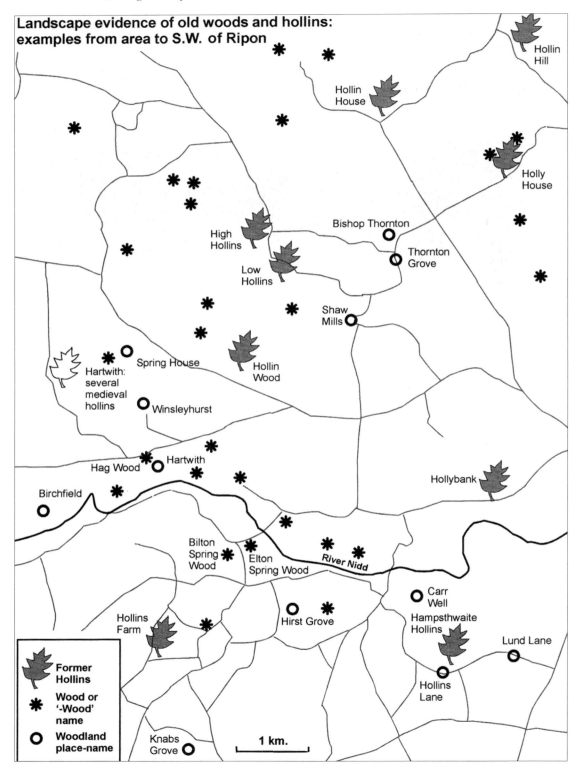

Landscape evidence of old woods and hollins:
examples from area to S.W. of Ripon

Hollin
Hill

Hollin
House

Holly
House

Bishop Thornton

High
Hollins

Thornton
Grove

Low
Hollins

Shaw
Mills

Spring House

Hollin
Wood

Hartwith:
several
medieval
hollins

Winsleyhurst

Hag Wood

Hartwith

Hollybank

Birchfield

Bilton
Spring
Wood

Elton
Spring Wood

River Nidd

Carr
Well

Hampsthwaite
Hollins

Hollins
Farm

Hirst Grove

Lund Lane

Hollins
Lane

**Former
Hollins**

**Wood or
'-Wood'
name**

**Woodland
place-name**

Knabs
Grove

1 km.

The medieval hollins of Hampsthwaite in Nidderdale is commemorated in this road name

farming economy. This is evidenced by the wealth of 'Hollins/holly/husset' place names and by the special status accorded to hollins in leases issued by monastic landlords. These were often leased by tenants separately from their holdings, such was their value (Michelmore, p.lxiii). Sometimes the tenants and keepers of dairy farms were allowed to cut the leaf fodder, but conditions were strictly regulated. Thus, when Richard Atkinson leased a holding on the Fountains estates at Pott in 1536, he agreed

> … not to fell or cause to be felled any of the abbot and convent's wood "of warrante" without licence, except for "lefull fellynge of hollyng bowes and other bruchwode at seasonal tyme of the yere callyd brusyng [browse] for pastour of cattell, and also oke bowes, not tymber, for ther fewell and makyng of fensez" without waste (Michelmore, lease 280).

There appears to have been a convention on the Fountains holdings that holly and brushwood could be used as browse, while oak boughs could be taken from pollards for fuel and fencing and *watter bowes* (presumably water boughs or soft growth) could be cut for cattle.

Coniferisation

During the nineteenth century, with the gradual shift from growing hardwood timber to the cultivation/importation of alien softwoods, many new afforested areas were introduced. These were not woods, where trees are propagated

Coniferisation of an ancient North Yorkshire wood is evidenced in the old ground flora of ramsons growing between the introduced larch and beech

naturally, but plantations, where fast-growing timber was grown like any other crop. In some cases – and very commonly in the north of England – plantations were created by clear felling an old or ancient wood and replanting with alien trees. Such woods were most common on the larger estates, where the trees furnished fencing and constructional timber for the estate's own joinery workshop, and where they also, along with rhododendron, provided cover for pheasants. The conifers that found early favour were Scots pine and larch, while beech was often incorporated, being quite quick to grow (and to fall down) and providing a heavy shade that suppresses undergrowth. It also yielded a hard, white timber for more specialised uses, including cheaper furniture. Coniferised woods may be recognised by their irregular shapes that contrast with the rectangular forms of the plantations, the survival, sometimes, of ancient pollards or some old understorey or woodland edge shrubs, like hazel or bird cherry around their margins, and perhaps the presence of old woodland ground flora, like bluebells or ramsons, on their floors. Occasionally, the presence of massive glacial erratic boulders reveals a wood on ground that never experienced an episode of farming.

Forest

A Forest was a special type of administrative division that might have had loose origins in Anglo-Saxon England, that was formalised by the Normans and endured through the Middle Ages and into the post-medieval centuries. It was a royal hunting reserve subject to special conservational controls to reduce the poaching of game. It might be heavily or partly wooded, though there could be no woodland at all within a Forest. Here, capitals are used to differentiate between the administrative area, replete with its courts and its officials, like regarders and foresters, and the forest, a tree-covered expanse. While modern writers make these strict distinctions, in fact, at least in the North of England, the term 'Forest' was frequently applied to non-royal hunting territories, like the Clifford's 'Forest' of Barden, which in precise modern usage would be termed a 'chase'. In 1598, John Manwood (d.1610) wrote a treatise on the laws of the Forest and explained that:

> A forest is a certen territorie of woody grounds and fruitful pastures, privileged for wild beasts and foules of forrest, chase and waren, to rest and abide in, in the safe protection of the king for his princely delights and pleasure; which territorie of ground so privileged is meered and bounded with inemovable markes, meeres and boundaries, either known by matter of record or els by prescription...there are certain particular laws, principles and officers, belonging to the same, meete for that purpose, that are only proper unto a forest, and not to any other place....The king causeth it to be proclaimed throughout the county where the land lieth that it is a *forest*, and to be governed by the laws of the *forest*, and prohibits all persons from hunting there without his leave ...(quoted in Grainge, 1871, p.50)

Tree and woodland place names

Place names including field and wood names are remarkably common. They do not usually record countrysides that were continuously wooded. Rather, they provide windows on times when trees and woods featured more prominently in communal life and when ordinary people employed far broader and more specific vocabularies to describe the qualities and uses of trees. This vocabulary reflects the different Celtic or Old English origins of language, the introduction of Old Norse and Old Danish elements, the evolution of the English tongue into Middle English and then the language of Tudor and later times. So, in a very coarse sense, tree and wood names may be datable, and this gives them a use in the reconstruction of past environments. Some of the meanings are summarised as follows:

Name	**Source:** OW=Old Welsh; ON=Old Norse; OD=Old Danish; OE=Old English; ME=Middle English, OF=Old French	**Meaning**
Bere	*Bearu,* OE	A grove
Coed	*Coid,* OW	A wood
Coppice, copse, copy	Copis, ME	A coppice wood
Den, dene	*Denn,* OE	A woodland pasture for swine
Frith, freeth	*Fyrhth,* OE	Woodland
Grove	*Graf,* OE	Grove
Hagg	*Hogg,* ON	Coppice division, clearing
Hanger	*Hangr,* OE	Wood on a steep slope
Hay	*(ge)haeg,* OE	A small wood or hedge or a hedged assart
Hollins	holegn, OE	Holly grove
Holt	*Holt,* OE	Thicket
Hurst	*Hyrst,* OE	Wooded hill
Launde	*Launde,* OF	Glade, wood pasture, lawn
Ley	*Leah,* OE	Troublesome word – trees or clearing
Lound, lund	*Lundr,* ON	A small wood
Ridden, Ridding	*Ryding,* OE	Clearing, assart
Rode, royd	*Rodu,* OE	An assart
Sart	*Assart,* OF	An assart
Scroggs	*Scrogge,* ME	A place with brushwood
Shaw	*Sceaga,* OE, *skogr,* ON	A small wood
Spring	*Spring,* OE	A coppiced wood
Stock	*Stocc,* OE	Assarted land with stumps standing
Storth	*Storth,* ON	Brushwood or plantation
Stocking	*Stocc ing,* OE	Assarted land with stumps grubbed-up
Stubb, stubbing	*Stubb,* OE	Land with tree stumps
Thwait	*Thveit,* ON	A clearing
With	*Vithr,* ON	A wood
Wood	*Wudu,* OE	A wood

Trees frequently feature in place names and old documents, and the following is a guide to their Old English names:

Old Name	Tree	Old Name	Tree
Ac	Oak	*Lind*	Lime
Aeppel	Apple	*Mapul*	Maple – field maple or sycamore?
Aesc	Ash		
Aespe	Aspen	*Pirige*	Pear
Alor	Alder	*Salh*	Sallow
Beorc/birk	Birch	*Thorn*	Thorn
Boc	Beech	*Welig/withig*	Willow
Crabbe (ME)	Crab apple	*Werg (vernacular)*	Willow
Elm	Elm	*Wice*	Wych elm
Ellern	Elder		
Haesel	Hazel		

REFERENCES

Gainge, W., 1871, *Harrogate and the Forest of Knaresborough*, J.R.Smith, London.
Green, (Ted), 'Pollarding – origins and some practical advice', *British Wildlife*, **vol.** 8, no 2, pp.100-105.
Michelmore, 1981, *The Fountains Abbey Lease Book*, Y.A.S. Record Series, **vol cxl.**
Rackham, O., 1976, *Trees and Woodland in the British Landscape*, Dent, London.
Raymond, W., 1915, 'The war and the woods', *Country Life* April 3rd, pp.452-4.
Vera, F.W.M., 2000, *Grazing Ecology and Forest History*, CABI Publishing, Wallingford, Oxford.
Windle, B.C.A., 1897, *Life in Early Britain*, David Nutt, London.

2

Landmark trees

Communities of trees in woods, groves and hedgerows are important components in the countryside mosaic. There are, however, individual landmark trees which, by virtue of their special qualities, or significant locations, stand out from the arboreal crowd. They penetrate the public imagination and gain a special place in our perception of their localities. Such trees may be employed as territorial markers or as eye-catchers within a scene, and they may also become vessels for our imaginings and superstitions and conduits to a mythical past.

When using historical sources for landscape reconstruction, one mainly encounters fragments of a broader picture. One might discover a medieval reference to the destruction of a hedgerow by manorial tenants who were deprived of fuel in a bitter February, or who were resisting enclosures in communal farmland. Very frequently, the precise location of the hedge is difficult to establish, while the names and outlines of woods can change in ways that can be puzzling to the historian. There were (and are), however, a number of individual trees with distinct historical pedigrees. They were specimens that were prominent and notable in some way. They could be large trees standing on the margins of estates or administrative divisions and serving as boundary marks that would be recorded during successive perambulations of the bounds of the territorial unit concerned. Such landmark trees provide us with fixed points in the shifting sands of cultural history and historical ecology.

A tree could be mentioned because it was regarded as an unusually large or venerable example, or a remarkable example of its species. For example, with a girth of 18.7ft (5.7m), the Studley Royal Wild Cherry is thought to be the largest specimen of *Prunus avium* to be found in Britain, and is celebrated accordingly. In other cases, a landmark tree was associated with a particular and distinguished historical figure, a noteworthy event or a memorable occasion involving people of note. In all these circumstances, the tree concerned would be named and recorded in ways that generally make it possible to establish where it stood (in many cases such trees still stand). When they are unearthed in the records,

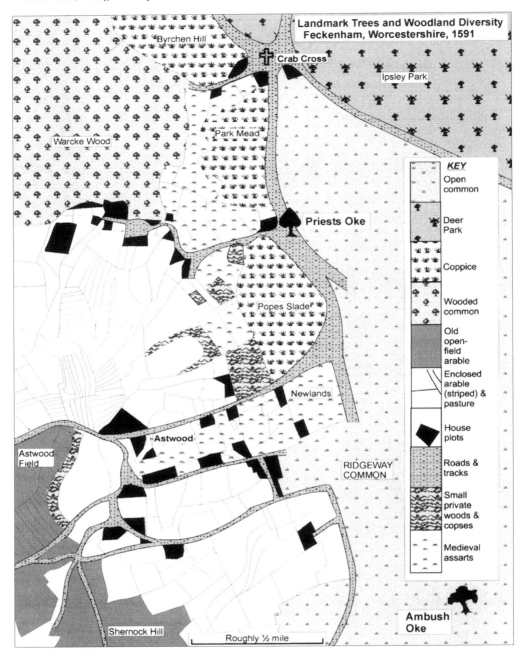

Landmark Trees and Woodland Diversity Feckenham, Worcestershire, 1591

Byrchen Hill

Crab Cross

Ipsley Park

Park Mead

Warcke Wood

Priests Oke

Popes Slade

KEY

Open common

Deer Park

Coppice

Wooded common

Old open-field arable

Enclosed arable (striped) & pasture

House plots

Roads & tracks

Small private woods & copses

Medieval assarts

Newlands

Astwood

Astwood Field

RIDGEWAY COMMON

Ambush Oke

Shernock Hill

Roughly ½ mile

Landmark trees at Fakenham. The survey of the locality in 1591 reveals the remarkable diversity of countryside types in Elizabethan England. The survey also identified several landmark trees that were standing at that time. There is nothing on the map to explain the designation 'Priest's Oak' of one tree at the common margin. Ambush Oak is more easily explained. It stands on the common well removed from settlement, by the Ridgeway and near to the places where several trackways enter the common. It is sited in an ideal place for use by roguish elements. Thus it is probably named after an ambush at this place

successive mentions of a specimen, occurring across a considerable time-span, can provide information about the longevity of trees of a particular type or they may assist the understanding of a landmark tree that still survives. Sometimes, they confirm the antiquity of a boundary.

The sources of relevant early information are diverse and unpredictable, making it difficult to research a particular locality and, generally, more likely that the researcher will stumble across the material while making enquiries about something else. An example of an unlikely source is the very interesting letter from a Louisa Charlotte Frampton found in the corrrespondence of William Henry Fox Talbot (1800–77), the pioneer of photography, who had apparently supplied her with dimensions of an old oak. She had been conducting research into noteworthy trees, but believed that three quarters of them no longer existed, many apparently falling in 1829 and 1836. She wrote:

> The latter was, I know, the year of the dreadful storm, which blew down the M.Q. of Scots [Mary Queen of Scots] Thorn at Duddingstone near Edinburgh, respecting which there was a most curious tradition of her planting it with the Regent Murray; & Professor Balfour says that the Regents Thorn in his garden in the Canongate (now called Moray House) was blown down the same year (*Lacock Abbey Collection* Doc.No. 02864).

While oaks tend to have captured the popular imagination, she mentioned other, now-forgotten, trees:

> Some of the Elms are wonderful. One at Northover House, near Ilchester, was a real curiosity, branching into 7 large limbs at 12 feet from the ground, & upon these was constructed a room which held 20 persons, where Mr Chicester used to hold his justice meetings. How undignified! To be dealing out justice up in a tree. This was blown down in 1833. There is or was, also, one in the passage leading to Spring Gardens, planted by the D. of Gloucester, brother to Charles 1st – As the King went from St.James's to execution, he pointed it out, & mentioned the circumference (*ibid.*).

She mentioned various other trees that were celebrated in Victorian times, some of which are now gone: the Carclew Oak, the Ampthill Oak, the Welbeck Oaks, the Aunus Thorn, the Tortworth Chestnut and the Chepstead Elm.

Early maps, like the beautifully executed and detailed large-scale maps commissioned by Elizabethan landowners to portray their estates, will sometimes have landmark trees plotted and named. However, only two trees are found to have been named on the early editions of Ordnance Survey maps: the Fortingall Yew, whose hollow trunk formed a breached shell, and the great Tortworth Chestnut. References to significant trees may appear in diaries or travel journals – though in scouring the archives one will have no means of anticipating when

Though much fewer than before, numerous trees of landmark status can still be found, like this remarkable lime pollard on Christmas Common, Oxfordshire

or whether such mentions will occur. Where such journals are concerned, they may sharpen an appreciation of the perception of landscape in one place, by contrasting it with such perceptions in another. Writing in 1832, Fanny Trollope recorded her impressions of the eastern USA: 'On first arriving, I thought the many tree covered hills around very beautiful, but long before my departure, I felt so weary of the confined view, that Salisbury Plain would have been an agreeable variety.' This sense of ennui was experienced quite frequently by travellers from the Old World to the New. Susanna Moodie described a Canadian forest:

> One wood is the exact picture of another; the uniformity dreary in the extreme. There are no green vistas to be seen; no grassy glades beneath bosky oaks, on which the deer browse, and the gigantic shadows sleep in the sunbeams. A stern array of ragged trunks, a tangled maze of scrubby underbrush, carpeted winter and summer with a thick layer of withered buff leaves…(1853, quoted in Miller, p.82).

The records of boundary marks and perambulations have been mentioned as promising sources, while medieval charters or manorial court rolls may make passing and often ambiguous references to trees. The local antiquaries of the post-medieval centuries can be promising sources of information, though any of their observations concerning landmark trees are likely to be buried within a mass of other data.

In order to function as significant landmarks, trees must be geographical features that are familiar to the population at large. The 'Hoar Apple Tree' that stood on Caldbec Hill on the Sussex Downs must have been such a tree. Encrusted with lichen to produce its hoary appearance, it was selected as a gathering place for the English army in 1066. It was to the hoar apple that Harold chose to march with his brothers, the Earls Gryth and Leofwine, his Huscarls and Fyrdmen after the forced march from Stamford Bridge to face the Norman invaders on Senlac ridge. Following the English defeat, Battle Abbey was built by the victors near the site of the celebrated tree. It seems likely that prominent trees served as gathering places quite frequently in the Dark Ages and in earlier times, and this role continued in the English hundreds and wapentakes and among the Scottish clan societies. A still surviving yew growing on the Knockie estate near Fort Augustus and the shores of Loch Ness has suckered to form a grove some 360ft (about 110m) in diameter. This was the place of assembly for Clan Fraser, a landmark role that may have been performed for much of the yew's seven centuries of existence.

One of the most intriguing examples of a tree with a historical biography was the 'Harte's Horn Oak' which stood close to the Eamont river, near Brougham church, in the old county of Westmorland. In his historical biography of Lady Anne Clifford, published in 1922, Williamson recorded a legend that had existed for seven centuries. In 1333, Edward Balliol, the puppet king of Scotland, in refuge and a fanatical slayer of game even by the gory standards of his day, was the guest of the Cliffords at their castle at Brougham. A deer hunt was organised, during which a celebrated dog, named 'Hercules', was said to have hounded a stag to the Scottish border (closer then) and back to Brougham. There, near Honby Hall, local legend told, the stag fell dead on one side of a wall and the hound on the other. To commemorate this epic hunt, the frontlet of the beast's skull bearing the antlers was nailed to an oak growing near the pale of Whinfield deer park. No matter how embroidered the legend may have become, both the tree and the antlers were real enough and Lady Anne recorded that as the centuries passed, the bark of the tree began to envelop the antlers. She noted that during the Civil War, in 1648, soldiers encamped nearby broke one of the antlers, while the other was broken by 'mischievous people coming in a summer night'. In 1658 she also wrote that: '… this Tree, with the Hartes hornes in it, was a Thing of much note in these parts' (reprinted in Williamson, p.10). As a notable landmark, the tree was mentioned in later writings, having a part of its trunk still standing in 1790 and having its roots still in situ in 1807. Assuming that the huntsmen chose a tree of some prominence as a place for the antlers, it is difficult to imagine that the Hart's Horn Oak was less than seven or eight hundred years old when it died, and it could have been much older.

Another remarkable feature of the tree was that it had *other* landmark trees as neighbours. When Thomas Machel wrote his Westmorland additions to the text of Camden's *Britannia* for the 1695 edition, he mentioned the legend of the Hart's Horn tree, but added: 'In the midst of the Park [Whinfield], not far hence is the three-brether-tree (so called because there were three of them, whereof this was the least) in circumference 13 yards and a quarter a good way from the root' (p.816). Presumably he meant that the tree with the massive girth was the smallest survivor of a trio of great trees.

Ancient giants

Great age and unusual size were likely to confer landmark status on a tree. However, the criteria by which local communities have designated certain trees as being very special, and those by which the wider community has 'adopted' such trees, are unpredictable and unreliable. The Major Oak in Sherwood Forest is now perhaps the second most celebrated tree in England after the Glastonbury Thorn, yet it is far from being the oldest, the largest or visually the most evocative. The oldest trees are not necessarily those that 'look' the oldest, while perceived height is an unreliable guide to age or real size, and girth is only reliably judged on the evidence of a tape measure. One might imagine that, given that all trees produce annual rings, the link between the variables of size and age would be very easily demonstrated. However, when hardwoods pass maturity they tend to become hollow, the tubular structure which results is probably creating a form that is better able to resist high winds. Hollowness is associated with the disappearance of the tree's heartwood and this robs the dendrochronologist of evidence of the earlier years of growth, both as evidenced by tree rings and by materials suitable for radiocarbon dating. In recent years, improvements to our understanding of tree growth patterns have resulted in the development of curves that can be applied to the task of relating the girth of a tree to its presumed age (see White, 1997, pp.222-6).

Age and girth vary from species to species and there are great differences in growth rates and longevity.

> A veteran beech will be far younger than an oak of the same size, and only a fraction of the age of an equivalent-sized yew. A 250-year-old beech is exceptionally old: beech seldom live for more than 300 years. Oak on the other hand survives for a much longer time as an old tree. Most are past their commercial prime after 250 years but many remain alive for another 200 or more years and some live to be one thousand (White, 1997 p.223).

Within the same species, the size of a tree is greatly influenced by environmental factors, while genetic ones must also play a part.

> Nine-hundred-year-old veteran oaks at Windsor are a good 10 times larger than even older oaks in Wistman's Wood on Dartmoor …. The same Windsor trees have basal areas not so different from modern 140-year-old (non-veteran) British grown Wellingtonias … size variation may also be an expression of genetic diversity within a seed population of a single species (*op. cit.* p.222)

Several curves linking tree girth to age have been produced, though their deductions are far from being in harmony. There is a general recognition that trees tend to grow rapidly in their early years, and that this phase later gives way to a flatter growth curve. However, trees do not have lifespans in the way that we understand them. 'Old age' is not achieved at a predictable age in years so that death or 'senility' can occur much earlier or much later than any mean value might suggest. In a tree's formative years, following germination, the plant will grow quite rapidly up to a stage where its canopy is fully developed. It then enters a mature phase, when the crown size remains stable and although its trunk continues to increase in girth, the annual rings begin to decline in width. As the

Annual growth ring counting by the author's former research student, Andrew Done. Such counts give accurate indications of the relationship between tree age and girth during the initial phase of rapid growth. However, as soon as the tree becomes hollow, the tree ring evidence vanishes

tree becomes a veteran, the size of its canopy diminishes and the declining leaf cover produces less energy and growth of the tree is very slow. It may remain healthy in this condition for several centuries, right up to the point where fungal attack, lightning strikes or human intervention to remove a supposedly 'dying' tree bring about its death (Read, pp.28-9). Some very old trees will experience a phase of shrinkage, so that trees alive today may display smaller girths than those that were measured in the eighteenth or nineteenth centuries. The shrinkage is not due to any general contraction of the trunk, but to the collapse of greatly hollowed sections or sub-trunks around the circumference.

A curve for calculating the age of trees by measuring their girth was produced by Mitchell (1974) according to the premise that 1 inch (*c.*25mm) of girth at chest height or 1.2m from the ground represents one year of growth for a tree standing in open ground while only 0.5 inch (*c.*13mm) of such growth would be produced by a tree in a woodland setting. This measure has been found unsatisfactory, and while it seems closest to reflecting growth patterns in middle-aged oak maidens it does not reflect the slowing down of growth in veteran trees which are producing very narrow annual rings. A much more refined curve was produced by White (1998) and this takes account of the growth stages in the life of a tree and can be calibrated for different tree species so far as real datable timber and dated trees are available to provide the growth rate inputs. However, such methods of dating trees will remain imperfect because of all the different calibrations that would be needed to allow for the peculiarities of a specific site, its geology, soil chemistry, shading by neighbouring trees, hydrology, climate and microclimate, latitude, exposure, human management, genetic characteristics of the particular tree concerned and so on. Tree ring samples from living wood can be related to the data accumulated by dendrochronologists, but cannot give dates for timber lost in the heart of a hollow tree.

Landscape history/archaeology may give some vital assistance. For example, where there are old hedgerow trees in association with land that the records show to have been drained and partitioned into fields by hedgerows about, say, four centuries ago, then there are good reasons to presume that the older trees date to this event. Later, with an aristocratic enthusiasm for commercial arboriculture and landscaping developing, the planting of specific trees or plantations was quite frequently recorded in diaries, estate books, gardeners' logs and so on. Among the entries for the thousands of trees planted at Ripley by John Ingilby we find one for October, 1783:

> Planted in the Park and walks 150 large Horse Chestnuts in High Rails [a farm formed out of the medieval deer park] a plantation of oaks and scotch firs one foot high and some oaks and Scotch fir the same height in the Kettlespring Closes 1400 firs and 1000 oaks …. Planted at the same time in the Park and behind the Park Wall 50 Larches and six Weymouth pines… (Ingilby MS 2838).

(The timber from these prolific plantings later saved the family from penury when an eagerly awaited dowry failed to materialise.) Armed with a record such as this, one can search in the specified places for survivors of a documented planting episode.

Specimen trees may be dated by historical inference – for example, the great London Plane in the grounds of the old Bishop's Palace at Ely is believed to have been planted by Bishop Peter Gunning in 1680, perhaps after conversations with John Evelyn, the great advocate of silviculture who had attended some of his services in London (Stokes, p.49). At the same time, it can sometimes be hard to identify a wood, let alone a single tree, in the medieval records and various traps await the unwary. For example, in 1285, Edward I issued the Statute of Winchester which sought to protect commercial activity so that

> … highways leading from one market town to another shall be enlarged where as bushes, woods or dykes be, so that there be neither dyke not bush whereby a man may lurk to do hurt within two hundred feet of the one side and two hundred feet of the other side.

Were the terms of the Statute to be taken literally, then we could claim that any tree in England found within a zone of about 400ft (*c*.122m) wide that had a medieval highway as its spine must be younger than 1285, or 719 years. In reality, the statutes or edicts of that time often amounted to little more than wishes. It is most unlikely that a really significant fraction of the English road-bordering territory was actually cleared according to the royal demands contained in the Statute of Winchester. The fact that a local or national policy relating to trees was extant by no means implies that it was observed.

The relationship between the size of a tree and its age varies greatly from species to species. Some achieve great size very rapidly, so that a sweet chestnut of 'landmark' proportions need not be more than a few centuries old, while, as noted above, beech quickly grow to great heights and the massive but shallow-rooted trees are likely to be blown over before reaching the three-century mark. Though superficially resembling oaks of twice their age, sweet chestnuts at Inchmahome in Stirlingshire, including the great, stag-headed Antlered Chestnut, may not have germinated until the end of the medieval period or shortly after. The famous sweet chestnut pollards in the park of Croft Castle, Herefordshire, may be no older than the mid-eighteenth century.

Age is hard to judge and a gnarled and moribund specimen may possibly develop some new growth and effectively rejuvenate itself. This occurred in trees like the Queen Mary's Thorn in the college quadrangle of that name at St Andrews (said to have been planted by the queen in 1563), that seemed close to death yet threw up vigorous new stems from ground level. Also, there are those self-perpetuating trees that self-layer, like the Great Yew of Ormiston or the Whittinghame Yew, two Scottish layering yews that may root and produce new

Yews are noted for their longevity and several very old and contorted specimens can be found on the slopes of Borrowdale in the Lake District. The group has been famed for at least two centuries

growth wherever their down-curving branches touch soil. Heralded by Peter Collinson in 1766, as the largest tree in England, with a girth of 52ft (15.8m), the sweet chestnut at Tortworth in Gloucestershire has layered from its trailing boughs to assume the form of a thicket. (The collapse of parts of its trunk now reduces its girth to 36ft (11m) (Stokes, p.93)). Then, too, there are the coppiced trees, each great stool an individual tree that was regularly rejuvenated by coppicing and which may possibly attain or pass an age of 1000 or more.

In the recent past, writers on trees seem to have conjured up ages for them using no criteria other than their apparent antiquity. Oaks and yew trees were the commonest recipients of amazing ages. Today, the Fortingall Yew, near Aberfeldy in Perthshire '… is believed to be the most ancient tree in the United Kingdom, and probably the oldest living thing in Europe' (Rodger, Stokes and Ogilvie, p.129) with an attributed age of 5,000 years. In 1769, the curving wall of the trunk had a circumference of 52ft (*c.*16m) (Barrington, p.23) and, though the tree was ancient then, this is not evidence of five millennia of preceding life. The older topographers seem to have employed folklore, intuition and aspiration in the ageing of trees. For example, in 1942, the woodland historian, Dowsett, produced a photograph of an ancient yew with a service tree growing out of it and claimed that this tree had been mentioned in Domesday Book (1086) when

Ancient, contorted oak pollards, like this example from Sherwood Forest, perfectly matched the mood of neo-Gothic literature and art

it already had an age of about 1,500 years (infra pp.146-7). One then asks how, in the late eleventh century, could anyone calculate the age of a tree and where were their deductions recorded? The Tortworth Chestnut was a huge tree in the mid-eighteenth century, but sweet chestnuts grow very rapidly and the legend that it sprang from a nut planted by King Egbert in AD 800 (Stokes, p.92) seems highly dubious. Why would the king go about planting chestnuts, a less than kingly pursuit, and who, in a time of total illiteracy for all bar the clergy, would have been there to record such an inconsequential event?

Some of the unfounded claims must have been stimulated by the gnarled and venerable appearance of the subjects, while discoveries of bog oaks and the finding of fossil leaves in coal may have helped to nourish speculation. In the nineteenth century, notions of twisted, hoary trees sat well with the enthusiasm for Gothic imagery inspired by the novels of Scott (1771-1832), the poems of Tennyson (1809-92) and much more. This mood probably found its purest expression in the book illustrations by Arthur Rackham (1867-1939), where the trees, with their tense and angular forms, seem to exert an ancient, brooding presence within their countrysides. The renditions owe part of their effectiveness to the manner in which real veteran tree forms have been carefully studied and then, just lightly, caricatured. There were also less romantic or aesthetic possibilities. A landed family seeking to legitimise their claim to their estates might have seen political advantages in having their parks and castles associated with trees of immense antiquity, for some of this venerability might have reflected on the dynasty.

Perhaps the last great flowering of this neo-Gothic tradition was created by J.R.R. Tolkien (1892-1973) in his *Lord of the Rings,* the author having moved from the Orange Free State to settle at Sarehole on the rural fringes of Birmingham at the age of four. The countrysides of Tolkien's childhood, their ethos intensified and tinted, resurface in the second book of the trilogy. Here, the massive, ancient trees provide more than a background or mood contribution, for in the form of 'Ents' they become leading players in the unfolding drama. The Ents of Fangorn display the Gothic characteristics established in Victorian and Edwardian times, but now the contorted, mossy giants have acquired an ability to bestride their settings and communicate. In anticipation of later twentieth-century environmentalism, they are united against the forces of evil, which have exploited and destroyed their setting and kin. There is something as powerfully appealing as it is ludicrous in the idea of giant trees advancing remorselessly over the landscape to exact their revenge. Most recently, the filming of the three *Lord of the Rings* stories has created the hitherto unimaginable circumstance of children directing some of their hero-worshipping capabilities towards animated trees.

It is in this developing tradition of literary and visual representation that accounts of the antiquity of landmark trees are embedded. The ages claimed become more than just statistics or rhetoric. More often than not, they prove to be unfounded speculations – yet they succeed in establishing a passion for the antiquity embodied in old countryside, permeating it and yet remaining elusive. The tree becomes a vessel for that antiquity and a channel for that yearning. It is both a presence and a passport to far-off 'better times'. That such times, despite their undoubted ecological superiority, may have been terrifying and packed with injustices is not admitted as an issue.

Exceptional dimensions endowed a tree with the possibility of commemoration in historical records. However, perceptions of what was exceptional depended upon what, of the kind concerned, one had seen before? Thus, when Ralph Thoresby composed his West Riding Additions to the 1695 edition of *Britannia* and wrote about the Roman fortifications at Temple Brough, near Rotherham, his attention was caught by '… another large bench, upon which are huge trees; and upon the side of the bench of the high-way, there grew a *Chestnut-tree*, that had scarce any bark upon it, but only some top branches, which bore leaves. It was not tall; but the Bole could scarcely be fathom'd by three men' (p.723). The description calls to mind a sweet chestnut rather than a horse chestnut and it seems to have gone by 1695, but to have figured in recent memory. Taking a fathom as 6ft, the tree would have had a circumference of about 18ft (5.49m). It may not have been remarkable as Thoresby imagined. A sweet chestnut with a girth, measured by the author, of 8.6m fell in Ripley deer park, North Yorkshire, about the winter of 1962–3, and the stump and trunk are still on view.

The Cowthorpe Oak, near Marston Moor to the west of York, was rather more impressive. It was described in 1894 by the generally reliable Yorkshire topographical writer, Harry Speight (p.138). He thought it (rather improbably) to be 1,600 years old and also the largest tree in England, with only the Shire Oak, near Worksop, as a rival. (One wonders if he meant the Three Shire Oak, mentioned below, or the Spread Oak in Worksop Park, thought able to shelter 1,000 horses?) He mentioned (p.139) that in 1768 the girth of the Cowthorpe Oak was measured at 40ft 6in (12.3m) at 4ft (1.2m) above ground, it had a height of about 85ft (25.9m) and limbs that extended for 16 yards (14.6m.) from the trunk. He identified the tree as a specimen of *Quercus Robor var. pendiculata* and noted that it was still producing acorns in the 1890s. Its girth in 1893 at 3ft (0.9m) was 44ft (13.4m), and at 5.25ft (1.6m) it was 36ft 10in (11.2m). At some time in the 1880s, Speight wrote, the hollow trunk had accommodated 95 children from St James's church, Wetherby, and their pastor. The next largest tree, he claimed, had been the D'Amorie's (or Damory) Oak from Blandford, Dorest, felled in 1755 with a hollow trunk some 68ft (20.7m) in circumference. It was used as an alehouse with a main apartment 16ft (4.9m) in length and a small bar in an alcove. A little Yorkshire partisanship seems to have been at work, as the Blandford tree seems demonstrably to have been larger than the Cowthorpe Oak. Local sources claim that the D'Amorie's Oak was at its finest in the reign of Edward III (1327–77) and had become hollow by the Civil War. When Blandford burned in 1731, two homeless families are said to have found shelter there. It grew on the D'Amorie estate, close to the family seat of Damory Court and is commemorated by The Damory Oak inn, standing close to the former site of the tree that ended its celebrated existence as fuel sold for £14.

Another of the immense English oaks of the eighteenth century appears to have been the Greendale Oak, which grew in the vicinity of Wellbeck Abbey, which was recorded as having a circumference of 35ft (10.7m) in 1790. At some stage in that century both dead and living wood are said to have been removed from its core in order to create a passage through which a coach and six was driven (Dowsett, 1942, pp.162-3).

Girth could secure a place in the archives for a notable tree, but so, too, could an association with an important figure. One of the less celebrated associations concerns the 'Warwick Oak', which stood in the deer park associated with Sheriff Hutton Castle, north of York. It had gone by the time that George Todd wrote about the castle in 1824. It might have been planted in 1335, when the Nevilles created a deer park from 'carr' (swampy alder woodland) and from the farmland of the deserted village of East Lilling, though it could have been incorporated as an established tree. Todd recorded that around the house

> … are many fine oaks of ancient growth and venerable appearance. One of these
> trees, which was blown down many years ago, is said to have been standing in the
> reign of Richard III [1483-5]; it was called the "Warwick Oak", from having been
> (according to tradition of the neighbourhood) the limit to which the unfortunate
> Earl of Warwick was permitted to extend his walks during the period of his
> confinement in the Castle of Sheriff Hutton (pp.39-40).

Had the Warwick Oak blown down around 1800, it was then probably about 500 years old and quite possibly much older.

Exceptional trees have always exerted a fascination, but they can also provide evidence concerning the landscape history of their general setting. To develop a large, spreading form a tree required space of a kind that is not available within tightly-packed woodland conditions. Therefore, when such a broad, old tree is found within a woodland composed of younger, narrower trees it is extremely likely that it has grown in a former clearing, or that it once stood as a free-standing tree surrounded by farmland. Thus, the tree could indicate a former agricultural phase, followed by an abandonment of farming and colonisation by woodland. In North America, such trees are known as 'wolf trees' and Spirn explains:

> A "wolf" tree is a tree within a woods [sic], its size and form, large trunk and
> horizontal branches, anomalous to the environs of slim-trunked trees with upright
> branches. It is a clue to the open field in which it once grew alone, branches
> reaching laterally to the light and up. With that field unmowed, unplowed, or
> ungrazed, younger woodland trees grew thickly together around the older tree,
> their branches finding light by reaching up (pp.18-19).

Where wolf trees form alignments within woods, they are likely to be the relics of old hedgerows. After the abandonment of pollarding, the trees growing on woodbanks could develop asymetrical forms, with the side shaded by the adjacent wood producing vertical, light-hunting branches, while those on the opposite side would spread horizontally. Following the coniferisation of an old deciduous wood, similar forms could develop when a row of old woodland-edge trees escaped the clear felling of the interior.

Boundary marks

The possession of a situation on a boundary greatly assisted the likelihood that a tree would be recorded. Such trees could have been amongst the landmarks along which a boundary was first strung, although the immense antiquity of so many boundaries argues that a high proportion of boundary trees must have grown – or been deliberately planted – upon existing divides. A map of Moulsham in Essex, drawn in 1591, identifies 'The Great Marke Oak' where a boundary traverses the old common, 'mark' being derived from the Old English *mearc*, 'a boundary'. The linking of trees to boundaries in place names is not unusual, as with the field name 'Mark Oak Close' noted by John Field at

In North America, trees that out-date and overshadow their neighbours are known as 'wolf trees'. These huge beech pollards are growing on a boundary bank engulfed by younger woods

Northington, Hampshire (p.134). The Old English *(ge)mære* is another boundary word and it can appear in combinations like 'Mere Ash', Bratton, Wiltshire or 'Merry Oak', Feckenham, Worcestershire. The Old English *scïr* often signifies a major boundary and can be linked to former landmark trees, like Shire Oak, Brownhills, W. Midlands.

The possession of a boundary location can enable stages in the life cycle of a tree to be recorded, as the author discovered during research on the township of Ripley, North Yorkshire. 'Godwin's Oak' is notable because it can be linked to a real historic personage. Godwin appears to have been a member of the lesser landowning gentry and his granddaughter, who was called 'Avice' was alive at the start of the thirteenth century. His small estate included the locality 'Godwinscales', which may then have included summer pasture and which became absorbed into a deer park towards the end of the Middle Ages. His name also attached and endured in association with a local bridge and a 'syke' or streamlet. It seems fair to assume that to be named after an owner living in the mid- to late twelfth century, the oak must by then have achieved the dimensions of a tree of some note. The boundary upon which it stood divided the King's Forest of Knaresborough, a royal hunting reserve, from the lay manors at Ripley, which amalgamated and became the home estate of the Ingilby dynasty. Because of the importance attached to the conservation of royal game, the Forest boundary was important and subject to periodic perambulations. The evidence of these perambulations provides information on the history of Godwin's Oak, as a boundary mark recorded in these surveys. Its name evolved along with the English language, so that in 1234-50 it was 'Godwy Ayc' and in 1577 it was 'Gawdewane oke'. It fell in the eighteenth century, but the 1770 perambulation by Enclosure Commissioners describes a former park pale '… in which are the remains of an old oak tree known by the name of Godwin oak, where stands the bounder stone marked 43 K.F. 1767'. To have been a noteworthy tree around 1150, the oak should, one imagines have been at least 250 years old, giving it an age of at least 800 when it died (Muir, 2000 p.106 and 2001, pp.56-7).

In Britain there are thousands of place names that describe woodland, with many more words formerly being employed to identify the particular characteristics of woodland than are understood today. Now, we use very few woodland terms and do not recognise the different natures of groves, spring woods, hags and so on. In Old English, the word used for an individual tree, *trēow*, could also be used for heavy timber, in the form of a post or beam. Allowing for a few misleading 'lumber' words, we can discover scores of places named after trees that may have stood over a thousand years ago. They can tell us about the former nature of places at the times when they gained their names. Appletreewick, Wharfedale, was probably 'Apple tree cheese farm', though whether the farm was sited beside an existing crab apple or whether the tree was a cultivar planted by the farmer can not be known. Many of the tree names will pre-date the Norman Conquest, and Margaret Gelling cites Elmestree in Gloucestershire, where the estate of this name is known to have been in existence in AD 962 (p.212). A great many names that mention particular trees have the landowner's name as the first element of the place name and the tree concerned as the second element. Thus we have Yarlestree or 'Earl's tree', North Yorkshire, Manningtree or 'Manna's tree' in Essex, Edwinstree or 'Edwin's tree' in Hertfordshire and Ottery or 'Oda's tree' in Devon.

It has been noted that a surprising proportion of such places combining owner and tree in their names developed into medieval towns of some substance. There are hints that the tree concerned could have been a landmark and a venue for important gatherings, though perhaps a preaching, boundary or market cross made of timber marked some meeting places. In other cases, the first component is a word that describes or specifies the nature of the tree. In this group there are many examples like Langtree, a 'tall tree', Mapletree, a field maple or perhaps a sycamore, a Hoartree, with its lichen, or the sinister Gallantree or Gaultry: the gallows tree. Heavitree near Exeter has a notable old yew in its churchyard. This tree might be a descendent of the 'head tree' or place where Saxon kings held court, which is the possible origin of the place name. However, such things are seldom certain and the tree could be the (gathering?) place of a Saxon called 'Hefa'. Trees could be notable for all kinds of landmark functions, with the Bishop of Worcester presiding over a hundred court twice yearly at 'Beorna's Tree' in Henbury (Hooke, p.22) or with lovers in Scotland meeting at trysting trees. There are, however, a few suggestive names that do not denote landmark trees but timber products, like Whippletree Lane in Whittlesford, Cambridgeshire, named after the little beam to which the traces are attached when harnessing to a cart or plough.

The employment of landmark trees as meeting places for courts seems to have occurred throughout western Europe. The court of the medieval Abbot of St Albans was held under an ash growing in the middle court of the abbey. In Germany the use of trees as venues was very common: 'The most numerous, beyond all comparison, are the lindens; there are six oaks, five hawthorns, two beeches, two hazels, one each of fir, elm, willow, walnut, pear, apple, and "the Red Tree"' (Coulton, 1925, p.70).

The surviving texts of boundary descriptions in Saxon charters show that 1,000-1,500 years ago trees were commonly adopted and employed as boundary marks. However, the boundaries that were marked will often have pre-dated the English ascendancy by many centuries. Since border zones were conventionally the places for public gatherings, the names of boundary trees frequently became attached to the main territorial subdivisions, the wapentakes or hundreds. Surprisingly often, these trees had personal name prefixes, like the one that gave its name to Wixamtree Hundred in Bedfordshire, translated as 'Wihtstān's tree' by Gelling (p.213). Sometimes, trees with special characteristics are noted in the boundary descriptions. In the Burton Abbey charter of 996, in which Aethelred II granted land to his thegn, Wulfric, part of the bounds ran from the boggy ground to the street, on to the *readan ácon* or 'red oak' and then across a wood and on to the ('snipe-' or else 'pear tree-' named) brook (Hart, p.207). Three years earlier, King Edgar granted Earl Gunnar lands at Newbald, East Yorkshire, with bounds that began at the 'withered tree' and continued via a thorn tree on their way around the estate (Hart pp.122-3). In some cases, trees that stood up above their fellows were noted, like the *greatan ac* or 'great oak' that towered in the 'hurst' (a wooded hill) in the boundary description of the grant of land at Madeley on the Shropshire/Staffordshire boundary by King Eadred to his thegn, Wulfhelm, in 957. This charter also mentions one *witena leage*, the wood of the witan or councillors and the coppice or *gyrd-leah*, the wood where poles were obtained (Hart, pp.95-6)

The boundary marks described in these charters had not just come into existence. Rather, the descriptions give the impression of units of property and administration marked out by long-established ditches, very ancient tumuli, mature hedgerows and imposing boundary trees, like the elm prominently standing on the Wetmore/Stretton boundary in the Staffordshire charter of 1012. Property was paramount and the landmarks tracing the limits of ownership had to be both obvious and unambiguous: a boundary linked to a nondescript tree standing in an assemblage of such trees could only lead to confusion and trouble. Taking a random selection of 50 boundary perambulations from the *Cartularium Saxonicum*, Rackham identified a total of 1,230 recorded boundary features (1976, pp.54-5). Setting aside the numerous woods, groves, spinneys, clearings and hedgerows, he found that 56 (4.5 per cent) of boundary marks were individual trees or free-standing small tree clumps. Rather surprisingly, he showed that while oak is most numerous in Old English tree place names, thorn trees were by far the most numerous boundary trees, amounting to 23 out of the total and oak numbering only three. Similarly, thorn trees often marked the meeting places of the hundreds and wapentakes and Hooke quotes *Celfledtorn* in Gloucestershire, *Goderestona* in Dorset, *Cicimethorne* and *Thornegraue* in Wiltshire and *Nachededorn* in Berkshire as examples (p.23). In the boundary description concerning a grant of lands in Derbyshire by Aethelred II to the thane, Morcar, in 1009, the boundary follows a dyke to '*pulfeardes þorn*', or Wulfheard's thorn before linking to another dyke. Today, hawthorn and blackthorn are very largely encountered as hedgerow shrubs, though hawthorn scrub may occasionally colonise mismanaged pastures, as in the Yorkshire Dales, and blackthorn may spread from hedgerows into neglected farmland. Single thorns, however, are seldom seen and the Anglo-Saxon landscape seems to have differed in this respect. It is improbable that a large proportion of the boundary thorns were derived from decayed hedgerows, so perhaps thorn trees, so easy to propagate, were deliberately planted on boundary locations.

The landmark significance of what, to modern eyes, is one of the less spectacular of native trees deserves serious consideration. Certainly the proximity of its blossoming to ancient festivals heralding the rebirth of the year must be

The hawthorn or may in blossom. Seeped in magic and myth, the tree was astonishingly popular as a boundary mark

significant. In ancient Rome thorn wood was used for the torches carried at wedding processions and illuminating wedding banquets. Tudor townsfolk went out to the surrounding countryside to gather may blossom to decorate their homes, while may blossom garlanded the maypole and crowned the maiden chosen as the Queen of the May. The coincidence of its flowering with May Day was closer under the old calendar, with the Day falling 10-11 days later than today. Some of the mystical associations of the tree are less easily attributed to pagan festivals and fertility rites, like the belief in Ireland and northern England that bad luck will befall anyone who grubs up an old thorn tree (Raistrick, 1991, p.42). A circlet of thorns had crowned the crucified Christ and in medieval folklore there was an association between the thorn tree and the Saviour's wounds. A Marian poem associated with the cult of the Virgin Mary related that

At a sprynge-wel under a thorn
There was a bote of bale [a cure for sorrow]
A lytel here a-forn';
There by-syde stant a mayde

Fulle of love ybounde
Hoso [whoso] wol seche trwe love,
Yn hyr hyt shal be founde
(quoted in Bennett, 1986, pp.373-4)

The spring under the thorn equated to the great wound in the side of Christ, while the maid standing beside it was the Virgin Mary.

As a place name, the thorn is plentiful – almost amazingly so in the Yorkshire Dales, where Raistrick speculates that the trees may have been abundant about 1,000 years ago, when so many names were given. He lists

Thornborough, Thornbury, Thorncliffe, Thorn and Thornes, Thorner, Thorngate, Thornhill, Thornholme, Thornethorpe, Thornthwaite with, perhaps, the very curious Thorngumbald … while Thorntons are so numerous that many examples of them have to have distinguishing suffix – Thornton-in-Craven, -le Dale, -le-Beans, -le-Clay, -in-Lonsdale, -le-Street, and Thornton-on-the-Hills do not exhaust the list. As a compound name, -thorn is less common, but can still be found as in Skyrethorns, Brockthorns, Paythorne, etc. (*ibid.*).

Also surprising was the presence there of three records of wild pear, which is an extremely rare tree today and must have been uncommon in Saxon times. A comparable survey of Saxon charters in Worcestershire by G.B.Grundy had revealed the predominance of thorn trees, used as 23 out of 73 markers, though oak, with 20 occurrences was more strongly featured. Here, the uncommon wild service tree was sited, and this, along with the five counts for lime and his own record of wild pear, led Rackham to suggest that there had also been a predilection for unusual trees as boundary marks. This point is echoed by Hook (p.95) when she quotes an 'ash-apple-tree' from a charter of Pendock in Worcestershire and wonders if it might be an introduced true service tree, *Sorbus domestica*? She also provides a perspective on New Age notions of ancient tree-venerating paganism by quoting the Taunton charter that identifies a boundary mark as the 'ash which the ignorant call holy'.

It is plain from the charter evidence that the first British people to be 'historical' in the sense of leaving a *substantial* documentary legacy, the Anglo-Saxons, Anglo-Norse and Anglo-Danish communities, made a considerable use of landmark trees as boundary markers, many of these trees and boundaries doubtless being inherited from earlier times. The use of trees as boundary markers did not end with the Norman Conquest. In the centuries that followed, new boundaries were established and marked in the landscape and the intensification of feudal control heightened the profiles of property and territory. A 'copped' or pollarded oak was mentioned in a Hampshire Anglo-Saxon boundary charter (Hooke, p.164) and for these medieval boundaries, chains of pollards were frequently employed as boundary features. Hornbeams,

The blossom of the wild pear, one of the rarest of trees. Perhaps its rarity explained its popularity as a boundary marker?

oaks and elms, many examples of them still surviving, were planted along property boundaries, such as those that marked the limits of village tenancies, commons and woods. On the whole, they did not serve to establish the precise position of an otherwise un-demarcated boundary which would be marked more accurately by the lip of the ditch between two village closes or by the woodbank and its ditch. Low-cut pollards aligned along the crest of a woodbank was a very common sight in the English countryside, and though less frequently encountered in Scotland, low pollards will sometimes be seen growing on old boundary dykes (Quelch, 1997, p.31). Boundary pollards would yield timber and browse just like other pollards, but were not needed physically to establish the position of the boundary. Perhaps, then, their presence was symbolic rather than narrowly functional. With the gradual disintegration of communal farming from Tudor times onwards, closely spaced pollards were included within the new hedgerows that partitioned the privatised countryside. These could not normally be regarded as landmark trees, and so the boundary symbolism of the pollard chain presumably diminished.

There are plenty of post-medieval records of the planting of solitary trees to mark the limit of an ownership or jurisdiction and the planting of chains of trees to demarcate a boundary line. In wet lands in the West Midlands, black poplars were popular for this purpose, while elsewhere oaks were generally favoured for their longevity and useful timber.

Rare today, the black poplar was favoured as a boundary marker in the wet lands of the English Midlands

Execution sites were frequently placed on the margins of parishes and townships, sometimes at roadside and crossroads sites. Both gallows, where victims were hanged, or gibbets, where the corpses of prisoners executed in an adjacent town were suspended, might employ boundary trees, though other trees were also used. The use of boundary locations may have symbolised the marginalisation of the criminal who had thus been evicted from the social and spiritual heartland of the territory. A tree, possibly a black poplar, growing at Gallows Bank, Ludlow, in Shropshire is known to have been the scene of several hangings in the late sixteenth century. Gallows often made use of a horizontal branch of a living tree, as in the western movies, though artificial gallows were frequently employed. These were sometimes erected on ancient barrows, resulting in the numerous 'Gallows Hill' place names, and the gallows could be superseded by gibbets erected in the same location, the gibbets also being artificial structures from which the decaying bodies were hung in cages or chains. Popular concerns about restless spirits focused particularly on suicides, their bodies being excluded from churchyards and frequently buried in roads and roadsides, where the traffic might deter their ghosts from wandering. It appears that the corpses of these unfortunates were sometimes transfixed by stakes that pinned them to the ground and local mythologies were attached to certain roadside trees which were reputed to have grown from such stakes (Whyte, 2003, p.35).

The use of trees as markers is not limited to the boundary-marking function. Some have been planted to mark incidents and occasions that hardly any survivors recall – like the one planted in Glengairn, near Ballater, to mark the spot where a child fell from a pony long ago. In the same now-desolate glen another large ash tree grows through the corner of a tumbled dwelling at the site of a former *clachan* or hamlet. Such trees can have an archaeological significance, for desertion could only have occurred before the germination of the tree. Deserted settlements have their botanical significance, as when rectangular patches of nettles are seen growing in the phosphate enriched soils of long-lost dwellings, often the portions of them that served as byres. In the case of trees, the stones of tumbledown walls could shelter seedlings from sheep and cattle. This was not the case with the tall ash tree at Clint, North Yorkshire, which stands in the middle of the lost village high street and demonstrates that it must have been disused since well back in the nineteenth century. However, at Chatsworth in Derbyshire trees grow in troughs that are wrongly identified as holloways; the 'trenches' are actually produced by sapping at the heads of parallel springs and so the trees have no particular historical significance. On Dartmoor the circles of moorstone which were dwellings in the Bronze Age still shelter hawthorn seedlings from grazing ponies and cattle.

Myths and magic

The relationship between humans and trees is one that is closer and more complicated than that between us and inanimate objects. We see parallels in the ways that we both live and die – even if the nature of the life-cycle is much different in trees – and we see parallels in the ways in which both tree and human communities compete to occupy space and exploit its resources. When paganism prevailed, the link between people and Nature was closer and more accommodating. There was no Christian mythology concerning a God-given dominion over natural resources. Instead, people considered themselves to be within Nature and to be inhabiting a world where everything was permeated by spirituality. Property and hierarchies were much less evident and, while saints and bishops described or invented the darker sides of paganism, it is hard to imagine that the impending environmental catastrophes would be so awesome had the antiquated beliefs prevailed. Today, so very late in the day, many thoughtful people are conscious of a sense of guilt concerning the human assault on the earth's forests.

Different associations between trees and guilt go back much further; the 'tree of the knowledge of good and evil' grew in the Garden of Eden, and Adam and

Eve were expelled for eating its fruit. Trees have figured prominently in classical mythology since at least the time of the legend of Jupiter, to whom the oak was sacred, and that of Apollo and his Daphne, who turned into a tree. Adonis was said to have been born from a tree, while after the Christian conversions Boniface was represented with his foot placed on a fallen oak, the tree sacred to the pagans, symbolising the victory over paganism, and Bishop Zenobius had a flowering tree as his attribute.

On the continent of Europe, as in Britain, pagan reverence for the natural world was constricted by the strictures of Christianity. The durability of the old beliefs is demonstrated by the testimony of Joan of Arc during her trial for heresy and sorcery in 1431. When asked about a tree growing near her village of Domrémy she replied that nearby there was a tree

> ... called *The Ladies' Tree*; and others call it *The Fairies' Tree*; and there is a fountain hard by. And I have heard say that those who are sick of fevers drink from that spring and go and fetch its water for health's sake ... I have heard that the sick, when they are able to rise, go to that tree for a walk. ... And there is a great tree called Beech [hawthorn?], whence cometh that which is called in French *le beau may*, and it belonged to the Lord Pierre de Bourlemont. When I went walking with other girls I made garlands at that tree for the image of St Mary at Domrémy. And I heard sometimes from old folk ... that the Fairy Ladies haunted there. ... I have seen girls hanging garlands on the boughs of that tree, and I have sometimes done so with them; sometimes they took the garlands away with them, and sometimes they left them. ... I do not know that I have danced by the tree since I came to years of discretion ... (quoted in Coulton, 1925 pp.262-3).

Similar beliefs, blurred by passing centuries, still permeated rural societies in post-medieval England. Phillip Stubbes, a writer inclined to Puritan perspectives on life, published an *Anatomie of Abuses* in 1583. He recorded how, at May or Whitsun-day people of all ages and sexes

> ... run gadding over night to the woods, groves, hills and mountains, where they spend all the night in pleasant pastimes, and in the morning they return, bringing with them birch and branches of trees, to deck their assemblies withall. And no mervaile, for there is a great Lord present amongst them, as superintendant over their pastimes and sportes, namely Sathan, prince of hell. But the chiefest jewel they bring from thence is their May-pole, which they bring home with great veneration, as thus. They have twentie or fortie yoke of oxen, every oxe having a sweet nose-gay of flowers placed on the tip of his hornes, and these oxen drawe home this May-pole (this stinking ydol rather) which is covered all over with floures and herbes, bound round about with strings ....

In former times the medicinal, magical and functional associations of every tree were embedded in popular lore. Hornbeam timber was hard and liable to split and so the trees were managed as pollards and coppards and the resultant timber used as fuel or as tough cogwheels, with some being converted to charcoal and gunpowder. These trees in Epping Forest helped to provide London with copious quantities of firewood

A special type of landmark tree is that which has its own particular mythology. Of these, the most celebrated must be the Glastonbury Holy Thorn. It is said to have grown from the staff that was carried to England by the biblical Joseph of Arimathea. Some versions of the myth have him accompanied by his nephew, the boy Jesus, and some have them prospecting for tin. Other versions claim that Joseph's staff came from the tree used to make the crown of thorns of the head of the doomed Saviour. Joseph, exhausted by his travels, stuck his staff into the ground of Worral Hill. Miraculously, the myth maintains, the staff rooted and grew into a tree that would only blossom on Christmas Day and so a church was built nearby, which grew into Glastonbury Abbey. The tree itself was real enough, being a specimen of *Crataegus monogyna var, biflora*, which flowered about the start of January. However, the setting is one where traditionally all rules of intellectual rigour are abandoned and where misrepresentation goes back to medieval times when a lead plaque inscribed 'Here lies the renowned King Arthur in the Isle of Avalon' was 'discovered', presumably in an attempt to invigorate the local pilgrimage industry.

In reality, the summit of Glastonbury Tor carried the timber buildings of a fairly high-status settlement (monastery or local capital?) in the fifth to sixth centuries AD, and later an Anglo-Saxon subsidiary of the Abbey at Glastonbury. The setting has, in its ethos and scenery, magical or inspirational qualities deriving from the plough-sculpted Tor which surges from the low Levels, and these might easily attract religious foundations, but there is nothing there that cannot be explained by geological principles and conventional archaeology.

The Glastonbury Holy Thorn died in June 1991, having grown in the churchyard of St John the Baptist's church for a modest 80 years. During the medieval period, pilgrimage became an increasingly important, indeed, a dominating aspect of the economy of the Abbey. However, it was not until the thirteenth century that any reference to the Holy Thorn was made and there is no evidence that the Thorn referred to then had winter flowering characteristics (Humphrys, 1998). The origins of the legend seem to go back to 1535, when the devious Thomas Cromwell, a key aide to Henry VIII, despatched a Dr Layton to Glastonbury to investigate rumours of a winter-flowering tree. Their confirmation marked the beginnings of a tradition which would have had far more commercial value had it occurred before the decline of pilgrimage and the Dissolution of the Monasteries, yet which is assiduously cultivated by modern commercial interests, as any internet search will reveal. The tree that Dr Layton inspected may have been cut down during the Civil War and subsequent claimants to the Holy mantle probably derived from cuttings, though cuttings taken in the latter years of the last thorn are said to have reverted to the May-flowering type. Louisa Charlotte Frampton wrote of how visitors had been mistaken or misled in the nineteenth century: 'I would not miss the Royal Oak nor Glastonbury Thorn, although neither of the original trees exist, & even a very old descendant of the latter, which Gilpin saw in 1801, & I saw in 1835, & both believed to be the ancient one, has now been gone [15?] years' (25 May, 1877, *Lacock Abbey Collection* Doc.No. 02864). If the visitors concerned had been looking in the same place, this suggests that an old claimant to the title of Glastonbury Thorn had died around 1860, been succeeded by one that may have lived until 1911, with this being followed by a thorn that lived until 1991.

The blossoming of the common hawthorn at a time when the countryside was greening after the long months of winter must have bolstered its mythical association with good luck, prosperity and renewal. In Germany, a pyre of thorn wood was thought to ease the departure of the souls of the dead and may blossom was conveniently available for May Day fertility rituals. Individual trees could be associated with special powers, like the thorn growing on the green of the Scottish Borders village of Polwarth. Newly married couples would dance around this tree for obvious reasons, and did so since at least the seventeenth century. The original tree has died but is succeeded by two of its saplings, which are protected by railings. Another noted thorn is at Appleton, Cheshire, where the original thorn is reputed to have been an offshoot of the Glastonbury Thorn and to have been planted by a returning crusader, Adam de Dutton, in 1178. The red-flowering tree seems unlike the Glastonbury Thorn, but is a last surviving venue for the 'bawming of thorn' ritual, when the tree is decorated with flowers and ribbons by local children who dance around it singing a May Day song. The origin of the term is not known to the author, though in Lowland Scots a bawm is a silly person.

May Day rituals persisted long after their place in the theology of pagan worship had been forgotten. On the eve of May Day, or in some places at Whitsuntide or midsummer, communities, or else the youths of a village, would go into the woods. They might return with a maypole, though in places as far apart as the English Midlands and Ireland a young tree as tall as a building was brought back for each household and set up in front of their house. Travelling in Westmeath in 1682, Sir Henry Piers reported on the practice of erecting tall slender trees and leaving them standing almost the whole year. It caused some confusion amongst the drinking fraternity, for a bush was the conventional sign of an inn (quoted in Rodgers, 1941, p.11). The Arbor Tree at Aston-on-Clun in Shropshire, a black poplar, is dressed with flags every Oak Apple Day (29 May), reputedly to commemorate the wedding of two local villagers in 1786. However, explanations diverge and the story seems to have become blurred with the passing years. Perhaps Mary Carter, the bride, endowed an existing flag-dressing custom that may have originated in a ceremony directed against witchcraft, or perhaps John Marston was anxious to avoid a second childless marriage (Morton, 1986 p.503)?

As well as the various trees that were supposed to provide a conduit that would relay the spirit of the dance or ritual to the realms of Supernature, there were a few that were thought to have innately magical powers. The Darley Oak, growing on the margins of Bodmin Moor, was said to cure boils and other diseases in those passing through its hollow trunk. Moreover, those who followed the path around the tree would, it was claimed, have their wishes answered. Most of the medicines available to pre-industrial societies were obtained from the plant kingdom and trees were associated with a wide range of therapeutic effects. Some products derived from trees had genuine pharmaceutical properties, while the remainder probably exerted considerable placebo effects. The black poplar was reputed to have several medicinal properties: water dripping from the trunk was said to cure warts and an ointment derived from its buds could be used to treat bruises. Certain landmark trees, like the Darley Oak, were thought to have particular powers, but normally 'cures' could be obtained from any individual of the relevant species concerned. Nail clippings from a fever sufferer should be sealed in a hole cut in an aspen tree; toothache could be cured by driving a nail into the painful tooth, and then hammering the nail into an oak (by which time, one imagines that the sufferer would have more than toothache to worry about), while some tree derivatives were said to endow one with visionary powers. Among the superstitious (minority?), trees and timber also served as charms, with ash repelling snakes and maple doing the same to bats – though these could hardly have been much of a household problem. Then, when all the cures and charms had been found wanting, a churchyard rowan protected a coffin left in its shade and, later, elder branches in the coffin gave the corpse protection against evil spirits. However, a measure of cynicism seems to have been present at all times, even among the advocates of tree-based cures. In his *Herball* of 1597 John Gerard commented on the suitability of the box for making boxes and dagger haftes, in contrast to its medicinal shortcomings '... though foolish emperickes and Woman leeches doe minister it against Apoplexie, and such diseases'.

It is plain that, in medieval and earlier times, trees had a wealth of mystic associations. Certain individual trees were thought to have supernatural powers or to serve as links to the spirit world. Other powers were shared across all the members of a species. Beech, it is claimed, had a name which derived from books formed from slivers of timber used as pages – and the tree was accorded symbolic links with learning as a result. Today, we may encounter the last remnants of ceremonies with half-remembered meanings or find hints of superstitions linked to trees in old documents. Yet it is certainly not clear whether tree cults, tree magic and mythology were part and parcel of ancient and medieval life, or whether those who were involved in such things were often regarded as 'ignorant' by their fellows, as suggested by the author of the Taunton charter quoted above.

Less speculative territory is occupied by the large numbers of landmark trees that have achieved celebrity through their association with a notable historical personage. In some cases, historical sources confirm the links concerned, though in others the connection may have been formed by the conflation of different legends, confusion or invention. Also, to the untutored mind it may sometimes have seemed that a tree with remarkable qualities must/should have a patron or planter of comparable stature in the human world. Usually, the tree concerned seems too young to fit the bill, like Kett's Oak at Hethersett in Norfolk, which appears too small to have sheltered the firebrand when he addressed protesters against enclosure in 1549 (Stokes, 2002, p.44). In contrast, the Sidney Oak at Penhurst Place, Kent, appears too old to have been planted to mark the birth of Queen Elizabeth's poet, campaigner and patron of the arts, Sir Philip Sidney. Had it been planted in 1554 is unlikely to have had a commodious hollow bole within less than 250 years, as the records show it to have had (Stokes, p.66).

Generally, the historical realities of landmark trees are shrouded and the stories that are conveyed are founded in folklore and in legends that evolve somewhat with each successive generation of tellers. As their origins were not recorded by reliable contemporaneous writers, they may be factually unrooted – and often there is a troubling gap between the supposed origin of the story and its first recorded mention. One case that is notable because it has been subjected to academically rigorous scrutiny concerns the Royal Oak at Boscobel in Shropshire. This tree, reputedly the one in which Charles II hid after his army was defeated at Worcester in 1651, gave rise to scores of inn names (inn names tended to change quite frequently and so the adoption of a new one was easily done). Recently, the legend was explored by Stamper (2002). The king fled from the battlefield with a host of about 60 and Lord Derby suggested that Boscobel might be a good destination. Charles thought that so large a party was bound to attract attention and he went first to White Ladies, held by the Catholic Cotton family and less than a mile to the south west of Boscobel. Charles then hid at White Ladies while his party rode off, soon adopting a rustic disguise and hiding in a wood called 'Spring Coppice' (both words mean the same thing). He then planned to take a ferry across the Severn, but found the crossing guarded and hid in a barn, later resorting to Boscobel. Having spent the night of 5–6 September there, he felt that both the house and the wood were too dangerous and he decided that, along with another Royalist fugitive, Maj. William Careless, he would pass the next day in the crown of an oak. In the account that he dictated to Pepys, the noted diarist, he chose a great oak that had been pollarded four years earlier and was now '… grown out very bushy and thick and could not be seen through …', though the tree did allow the refugees to prospect for danger. However, the tree was an uncomfortable perch and he returned to Boscobel House for the night, travelling to Moseley Hall for the following night and eventually sailing from Sussex to France and nine years of exile.

The character of the king's tree as a mature, recently pollarded oak is not in doubt, though its exact identity is. However, within a decade of the events one tree had been singled out for that designation and was identified in an engraving of the locality by Wenceslaus Hollar in 1660, the year of Charles's return. Shortly afterwards, the first visitors began to arrive, with bits of the object of their journey being hacked and yanked off as souvenirs. The then owners of Boscobel, the Fitzherberts, were obliged to take the novel action of building a high wall around the trunk, with access to it being gained via a door in the wall. This wall was replaced by another in 1787, and this by the still-surviving iron railings. However, Royalists delighted in possessing little boxes, stoppers or whatever made from the tree that had sheltered their king. By 1706, the attentions of the souvenir takers had apparently proved fatal, though a sapling, believed at the time to be a progeny of the Royal Oak, was growing immediately alongside it and inside the protective wall. This tree then assumed the mantle of its former neighbour, whose roots were now removed and fragmented for the market in mementoes. The younger tree appears to be the current Royal Oak, now in its middle age and enjoying the guardianship of the state, though this could not save it from rot and the lightning strike that badly damaged it in October 2000. It is pleasing and fortunate that the most interesting of the stories concerning celebrity-linked landmark trees is a story that is much better grounded in historical facts than most of the accounts that confront historians.

A point that emerges from these case studies of landmark trees is that each one is regarded as having special powers, antiquity or associations. When these trees reach the end of their natural lives, society and tradition are often not prepared to countenance their death and disappearance. Instead, they are endowed with a kind of immortality. The Glastonbury Thorn survives in numerous places in the forms of cuttings from the tree that was itself a successor of successors. Similarly, the Royal Oak was perpetuated by a seedling developing inside the protective wall that surrounded the trunk of the old tree and gave the (probable) progeny immunity from grazing beasts. The Hunter's Oak at St Dominic in Cornwall is another successor tree and the Shire Oak had a title that seems to have been inherited through generations of trees. The place name 'Schirokes', including the Old English term for a boundary, was recorded in 1160, suggesting a tree or trees that were precursors of the famous Shire Oak that died around 1800. It seems to have passed its mantle to a tree that was mature when the original tree died for, in 1874, Louisa Charlotte Frampton wrote: 'I have 71 Oaks. Three, remarkable only for size, are the Three Shire Oak, which drips over 777 square yards, & shades a part of 3 counties, York Derby, & Nottingham; the Spread Oak in Worksop Park, which could shelter 1,000 horse, & the Newnham Courtenay, which sheltered 2,420 men' (*op.cit.*). It is not clear whether she was quoting from old records, for a new Shire Oak, planted some time before 1864, was said to have been felled by vandals and there was no official Shire Oak until 1951, when the Mayor of Worksop planted a sapling, which died, but was succeeded by one planted by local residents.

In Britain today, the landmark tree in some respects enjoys better protection than before. The rise of the environmental movement in the second half of the last century created a popular emotional and political climate in which organisations concerned with trees, like *The Woodland Trust* and *The Tree Council*, could enjoy the advantages of mass support and sympathy. Equally, the development of nationwide television broadcasting allowed items of tree-related news that might previously not have extended beyond a village community to engage the attention of millions. At the same time, mass travel capabilities linked to the media interest in heritage topics have stimulated awareness. Meanwhile, however, and largely in imitation of habits in the USA, this has become an extremely litigious society, with television and other advertisements encouraging legal actions at the least provocation. In countless offices and transport departments there are officials who would far rather fell a largely harmless tree than see their employers risk incurring damages as a consequence of falling branches – no matter how small these risks may be (for potential risks, see Griffin, 1997, pp.227-30). These problems are compounded by widespread ignorance concerning the nature and management of trees. Oaks that are hollow and stag-headed are frequently considered to be on the verge of death and a dangerous collapse, though stag-headed trees can live for century after century. Similarly within what might be called a 'jobsworth culture' trees that could be made safe and stable by re-pollarding are often felled to the ground. To the damage caused by poorly founded fears of litigation are added those concerning a simpler form of selfishness. There are means by which a landowner/householder can get rid of a tree shading a garden or standing across a view no matter how much official designation and supposed protection it may enjoy, and the less scrupulous of 'tree surgeons' are not slow to proffer their advice on how this can be done. Countless trees with centuries of life in them and which pose no conceivable threat are removed on the basis of false premises. For all the alarmism, trees are not disposed to fall apart and '… on sound stems or trunks it was difficult to determine the extent of the cutting required. We found that at least 95 per cent of a stem's cross section had to be severed before it gave way and fractured' (Finch, 1997 p.236 quoting Finch, 1996).

It is clear that the more the litigation culture is allowed to flourish, and the more that the legal system favours the trespasser and the fool rather than the owner or tenant of land, then the more landowners who would otherwise be content to preserve veteran trees will have them cut down. It seems ridiculous that the owner of a tree should feel obliged to prop up the drooping branches of an ancient tree with expensive posts in case a bit of a bough might land on a person who had no business being there. Surely people who are sufficiently talented as to avoid sticking their fingers in electric sockets or drowning in the bath will recognise the risks of standing under sagging branches – but faced with a choice between engineering, litigation and felling, many tree owners will choose the easiest option.

In the past, landmark trees featured prominently in the perception of landscape by communities whose lives were shaped by property rights, obligations and the political geography of the local countryside. Today, trees symbolise the wholesome character of the natural world to societies threatened by toxins of their own creation. In the USA, 'Landmark Tree' has become an official designation provided to honour and protect selected trees. Public authorities have appointed special committees to review appropriate trees for inclusion in this category. Choosing from the multitude of examples, in south-east Alaska, Landmark Tree sites are scored according to the dimensions of the largest tree and the wood volume of the surrounding acre. Beginning as an effort to broaden Alaskan eco-tourism that was focused on whales, bears and glaciers, the project found success in deepening environmental awareness among Alaskan residents. In the very different environment of Monterey in California, Local Landmark Trees have been designated because of their health and unusual size or prominence, the selection being made following field review and discussion by members of the city's Architectural Review Committee.

But we must not allow localised successes to blur the broad view, for the last century has been a woeful period for old trees:

Most of the first half of it was taken up by resource-draining wars. The middle years saw the development of revolutionary mechanised tree-cutting equipment, earth moving and grubbing-out machinery and powerful herbicides. Finally, ground water removal, chemical-fertiliser enrichment and the unprecedented scale of fossil-fuel burning have made the environment hostile for them; especially those which have spent nine tenths of their lives in the relative tranquillity of the past (White, 1997, p.226).

There is a powerful, utilitarian branch of the heritage industry that cannot see an object of interest without wanting to stick a visitor centre in front of it, and which often seems blind to the value of anything that lacks a visitor centre. However, trees do not flourish as tourist attractions and the compaction of their sites by trampling, the building of hard-surfaced car parks, climbing, cutting, carving and swinging all cause trouble. Sadly, even the ancient trees slumbering out in the pastures are unsafe and, as a commentary on modern society, cattle are now pumped so full of powerful chemicals that their very dung scorches and scars the bark on which it lands.

REFERENCES

Barrington, D., 1769, *Philosophical Transactions of the Royal Society*, 59, p.23.
Bennett, J.A.W., 1986, *Middle English Literature*, Clarendon Press, Oxford.
Coulton, G.G., 1925, *The Medieval Village*, Cambridge University Press, Cambridge.
Dowsett, J.M., 1942, *The Romance of England's Forests*, Gifford, London.
Field, J., 1972, *English Field Names*, David and Charles, Newton Abbot.
Finch, R., 1996, 'Veteran trees', A paper presented to the 30th National Arboricultural Conference and Technical Seminar, Exeter, September 1996.
Finch, R, 1997, 'Caring for veterans, the practicalities', *Quarterly Journal of Forestry*, 91, 3, pp.231–236.
Gelling, M., 1993, *Place names in the Landscape*, Dent, London.
Griffin, N., 1997, 'Problems from a slippery slope? Veteran trees and the law', *Quarterly Journal of Forestry*, 91, 3, pp.227–230.
Grundy, G.B., 1931, *Saxon Charters of Worcestershire*, Birmingham Archaeological Society, Birmingham.
Hart, C.R., 1975, *The Early Charters of Northern England and the North Midlands*, Leicester University Press.
Hooke, D., 1998, *Anglo Saxon England*, Leicester University Press, London.
Humphrys, G., 1998, 'Glastonbury's Christmas Tree', *History Today*, **Dec.** 1998.
Machel, T., 1695, Westmorland Additions to Camden's *Britannia*, reprinted by David and Charles, Newton Abbot.
Miller, C., 1994, *Early Travellers in North America*, Alan Sutton, Stroud.
Mitchell, A.F., 1974, *A Field Guide to the Trees of Britain and Northern Europe*, Collins, London.
Morton, A., 1986, *The Trees of Shropshire*. Airlife Publishing Ltd., Shrewsbury.
Muir, R., 2000, 'Pollards in Nidderdale: A Landscape History' *Rural History*, 11.1, pp 95–111.
Muir, R., 2001, *Landscape Detective*, Windgather, Macclesfield.
Quelch, P.R., 1997, 'Ancient Trees of Scotland', in *Scottish Woodland History* (edited by Smout, T.C.), Scottish Cultural Press, Dalkeith.
Rackham, O., 1976, *Trees and Woodland in the British Landscape*, Dent, London.

Raistrick, A., 1991, 'The Thorn Tree' in D. Joy, (ed.), *Arthur Raistrick's Yorkshire Dales*, Dalesman, Clapham.

Read, H.,1999, *Veteran Trees: A Guide to Good Management*, English Nature, Peterborough.

Rodger, D., Stokes, J. and Ogilvie, J., 2003, *Heritage Trees of Scotland*, The Tree Council, London.

Rodgers, J., 1941, *The English Woodland*, Batsford, London.

Speight, H.,1894, *Nidderdale and the Garden of the Nidd*, Elliot Stock, London.

Spirn, A.W.,1998, *The Language of Landscape*, Yale University Press, New Haven.

Stamper, P., 2002, 'The Tree That Hid a King: The Royal Oak at Boscobel, Shropshire', *LANDSCAPES*, 3.1, pp.19-34.

Stokes, J., 2002, *Great British Trees*, The Tree Council, London.

Stubbes, P., 1583, *Anatomie of Abuses*, London.

Todd, G., 1824, *Some Account of Sheriff Hutton Castle*, no publisher listed.

Trollope, F.,1832, *Domestic Manners of the Americans*, Whittaker and Treacher, London.

White, J., 1997, 'What is a veteran tree and where are they all?', *Quarterly Journal of Forestry*, 91, no.3, pp.222-226.

White, J., 1999, 'Estimating the Age of Large and Veteran Trees in Britain', *Forest Information Note 250*.

Williamson, G.C., 1922, *Lady Anne Clifford*, Titus Wilson, Kendal.

3

Ancient trees and hedgerows

People accustomed to the more recent countrysides tend to imagine hedgerows as alignments of shrubs that are all trimmed to a uniform height and will tend to overlook the importance of mature trees as hedgerow components. This popular perception of the hedgerow fits most, though not all, Parliamentary Enclosure hedgerows, but it certainly does not accord with those inherited from pre-Georgian times. Moreover, the old hedgerows that we see today contain far fewer standard or pollarded trees than they did in early Victorian times. There is possibly no facet of the countryside that has been the subject of more confusion and misunderstanding than the hedgerow. A large portion of this misunderstanding derived from the enthusiasm for 'hedgerow dating' that was current in both academic and amateur enthusiast circles during recent decades. Since the 'technique' is not only flawed, but fundamentally wrong, it has led to a misdirection of effort and badly confused interpretations of hedgerows. The best understanding of traditional hedgerows derives not from counting remaining species but from examining real historical evidence, such as the old pictorial representations of them and the manorial documents that reveal their nature and uses.

From early maps and pictorial images one gets a picture of pre-industrial lowland countrysides that were tightly enmeshed by hedgerows, with the short lengths of hedgerow shrubs being punctuated by tall, quite closely spaced trees. Meanwhile, however, written records were slanted for the humbler resources of the hedgerows; their trees and their herbs were exploited by the common people who were illiterate. The lords of manors, whose views the clerks recorded, were largely interested in hedges in terms of their proper maintenance, their role as property boundaries, their ability to keep horn out of corn and the need to trim them to prevent the obstruction of lanes and trackways. Fuel and dead-hedging materials to the feudal tenant were theft and vandalism to their lord. Consequently, the detailed structure, management and contents of hedgerows tend to be poorly documented. Terminology can be confusing and in the period

Above Hedge laying in progress. The pleachers have been severed, leaving just a living hinge of tissue, and woven between posts and the heathering is being twisted into the top of the hedge

Left An excellent newly-layed Cambridgeshire hedge

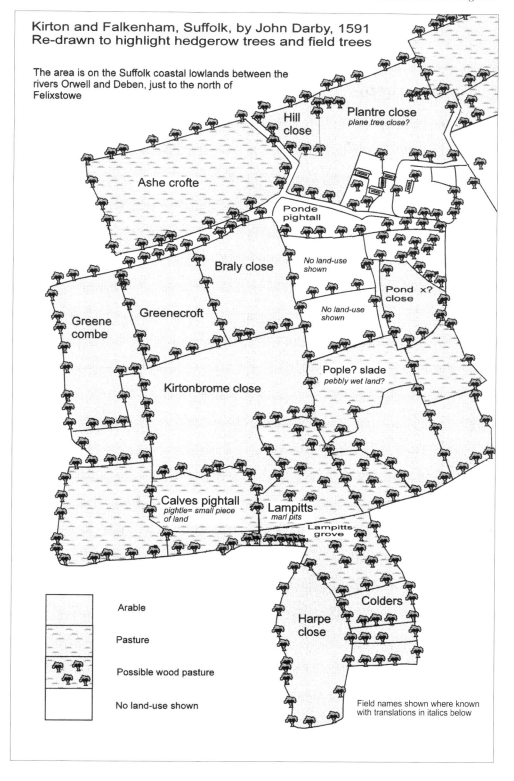

Kirton and Falkenham, Suffolk, by John Darby, 1591
Re-drawn to highlight hedgerow trees and field trees

The area is on the Suffolk coastal lowlands between the
rivers Orwell and Deben, just to the north of
Felixstowe

Hill
close

Plantre close
plane tree close?

Ashe crofte

Ponde
pightall

Braly close

No land-use
shown

Pond x?
close

Greenecroft

Greene
combe

No land-use
shown

Kirtonbrome close

Pople? slade
pebbly wet land?

Calves pightall
*pightle= small piece
of land*

Lampitts
- marl pits

Lampitts
grove

Colders

Harpe
close

Arable

Pasture

Possible wood pasture

No land-use shown

Field names shown where known
with translations in italics below

around the Norman Conquest the term 'haie', deriving from an Old English 'hedgerow' word, could be used to describe small woods or hedged assarts or even parks as well as hedges themselves. In 1285, Sir Robert Plumpton was granted rights of pannage and allowed to assart the woods of Bircom, Loxley, and Hadlaugh, in the Forest of Knaresborough, and was also allowed the right to assart the hays growing in the 'cultures' or furlongs of ploughland on the east side of a ditch and hedge running from Plumpton to the banks of the Nidd (quoted in Grainge, 1871, p.58). These hays are unlikely to have been hedgerows and were more likely to have been small woods interspersed among the plough strips. Often, it is difficult to deduce whether a hedge referred to in a manorial document was a 'quick' or living one, or whether it was a dead hedge – a short-term barrier of cut and woven brushwood and thorns used, say, to exclude livestock from a field at a particular period, or to pen them in a certain place. To add to the complexity, materials for dead-hedging were obtained from pollarded thorns in living hedges. Whether a hedge was treeless or packed with pollards would normally go completely unremarked in early documents, though the early pictorial representations – on Elizabethan estate maps, for example – show most hedgerows as being packed with trees. Most had probably been thus for quite some time.

Like the free-standing 'landmark' trees, hedgerows featured frequently as boundary marks in Anglo-Saxon charters. Commonly, boundaries will have followed hedges, or the ditches at their feet but, although mentions of hedgerows in these charters are very numerous, the nature of the hedges themselves is not described. Undoubtedly, the hedgerows were managed in accordance with some of the systems still current in the medieval and later centuries. In his campaign against the Nervii, who lived on what are now the marchlands of France and Belgium, in 57 BC, Julius Caesar described encountering strong hedges that could only have been produced by effective laying techniques. Informers told him of

> … a tactic of the Nervii developed long ago because their cavalry was almost non-existent – indeed to this day they pay no attention to that arm, preferring to rely entirely on their infantry forces – and they had to find a way of thwarting the cavalry forces of neighbouring tribes when they made plundering raids on them. They had succeeded in making hedges that were almost like walls by cutting into saplings, bending them over, and intertwining thorns and brambles among the dense side branches that grew out. These hedges provided such protection that it was impossible to see through them, let alone penetrate them. Since the march of our column would be hindered by such obstacles, the Nervii thought that the proposed plan should be tried (Julius Caesar, *Battle for Gaul*, translated by Wiseman and Wiseman, p.50).

In the course of the battle, some legions were unable to adopt proper formations as: '…their view was hampered by the very thick hedges described above; it

Trees may not be as old as the boundary on which they stand. When the two hedgerow trees were very young, this lane was part of the main road from York to Lancaster, but the route itself is Roman in age

was impossible to find fixed points at which to position our reserves, or to see ahead what was needed in each part of the field, or indeed for any one man to give all the commands that were necessary' (*op. cit.* pp.51-2). Perhaps Caesar was exaggerating the problems posed by a network of dense but unexceptional agricultural hedgerows? They can scarcely have been objects of mystery, for the classical sources are packed with references to the use and planting of hedges and the Roman writer Cato implied that trees were included when he advocated boundary hedges of elm and poplar, which would produce both timber and browse. In Britain, it is known that when the Roman fort at Bar Hill on the Antonine Wall was built, around AD 142, pre-existing field ditches were infilled with turves and bundles of brushwood from managed hawthorn hedges. Environmental and circumstantial evidence carry hedgerows back into the Bronze Age and beyond, though, as before, the presence of a tree content is harder to demonstrate.

Hedges are frequently mentioned in the boundary clauses of Anglo-Saxon charters. For example, in the grant of land at Rolleston, Staffordshire by Aethelred II to Abbot Wulfgeat in 1008, boundary marks include a 'great thorn', a hedged pen or '*haeg stowe*', a '*scid haege*' that was perhaps a fence of split boughs or a dead hedge, another hedge and a '*dic haege*' that might have been a ditched, or hedged and ditched, enclosure and another hedged pen, pound or enclosure.

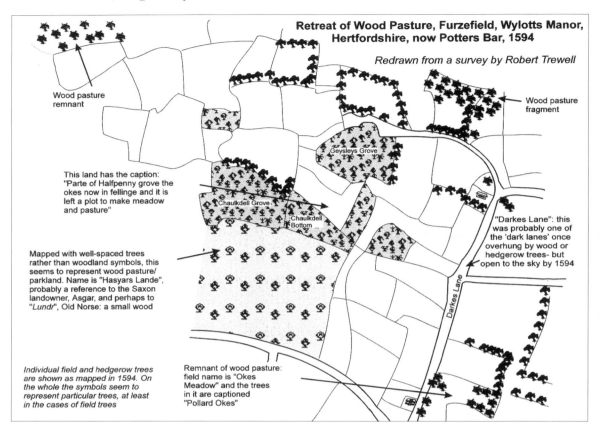

Retreat of Wood Pasture, Furzefield, Wylotts Manor, Hertfordshire, now Potters Bar, 1594

Redrawn from a survey by Robert Trewell

Wood pasture remnant

Wood pasture fragment

This land has the caption: "Parte of Halfpenny grove the okes now in fellinge and it is left a plot to make meadow and pasture"

Geysleys Grove

Chaulkdell Grove

Chaulkdell Bottom

"Darkes Lane": this was probably one of the 'dark lanes' once overhung by wood or hedgerow trees- but open to the sky by 1594

Mapped with well-spaced trees rather than woodland symbols, this seems to represent wood pasture/ parkland. Name is "Hasyars Lande", probably a reference to the Saxon landowner, Asgar, and perhaps to "*Lundr*", Old Norse: a small wood

Darkes Lane

Individual field and hedgerow trees are shown as mapped in 1594. On the whole the symbols seem to represent particular trees, at least in the cases of field trees

Remnant of wood pasture: field name is "Okes Meadow" and the trees in it are captioned "Pollard Okes"

Here we see the difficulties of discriminating between living and dead hedges, fences and 'sikes' or ditches that may or may not have followed hedges. After the Norman Conquest the documentary evidence for trees standing in hedgerows is surer, though the mentions of trees are often oblique. The use of dead-hedging continued during most of the period, though it cannot always be differentiated from quick-hedging. In 1175/85 nuns of Syningthwaite, West Yorkshire, had a grant confirmed of a house in Guiseley, a large area of common pasture and dry wood from two townships 'for burning and hedge-making' (Farrer, 1914 pp.169-70). It seems certain that the wood was for use in dead-hedging, though cut posts as well as wands for weaving in the heathering along the top of a new hedge were often employed in laying a living hedge. Manorial tenants often enjoyed the right of heybote or of taking stakes and brushwood for the making of impermanent barriers. These were useful in fencing-off crops and could be removed to allow beasts to graze the stubble and aftermath. Numerous cases and disputes concerned the operation of the system and at Minchinhampton in Gloucestershire in 1273, one Adam of Forwood was charged that: '… he had his fences around the field of Westfield carried off before the term'. He replied that: '… the reapers and others carried off part of the hedges so that in many

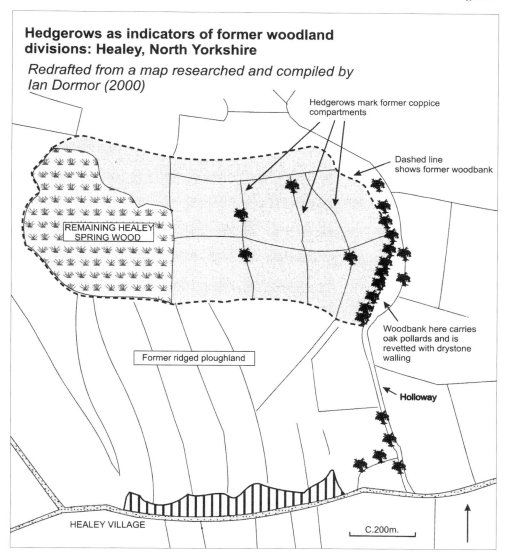

Hedgerows as indicators of former woodland divisions: Healey, North Yorkshire

Redrafted from a map researched and compiled by Ian Dormor (2000)

Hedgerows mark former coppice compartments

Dashed line shows former woodbank

REMAINING HEALEY SPRING WOOD

Woodbank here carries oak pollards and is revetted with drystone walling

Former ridged ploughland

Holloway

HEALEY VILLAGE

C.200m.

places there was an entry, so that cattle had a common entry before he carried off anything' (Homans, p.66).

Living trees were important as sources of materials for dead hedges and sometimes this was the sole cutting tolerated by the manor courts. Thus, at Waterbeach cum Denny in Cambridgeshire in 1349, a marshy enclosure was granted 'Excepting all trees thereon growing or which should grow, saving the lop of the said trees for hedgbote' (court book, 22 Ed. III). A high proportion of references to trees in manor court rolls concerns their conservation and the punishment of illegal felling. At Ripley in the years around 1600 there was a spate of hedge-breaking for the manor court to deal with. It is not clear if this represented opposition to enclosures or a need for fuel. In one case, a specific tree is mentioned: Thomas Holdsworth was at the mercy of the court on 16 April 1649 because he: '… cut down a tree called in English *a Crabtree* in Robert Bransbye's hedge' (Ingilby MS 1607, no.13). Hedges were plainly subject to the illegal incursions of humans, and the activities of a man employed in stealing masses of dead-hedging materials, seemingly to hedge coppiced stumps, were reported to his master by William Bywell of Middleham in Wensleydale: 'Sir I am sory to inform you that Joseph Courts has a man cutin the quick fences in a destructive manor and in unproper tim of the year wich is A nuf to Distroy them' (Ian Dormor, pers. comm.).

The courts, which were responsible for local routeways, took a different attitude towards trees when their branches obstructed highways and tracks, and it is in this context that we find clear references to hedgerow trees. Manor courts devoted much of their time to the imposition of fines on those who had failed to scour ditches or cut back the growth of road- and track-side trees and hedges. The frequency of their fining demonstrates the extent to which their demands were ignored. An acquaintance with these records creates a picture of travellers whose journeys were frequently made unpleasant or, indeed, dangerous by overhanging boughs, snagging thorns and flooding. Thus, in 1537, tenants were required to clear trees overhanging a lane near West Hall (West House, Cringlesworth, West Yorkshire) that led to a ford on the R. Calder – the fact that they had neglected to do so was shown by a repeat of this demand later in that year (Darbyshire and Lumb, p.202).

There are sufficient references to roadside trees to show that medieval routeways were frequently lined by trees/hedgerow trees. For example, in West Yorkshire:

> A number of well defined holloways in the country are tree-lined, the branches blocking out the daylight along the path resulting in their being described as 'dark lane'. At least three such survive as public footpaths. The eastern part of the 'Wakefield Gate' in Southowram township is called Dark Lane where it climbs the approaches of Beacon Hill, the section on the plateau of the hill being known by the name Barrowclough Lane, taken from a deserted medieval settlement beside the route. Dark Lane in Barwick in Elmet runs east-west to the north of the village, providing access to the medieval fields which lay on either side of the medieval route, and covered for much of its length by an umbrella of trees. Leak Hall in Cumberworth township has a well pronounced holloway called Dark Lane running north from the site, also overhung by trees (Faull and Moorhouse (eds), pp.631-2).

These 'dark lanes' or 'hidden roads' were a source of concern to the authorities, partly because of the out-grown branches that obstructed movement, and also because the shade and gloom could harbour wrong-doers. However, the trees will also have served a number of uses, including some relating to the road itself. There are medieval and slightly later references to 'brigtrees'. These seem to have been rough-hewn planks that were placed across roadside ditches to provide bridges to adjacent dwellings and fields. Sometimes, they seem to have been used to provide firmer going for wheeled vehicles on rutted, muddy roads. (*ibid,* p.161).

Throughout the medieval period and its immediate aftermath, our perceptions of the landscape are constructed by inferences from the highly localised information derived from manor court rolls, leases, boundary perambulations and so on. One may seem to be peeping at places through keyholes, with most of the setting hidden in the shadows and with even the tiny areas that can be viewed being seen in hazy and partial manners. Then, with the appearance of the estate maps commissioned by landowners in Elizabethan times, it is as though great floodlights have been trained on swathes of historical countryside and we see whole landscapes in such detail that individual trees are marked. Cartographers had gradually been acquiring skills during the closing phases of the medieval period. The Boarstall plan of 1444 is said to be the earliest surviving representation of an English village and its setting. It shows the Buckinghamshire village (that was destined to wither) set in a well-wooded countryside. Hedges surround the settlement, its open fields and its pastures. Beyond them are woods and the boundary of one, labelled 'Frith', is marked by a hedge punctuated by pollards, two of which seem to have blossom or crops of fruits, with one seeming to have oak leaves.

The Boarstall map combines a plan view with pictorial images of trees, deer, buildings and so on. The convention of combining spatial relationships with pictorial representations was also employed in a symbolical plan of York of the early fifteenth century (*British Library Harley MS* 1808 fol.45v). The map would have been of little use in navigating around the walled city, which was dominated by images of the archbishop and of three maids bathing in the open air. However the area outside the walls was filled with illustrations of trees, including elongated ones around the walls which were apparently shredded, while in the surroundings were pollards, some shown as ancient and stag-headed, as well as spiky symbols, probably representing coppiced trees. The tendency to combine plan views with side-on images of buildings and trees continued, but with more attention to proper scale and with greater accuracy in the chain-based surveys. In 1607, John Norden, one of the advocates and exponents of good cartography, posed the question of whether the landowner might not do better to look at the real estate than at a painted replica but answered:

A plot rightly drawne by true information, discribeth so the lively image of a mannor, and every branch and member of the same, as the lord sitting in his chayre, may see what he hath, and where and how he lyeth, and in whole use and occupation of every particular is upon suddaine view (pp.16-17).

The aspiring cartographers of the late Middle Ages seem to have been groping for ways to convert the skills and conventions associated with the illumination of

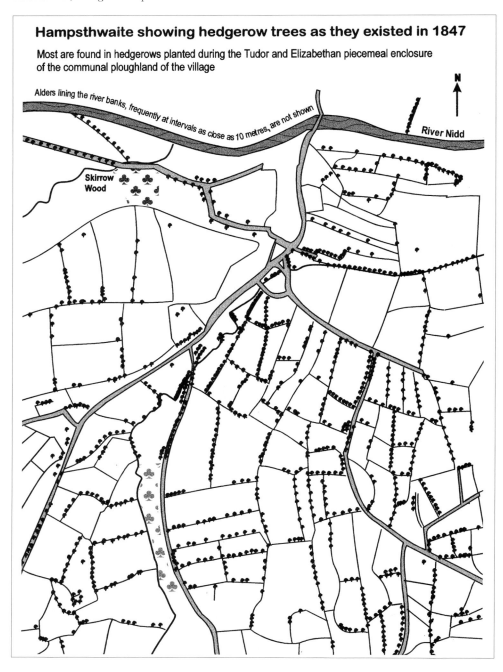

Hampsthwaite showing hedgerow trees as they existed in 1847

Most are found in hedgerows planted during the Tudor and Elizabethan piecemeal enclosure of the communal ploughland of the village

Alders lining the river banks, frequently at intervals as close as 10 metres, are not shown

River Nidd

N

Skirrow Wood

manuscripts into efficient maps. The earliest attempts to represent topographical features, appearing around 1300, were crude sketches associated with issues and disputes concerning the ownership of small pieces of territory. By about 1450–1500 this technique had been developed so that the plan of the demesne lands of Chertsey Abbey (probably the most frequently reproduced English medieval

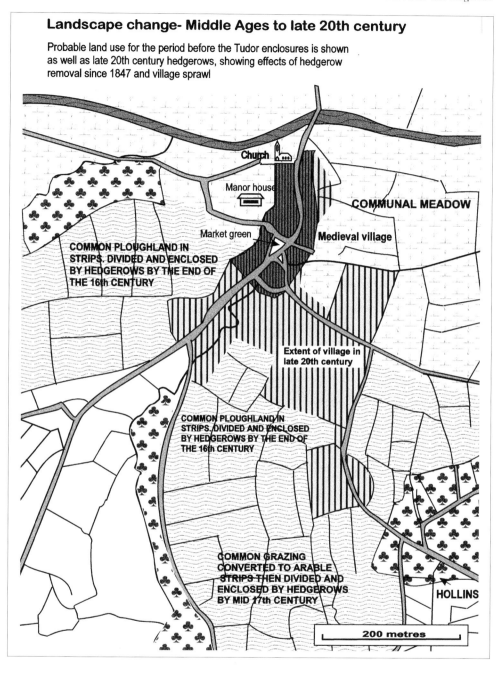

Landscape change- Middle Ages to late 20th century

Probable land use for the period before the Tudor enclosures is shown as well as late 20th century hedgerows, showing effects of hedgerow removal since 1847 and village sprawl

Church

Manor house

COMMUNAL MEADOW

Market green

Medieval village

COMMON PLOUGHLAND IN STRIPS, DIVIDED AND ENCLOSED BY HEDGEROWS BY THE END OF THE 16th CENTURY

Extent of village in late 20th century

COMMON PLOUGHLAND IN STRIPS, DIVIDED AND ENCLOSED BY HEDGEROWS BY THE END OF THE 16th CENTURY

COMMON GRAZING CONVERTED TO ARABLE STRIPS THEN DIVIDED AND ENCLOSED BY HEDGEROWS BY MID 17th CENTURY

HOLLINS

200 metres

map) had a refined appearance even though the spatial relationships were but sketchily shown. The abbey, watermill, bridge and other buildings were drawn with fine draughtsmanship; field names and crude boundaries were shown. Pollarded trees were drawn at either end of a mill outbuilding, one of them having recently been partly lopped for fodder or fuel.

During the sixteenth century, improvements to cartography accelerated. In its last two decades, a stage was reached whereby the owners of estates were able to commission surveys of their lands at large scales that were drawn to a good standard of accuracy; that showed the countryside in considerable detail, and that reasonably represented the relationships between places. The abundance of maps surviving from the years around 1600 demonstrates the considerable demand that existed for them. Such maps could be attached to written documents concerning the ownership of lands; the holdings and duties of tenants' and the evidence relating to property/boundary disputes. A 'terrier' or other document concerning the ownership of property carried more weight when linked to a map that clearly outlined its location and bounds. Some of the surveyors and cartographers were freelance operators, like Christopher Saxton and his son, Robert, though some benefited from positions of privilege, like the other father-and-son duo, John and John Norden, who jointly held the Surveyorship of the Duchy of Cornwall. Subsequent events ensured that the demand for estate plans remained buoyant. In Ireland, the seventeenth-century Plantation of the Gaelic lands by Scots and English colonists produced a hunger for maps of the forfeited lands. In Scotland the defeat of many of the Highland clans at Culloden in 1746 also resulted in the alienation of estates, while in England the accelerating agricultural changes brought a need for updated surveys.

While these estate maps were produced (at large but varying scales) to workmanlike standards of accuracy, their conventions were not standardised. Generally, the area of each field in acres/perches was shown and sometimes the name of the tenant concerned was written on the field or identified by a code letter linked to a key in the margins. For our purposes, some of the maps had special value, as when the numbers of trees in each field (usually hedgerow trees allocated to one field or another) are given in tables or, in cases like the Feckenham map of 1591, where there is a differentiation between the old demesne and assarted land. Woodland was normally represented by carefully drawn tree symbols. However, there is often no symbolic differentiation between wood pasture, coppice and un-coppiced woodland – or else a variation in symbols is not explained and might be lost in an accompanying document. In these cases, names on the map, like 'coppice', 'fall' or 'spring', are needed to designate types of management.

These maps almost invariably indicate field names and they demonstrate the universality of the practice of naming of fields. By providing a record of names in a locality at a cross-section in time, the estate maps are useful historical records. More importantly, the names also contain information about the evolution of the countryside. All the 'royds', 'stubbs', 'riddings' and 'sarts' incorporated in field names tell of lands that were cleared of trees during the medieval era, while some fields were named after then-remarkable trees standing in them, like plane trees, walnut trees or landmark oaks.

Hedgerows and hedgerow trees are also marked. Sometimes the hedgerow is just a line, sometimes a rather bobbling line, suggestive of a row of shrubs.

Trees are often shown standing well above the line of shrubs but there may be uncertainty about whether the cartographer was employing symbols to represent an unspecific tree/shrub combination, or whether each tree plotted was a real individual. The latter seems to be the case in the many examples where the trees are mapped at irregular intervals. Where there are two, three or more quite closely spaced trees separated by a broad gap the mapping seems representative of reality. Yet whether the representation of trees and shrubs is precise or stylised, one is left in no doubt that the hedgerows of England, Wales and the Scottish lowlands were usually heavily punctuated by trees. The illustrative and documentary evidence implies that the tree component of the hedgerows was generally pollarded, though shredded examples can sometimes be recognised.

One may wonder where all the tree-rich hedgerows that were mapped by the seventeenth-century cartographers had come from? In Britain today, those hedgerows that survive are essentially of two types. There are those which result from the Parliamentary Enclosures taking place mainly in the eighteenth and nineteenth centuries and there are the others, almost entirely older and sometimes very much older. Generally, the Parliamentary Enclosure hedgerows were planted as a monoculture of nursery-grown quickthorn, at about seven to the yard, though, not too infrequently, a tree component was included. Writing of north-western England, Whyte notes that: 'Hedges often had trees planted in them at regular intervals — at Skelton (Cu) these were mainly oak and ash. In the Eden valley there was a tradition of planting fruit trees — apple but also pear — at regular intervals in the hedges as well' (2003, p.65). The old and ancient hedgerows had a variety of origins. Some could be boundary features of pre-Norman, Roman or even prehistoric vintage. Some definitely resulted from the medieval process of enclosing farmland at the expense of woodland (though the notion that they resulted from alignments of trees left standing by the assarters defies belief). Some must be field boundaries of great antiquity, while others bound roads and lanes of undefined age.

In all such cases, one must avoid the folly of confusing the ages of a boundary with those of its current leafy occupants. In 1998 the author discovered the traces of an abandoned road traversing pastures near Nidderdale. It was successfully identified as a monastic right of way that could be precisely linked to a charter of 1153–73 by which a local landowner granted a right of way to a crossing on the river Nidd at Hampsthwaite to the abbot of Fountains (Muir, 2001, pp.58-9). Alignments of (mainly) old oaks marked each side of the lost 40ft (12.2m) cart road — but there was no question that they could be almost 850 years old like the road. The youngest of them, existing only as a stump, had been less than 200 years old when it was cut down. They had descended from the old roadside hedges and were simply the last survivors of successive generations of roadside trees. (On taking a party from the *Ancient Tree Forum* to see these trees in 2003 it was found that contractors had driven a deep ditch through the roots of the trees.) There

When large, ancient oaks like this one are found aligned along field walls it is likely that the walls have replaced the hedges in which they formerly stood

are, however, some cases where the hedgerow trees now standing are, at least in part, the original trees planted in a medieval hedgerow.

This can be established, for example, by a careful examination of the landscape and its history at Hampsthwaite, lying just across the river from Ripley. Here (and in neighbouring townships) we find hedgerows and the archaeological traces of lost hedgerows that are punctuated by veteran oak trees. There are a few younger oaks, some deriving from the Parliamentary Enclosure era, but the majority are old trees dating, according to the best calculations, to the last phases of the Middle Ages and its Elizabethan aftermath. Landscape research is at its best when field evidence can be combined with historical sources. In this case, the presumed appearance of these now-venerable trees can be tied exactly to a virtual revolution in the countryside when the traditional open fields of communal farming were being eradicated, though on a piecemeal basis, and replaced by networks of privately tenanted fields.

This process began during the fifteenth century and continued through the following century. Often, it involved arrangements between the tenants of neighbouring, open field, arable or meadow strips, who bought, exchanged and reorganised land holdings in order that each should acquire blocks of land that were consolidated in place of the scattered and fragmented patterns of communal farming. Thus, a little further up the dale at Thornthwaite in 1602-3,

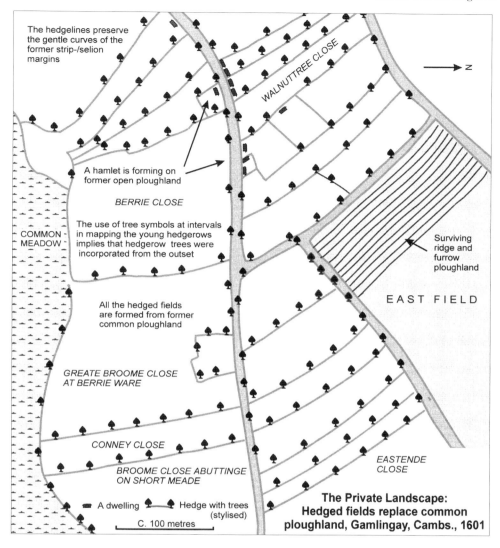

The hedgelines preserve the gentle curves of the former strip-/selion margins

WALNUTTREE CLOSE

N

A hamlet is forming on former open ploughland

BERRIE CLOSE

COMMON MEADOW

The use of tree symbols at intervals in mapping the young hedgerows implies that hedgerow trees were incorporated from the outset

Surviving ridge and furrow ploughland

EAST FIELD

All the hedged fields are formed from former common ploughland

GREATE BROOME CLOSE AT BERRIE WARE

CONNEY CLOSE

BROOME CLOSE ABUTTINGE ON SHORT MEADE

EASTENDE CLOSE

A dwelling   Hedge with trees (stylised)

C. 100 metres

The Private Landscape: Hedged fields replace common ploughland, Gamlingay, Cambs., 1601

Walter Holme gave John England his tiny holdings called *Burntacredale, Lungriggs, Burtredales, Middlestackland, Botholmes, Ing* and *Dale under holme*. In return he got from England ones called *Pickell, Intack, Brodedayle, Fayrepece, Brotts, Phedren and Little Stackhead Land* – and the consolidation process advanced another step (Jennings, 1983, p.131). Larger tenants were emerging who sought to sublet their holdings in coherent units, while lords of manors had been working to disentangle the demesne from the strip networks for quite some time. As these processes proceeded in a piecemeal fashion, the communal landscape was gradually replaced by a privatised one. Boundaries that had previously been marked by a balk, a furrow or a meerstone now had to be made stockproof and this produced a ever-increasing network of hedgerows. At Hampsthwaite it was not just the plough strips or selions that were bundled-up and hedged around.

The 'holmes' or common meadows down on the floodplain of the Nidd were also parcelled out, as, too, were the 'rakes' at Rowden, where rough cow pasture had been held in strips (Jennings, p.130).

Though drystone walls and quick hedges had always existed, the new hedgerows also supplanted the dead hedges of hurdles and thorns that had been used to provide temporary barriers, like those that could be opened to let cattle graze the aftermath on open fields. The privatisation of the landscape disrupted traditional arrangements, affronting rights to commons and freedom of access. As the old commons were fragmented and closed and movement became channelled between the hedgerows defining the narrowed rights of way, so instances of hedge-breaking became more common. At Hampsthwaite, and in countless other places, one can see how the new hedgerow patterns were conditioned by existing countryside features – the snaking margins of old open field selions, the edges of a highway, the sinuous swell of a headland, and so on.

On the modern map we can see how facets of the medieval countryside influenced the patterns of boundaries that we see today. Given that the documents of the Tudor and Elizabethan eras tell us what was happening in the localities and given that one can date many surviving hedgerow trees to that era, it is not unreasonable to presume that these trees were planted as elements in the new hedgerows. Where the materials for the 'quick' or living hedgerows came from (seeds or cuttings?) is often uncertain, but the local woods will have provided oak, ash and elm seedlings and saplings for the tree components. Moreover, oak seedlings can still be dug from the local meadows. Members of the crow family peck and hammer acorns into the ground, where they germinate and their soft stem and leaves endure until the hay crop is cut and livestock come in to graze. In many places, traditional arable land was converted into pasture, while on the new tenancies, release from the communal field/furlong rotations allowed flexible mixed farming rotations to be practised on the old arable lands. Tall hedgerows and their associated trees had value for pastoral farming, sheltering both the pasture and the livestock.

Hedgerows could be crucial sources of timber for burning or for construction works. Turner writes:

> By the late nineteenth century in much of Devon and Cornwall woodland was found most commonly on the steeper valley-sides, and often in relatively small patches. If many areas, like west Cornwall, were largely without extensive woods, the lack of material for fuel or building could be partly remedied by growing crops such as hazel, ash and oak on top of the huge hedge-banks that divided the ancient farmland into fields (2004, pp.22-3)

While the partial privatisation of the countryside greatly increased the need for more property boundaries, hedgerow trees had a long-standing value. When pollarded or shredded, oaks, elms and other common trees produced leafy browse that could conveniently be lopped and tossed down to livestock. If cultivated as a part of the hedgerow, holly would yield only thorny, unpalatable leaves, though when growing tall above the hedge, the thornless upper branches could provide useful winter fodder as described in Chapter 1. Oak was exceptionally useful, with old hedgerow pollards and standards producing the spreading, curving boughs that were ideal sources for the braces of timber-framed buildings. By scrutinising a selection of hedgerow oaks a housewright could discover just the piece of timber that was needed for a particular task. The medieval shipwrights, still producing relatively small craft in fairly modest numbers, looked to the hedgerow oaks for the curving timbers for ribs and prows. Oaks could also be prodigious sources of domestic fuel. In 1392, a man was fined at West Donyland, Essex, manor court, having cut almost 2.5 tons of billets of firewood from the boughs of what must have been an enormous oak (quoted in Rackham, 1986, p.213). In addition, the bark of the oak was a source of tannin, which was used in countless local tanneries. The great value of oak timber was its weatherproof qualities, shared only with the black poplar until the invention of coal- and oil-based preservatives.

All other timbers had their particular uses: hedge-grown ash, with its springy resilience, was preferred by wheelwrights, while the wych elm yielded pliant timber for cart shafts, leaf fodder relished by livestock and an edible inner bark that could be pounded to produce fibres. Perhaps the most potent of the hedgerow trees in terms of rural mythology was the 'shrew ash', an ash whose twigs or branches were believed to effect cures when applied to injured limbs of cattle. These injuries, it was thought, were caused by shrews which, being baneful creatures, had run over the bodies of the afflicted animals to cause them pain. A shrew ash was created by gouging a deep hole in the trunk of an old tree and incarcerating a living shrew in it (Rodgers, 1941, p.14). Ashes were also thought rather good at producing sticks for killing snakes.

The hedgerow trees also provided food in the form of crab apples, wild pears and the fruits of various members of the wild plum family, like the cherry plum (*Prunus cerasifera*), damson (*Prunus domestica*), bullace (*Prunus insititia*) and wild cherry (*Prunus avium*). John Gerard's *Herball* (1597) revealed a wide spectrum of fruit trees growing in the gardens of Elizabethan England – four types of medlar, six of pear, four of crab and numerous cherries. Some of these were deliberately cultivated in hedgerows – he mentioned the quince and pears. Rural societies whose only other experience of sweetness came from honey – also often a hedgerow tree resource – will particularly have valued the presence of fruit trees in their hedgerows. How much of their crop remained after the wild birds had had their fill and how many of the trees were deliberately planted rather than being propagated via the birds, we will not know. It is sometimes said that these hedgerow trees appeared where village labourers had lunched and discarded pips and fruit stones – though this would be very hard to prove. It is plain from the records that hedgerow fruit trees and their products were locally well known,

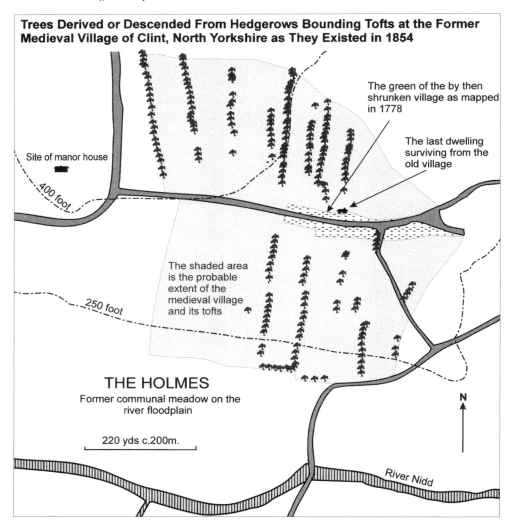

Trees Derived or Descended From Hedgerows Bounding Tofts at the Former Medieval Village of Clint, North Yorkshire as They Existed in 1854

The green of the by then shrunken village as mapped in 1778

The last dwelling surviving from the old village

Site of manor house

400 foot

250 foot

The shaded area is the probable extent of the medieval village and its tofts

THE HOLMES

Former communal meadow on the river floodplain

220 yds c.200m.

N

River Nidd

valued and protected. Some useful trees were deliberately planted in hedgerows, but others could be unplanned assets. Camden's *Britannia* of 1695 quoted William of Malmesbury's book *De Pontificibus* on the subject of Gloucestershire hedgerows: 'Here you may behold the high-ways and publick roads full of fruit trees, not set, but growing naturally'(p.231). Finally, as the practice of pollarding was petering out, the makers of fine furniture began to exploit the tightly swirling patterns in the burr timber of oaks and elms, the scar tissue formed around the pollarding cuts. Wood turners still relish this timber, though with the long abandonment of pollarding the source will eventually be exhausted.

Countless trees were planted in hedgerows and pollarded shortly afterwards during the great enclosures of the Tudor and Stuart eras. By the onset of the age of agricultural reform these trees will have reached maturity – in time only to become the targets in campaigns to 'reformed' farming. However, such was their usefulness that in 1796 even a leading apostle of change, William Marshall, felt obliged to write (see References, 1796a) that the old enclosed lands in Wensleydale looked like woodlands when seen from a distance, the enclosures being narrow and packed with hedgerow timber. He thought that these trees were about 50 years old, and if left to grow for a further 50 years or more then the value of the timber in some places would be equal to that of the land.

Not all the plants with a value that extended beyond boundary- and barrier-making overshadowed the hedgerow shrubs. Useful plants formed part of the hedgerow itself or could be found weaving amongst the shrubs or amongst the herbage at their foot. Brambles, sloes, gooseberries and raspberries might be found among them, some having escaped from nearby gardens, some spread by birds and some, perhaps, planted. Hazel was a common hedgerow shrub, while Gerard noted that walnut trees could be found growing on fertile ground near highways. Not all fruit trees were unqualified successes. The elder produces copious amounts of fruit for the wine-maker but was something of a problem in the hedgerow, being brittle and short-lived and therefore likely to produce a weak spot that bullocks could barge through. Elder was often grubbed out during hedge-laying, though perhaps not by the superstitious – who believed that Judas had hanged himself from an elder and that the tree bled when cut. Bird cherry abounds in some northern English hedges and can be very competitive, though its fruit is bitter and unappealing. There were plants with medicinal value, like the privet, which seems to have been spreading in the Elizabethan hedges of south-eastern England and was thought to ease mouth ulcers, while those with sore gums chewed beech leaves. The nuts of the hazel were employed for divination rituals, while its wands were favoured by water diviners. They were also sought by thatchers seeking 'sways' to staple down the thatch, though most of these came from coppices. Rowan, sometimes seen in northern hedges, was said to have good anti-witch properties and it was incorporated into the furnishings of cow houses to stop witches from turning the milk sour. A less familiar use for the hedgerow pollard was described by Green, who cited a personal communication from D. Hughes: 'At the National Trust property of Croft Castle in Herefordshire, there are several ageing Hawthorn, *Crataegus monogyna*, pollards that are still cut and the branches used to "gap up" damaged hedgerows' (p.103).

Before concluding this section we may mention the hedgerow trees that were planted to produce a scenic *tour de force* rather than to enforce a boundary or provide resources of timber, browse or fruit. In Scotland, there are beech hedges in which the trees rather than the shrub layer constitute the curtain. Millman (1975, p.144) notes that beech, which '... was used by the Improving lairds to produce the trimmed beech hedges and beech avenues whose rusty-gold leaf cover [helped] to protect the buds through the winter forms a very distinctive feature of the high farming landscapes of the central and eastern Lowlands, North-East and Moray Firth district [sic] today'. The Meikleour beech hedge, flanking the A93 near

The Meikleour Beech Hedge near Blairgowrie – said to be the tallest hedge in the world

Blairgowrie, Perthshire, is said to be the tallest such hedge in the world. Planted in 1745 by Jane Mercer, destined to be a Culloden widow in the following year, what may have been intended as a conventional beech hedge could have grown unattended when she moved to Edinburgh after the battle. Existing as a row of slender, closely spaced trees, the hedge overtops the free-standing trees on the other side of the road and has attained a height of 120ft (36.6m).

An even more specialised form of a hedge was the kind that formed a maze. References to labyrinths were made from time to time during the medieval period but the first well-documented example appears to have been a labyrinth made by one Giovanni Fontana in the third decade of the fifteenth century and mazes seem to have become established in the repetoire of garden features in the sixteenth century. A later but much-discussed English hedge maze, now the most famous example in the world, was at the royal palace of Hampton Court, although the original trees were replaced by yew in the 1960s. The first hedge was planted in hornbeam for William III in 1690, with his royal gardeners, London and Wise, presumably being involved. In the Queen's collection of paintings at Hampton Court there is, appropriately, a detailed illustration of a hedge maze 'Labyrinth of Love' of the school of Tintoretto and dated to 1550-60. The hedge maze was anticipated by the intricate patterns formed by low

Scots pine providing an unusual tree component in a Devon hedge

box hedges in the knot gardens associated with the last baronial castles and first generations of stately homes. The Hampton Court maze formed part of a then fashionable 'Wilderness' and similar labyrinths were created at various other important residences. This continued until the eighteenth century, when Lancelot 'Capability' Brown (1716-83) dispensed with parterres and other aesthetic details and brought the park lawns sweeping up to the walls of England's mansions. He became Royal Gardener to George III, but was forbidden from tampering with the maze that lay beside his house.

While the Hampton Court maze of 1690 is claimed as the first example of its kind in England, Thomas Platter from Basel visited England in 1599, and recorded his visit to Nonsuch palace near Tooting, London. He mentioned the pavilion where the Queen would sit to watch the game being coursed in the park; an avenue cut through the woods, and a boarded area in the wood like a tennis court where ball games could be played: 'From here we came to a maze or labyrinth surrounded by high shrubberies to prevent one from passing over or through them. In the pleasure gardens are charming terraces and all kinds of animals – dogs, hares, all overgrown with plants, most artfully set out, so that from a distance, one would take them all for real ones' (quoted in Fleming and Gore, 1979, p.34).

The ages of hedgerows and their trees

An old garden is not likely to be the same age as its rhubarb patch or Wendy house, and, as noted above, boundaries need not be the same age as the things seen growing along them. Equally, there is no reason to believe that the age of a hedgerow can be gauged by counting the species in it, any more than the age of a bus is signalled by the number of passengers travelling in it. As a geographer turned landscape archaeologist, it does strike the author as strange that botanists, having developed a science of ecology that focuses on the intricate relationships between species and their habitats, should then subscribe to a doctrine of 'hedge dating' that offends all ecological beliefs. Even so, the notions have become so deeply ingrained that another rebuttal is necessary. Here are some of the objections to the idea that each 30-yard (sometimes 30m) section of hedgerow gains a new species every century:

1 *Where is the gatekeeper?* Where is the mechanism that opens a hedgerow to a colonist of a new species just once every century? Who or what is there to prevent two, three or more species getting in during a particular century? Who or what is there to rustle up the required new colonist if 'Nature' has failed to provide one at the end of a century? Where is the mechanism to override the fact that, with a fixed number of potential colonists and a limited and progressively declining amount of hedgerow space available, statistics determine that it will become progressively more difficult to find and admit a new colonist each century? The time intervals for species establishment should become markedly longer at each stage. Where is the mechanism that will prevent any representative of a species from dying and thus depressing the species count? What mechanism is there in place to override the fact that some settings support a much broader spectrum of potential colonists than others?

2 *How can one disregard ecological principles?* Ecology reminds us about the sensitive relationships between plants and their environments and about the competitive nature of the coexistence between species. The environments of southern Britain are found favourable by a much wider range of hedgerow trees and shrubs, and calcareous soils support various shrubs, like the wayfaring tree, that do not flourish elsewhere. Therefore, the southern chalk countrysides contain a much larger range of potential colonists and must therefore be more ecologically disposed to multi-species hedgerows. Their hedges are, indeed, rich in plants while those of acidic northern soils are deprived, with the diversity reflecting environmental factors rather than age. Moreover, if, as ecology shows, some species are more competitive in a given setting than others, then should not shrub numbers in a hedgerow decline rather than increase, as explained below?

Scots pines planted as shelterbelts in the poor, sandy country of the Brecklands on the Norfolk/ Suffolk borders provide the main eye-catchers in the landscape

Elm is invading ever-lengthening sections of this North Yorkshire hedge, turning it into a monoculture, to the consternation of 'hedgerow dating'

Beech hedging beside a Roman road in Cambridgeshire, the most recent of a long succession of hedgerows

3 *Invasion and the diminution of species.* Even a basic familiarity with ecology tells one that a species that is singularly well adjusted to its environment will flourish and expand at the expense of less well adjusted neighbours. Obviously, this is as true in a hedgerow as it is in a pond or on a railway embankment. If one particular shrub is particularly 'happy' in a hedge then over time, and as long as the environmental conditions are stable, it can be expected to advance along that hedge, displacing competing species that are less 'at home' there. In this way, a species-rich hedgerow does not become richer, but poorer in species. Various shrubs found in hedgerows have forms of propagation other than the production of seed that equip them very well for the advance along a hedge. Holly can be seen to self-layer, which explains many of the long stretches seen in northern hedges that are monopolised by holly. Blackthorn and elm are among the shrubs that can sucker aggressively – as represented by Roman roads like the *Via Devana* in southern England where blackthorn has advanced from and along roadside hedges to form a dense tunnel shading the route, or by the sometimes encountered stretches of medieval hedgerow 50m or more in length containing nothing but elm.

4 *Where are the controls?* The fact that this writer wrote about the Hampsthwaite hedges in the spring of 2004 does not prove that this is when they were planted. Publications based on hedgerow dating frequently invoke 'dated' hedgerows to validate their findings. Here two factors, particularly, come to mind: (a) The fact that a hedge is mentioned at a particular time is *no indication that it had just been planted*, and (b) Even if a hedge was precisely dated in an medieval document, *it is unlikely that one could identify it on a map today*. Only a small minority of hedges can be dated with any degree of confidence. These are (a) Parliamentary Enclosure hedges, datable to the year, but seldom older than the eighteenth century and often much younger; and (b) hedges, datable, though sometimes with less certainty, that can be linked to particular historical occasions, like the Tudor enclosures at Hampsthwaite or the emparking of countryside for a deer park that was soon ringed by new hedges, like the new deer park at Wilstrop near York, partly ringed by a quickthorn hedge about 1490. Hedgerows associated with Saxon boundaries are often invoked in the hedge-dating literature. Yet sometimes the course of their boundaries is uncertain and in all cases the boundary mentioned might have been Roman or prehistoric in origin. After all, we know of a few extant boundary hedges that existed in Saxon times, so a hedge mentioned by Saxons might well have been of Iron Age or even Bronze Age origin. Hedge dating claims might be easier to test if ancient records took the following form: 'In the second year after his coronation, King Cnut caused a hedge consisting of a blackthorn monoculture to be planted between what will come to be known as Ordnance Survey grid references SE 25615802 and 25635803.' Of course, the flimsy evidence lacks this reliable form and the identification of hedges mentioned in old documents is a matter fraught with uncertainty.

5 *Who tampered?* When working on a book on hedgerows (1987) this writer made an intense study of the hedges bounding a lane just across the Nidd from Hampsthwaite, in Clint township. The lane served as a spur linking a small Roman road to the (deserted medieval) village of Clint and places beyond, and it and, presumably, its hedges, must have been very old. Although of one age originally, the roadside hedges fell into three distinct groups: those heavily invaded, mainly by elm and sometimes by holly, to become virtual or total monocultures; those consisting of little or nothing but hawthorn; and those containing other species, like oak and field maple, normally associated with more mature hedges. It was clear that each of the hawthorn stretches had resulted from the grubbing-up of a 'gappy' section of an old hedgerow and replanting with hawthorn. Presumably, this would occur when the hedge had become broken by gaps with exhausted soils in which solitary seedlings would not 'take' and was failing to provide a stockproof barrier. Thus, invasion and replanting had given hedgerow sections with a common origin different hedge-dating 'ages'. The late Tudor hedges of Hampsthwaite and adjacent townships generally fail to yield the 5-6 species

required by the dating dogma and many stretches offer little but hawthorn. One suspects that this is often due to the patching of the original hedges. One can recognise a hedge that was patched by replanting 20, 30 or, maybe, 50 years ago. But what about patching that occurred two, three, four or five centuries ago?

6 *Who counts what?* Different hedge-daters have counted different things. If one splits up all the different members of the plum or rose families, should one not do the same with the great multitude of blackberry sub-species? Some practitioners have counted all the various plants that twist and twine in a hedgerow, like honeysuckle and old man's beard; some of them have counted some but not others, while some count none. Consequently, not only is the activity rather a waste of time but also it produces results that are not comparable. It is something like a farming survey in which some of the data collectors had ruled out pigs, some had grouped all chickens together, while others still listed Rhode Island reds, black leghorns and Wyandottes separately.

7 *How were they planted?* Hedge dating assumes that hedgerows originated as single species plantings that then acquired new species at the 'prescribed' rate. There are various ways of creating a hedgerow. Firstly, we may disregard the notion that a hedge can be produced by leaving a convenient alignment of shrubs and trees when clearing a wood. (Anyone disagreeing should go into an old wood with a tape or length of string to discover how very little grows along a designated alignment. Hedges with gaps of 10m or more between trees/shrubs are somewhat unhelpful.) One could propagate suitable hedging material by seed. Various Classical writers described ways of doing this and Columella advocated collecting berries – from thorn trees, holly, briars and wild eglantine – mixing them with meal and plastering the mixture on an old wet rope which was then stretched along the intended line in a furrow. *The hedge resulting from this practice would begin life as a multi-species one.* Alternatively, one could obtain cuttings, with common hawthorn, always a popular choice, striking quite easily from cuttings. Rooted cuttings or quicksets were apparently available at rural markets in the time of Tomas Tusser in 1573, 'new gathered and small', and he also recommended sowing the seeds of bramble and hawthorn. Earlier, in 1534, Fitzherbert had advised his readers from the wooded country to get quicksets of hawthorn, crab apple, holly and hazel, while dwellers in the plains should get ash, oak and elm – apparently for the future value of their timber. An alternative to these methods, which required a measure of forward planning, was to go out and gather material that was already rooted. In 1748, Pehr Kalm paid a visit to England and later recorded how, in the Chilterns of Hertfordshire, farmers would plant hedges of hawthorn and sloe and also incorporate willow, beech, ash, maple, lime, elm and other tree species at intervals (quoted in Williamson, 2002, p.79). Oak seedlings, as mentioned, could be found in ungrazed meadows, woodland holly trees often yield offspring from self-layering and all trees and

shrubs began as seedlings and saplings that could be dug in the woods. Because country folk were practical people who survived by making the best use of rural resources, most old hedges began by having numerous species. Thereafter, they might gain a few as new species colonised the hedgerow, or lose many of their species as a consequence of invasion. It was only once commercial nurseries became established that mass-produced quickthorn could be widely exploited. They had appeared in some numbers in the seventeenth century and became numerous in the eighteenth century, when single species hedging generally became an attractive proposition. Even so, traditional ways of collecting hedging shrubs were not completely extinguished.

There is one other significant way in which a hedgerow could materialise: by spontaneous development. The great majority of hedges are the results of deliberate choices by landowners and tenants. There are, however, other hedges that appeared by more natural processes and were subsequently adopted by those working on the land. When a neglected wall tumbles, the seeds of shrubs may germinate in the shelter of the stone litter, so that a potentially valuable yet spontaneous hedge is adopted as a successor to a wall. Stone rubble can quite often be found in the bottom of a hedge. Probably it most usually derives from discarded field-stones tossed to the field margins by successive generations of ploughmen; though sometimes, an abandoned field wall or dwelling provided a nursery for the hedge. Fences offer a lower level of shelter, while any unused ground beside a track might generate a line of shrubs if browsing levels were low. Spontaneous hedges will advance from the margins of a hedged/fenced/walled lane or track if traffic levels decline. However, the relationship between hedgerows and drystone walls is a difficult one. It is certainly true that in the Yorkshire Dales in the zone where hedges and walls overlap one can find spontaneous hedgerows that have grown in the protection of field walls (extant or decayed) in fields adjacent to those with walls that were built to supersede hedgerows. To complicate matters further, in areas like Wensleydale one will also find hedgerows planted on stone-revetted banks or ditch-sides. In the case of one field boundary that runs off from a medieval pack horse road in Nidderdale, the relative 'freshness' of the angular stones in the field wall and the presence of old trees along its alignment tell of a wall that has replaced a hedge. However, the ramshackle walls of the lane that this wall joins are providing shelter in which a 'natural' hedgerow is developing spontaneously. Post-medieval examples like this are not hard to discover, but one is left to wonder how many quick or living hedges began with seedlings that had germinated in the shelter of a decaying dead hedge of thorns and brambles? Haws, berries and rose hips could drop to the bottom of such a dead hedge, while with some defences against the tender snouts of grazing stock, such places would be ideal refuges for birds as they digested the fruits of wild fruits and passed their tough seeds.

An excellent example of a spontaneous hedge was provided by Beresford (1954, p.35) who quoted the case of the boundary mound and ditch at the site of the deserted medieval village of East Lilling, North Yorkshire:

> The vertical distance from ditch bottom to bank top at Lilling is in places 8-9 feet and the slope of the banks has harboured seeds and protected young scrub until they are now lined with hawthorns and blackberries. These thorns follow the perimeter of the village, and at a distance give the false impression of a hedge. The thorn-grown depression is a common feature in hollow-ways of other sites.

Having posed the question of how a hedge and its shrubs originated, let us now consider the origins of hedgerow trees. These could either be additions to an older hedgerow or components of the original planting. There is important evidence from the early advocates of good husbandry, who advised that useful trees should deliberately be included in hedgerows. Within 20 years of hedgerows being planted across lands (previously depopulated of peasant tenants around 1499) at Wormleighton in Warwickshire, these hedges were recorded as being '… grown full of *all manner of wood*, and one of the greatest commodity in the country'(Fisher, 1954, p.105, my ital.). Plainly, these hedges had been planted with the intention of creating a diverse resource of commercial timber products.

Not surprisingly, the multiplication of nurseries offering cheap, mass-produced hawthorns for hedging coincided with the rise of the mono-species hedgerow, but mixed plantings did not end completely. Even the rare black poplar was deliberately included in hedgerows and was, for example, frequently incorporated in hedgerows in West Yorkshire and Derbyshire, where the tree was probably an alien, and in the Severn valley, where hedging plants were obtained from indigenous woodland stock. The selection of hedging trees and shrubs from 'wild' communities seems to have been the traditional practice, as when, in 1376-8, tenants were described as 'pulling' ash and thorn plants to set along a ditch to the east of the manor house at Forncett in Norfolk (Davenport, 1967).

The relics of hedges

Hedgerows of the traditional kind – recently layed, trimmed regularly by sharp billhooks and, where appropriate, with their ditches scoured and their banks turfed – are seldom seen today. Instead, we encounter hedgerows in various stages of neglect and terminal decline. As a result, the impressions that we form of them are not accurate reflections of the hedges as they existed in their heyday, a heyday that continued until the age of farm mechanisation and balance-sheet farming. As the nineteenth century drew towards its end, it became ever less practical for farmers, now competing in a semi-global economy, to find winter work for forces of semi-destitute labourers. Thus, hedging and ditching were at least partly abandoned. The neglect of the hedgerow was paralleled by that of its

Jumbled boughs from a bulldozed hedgerow oak

An early stage in hedgerow decline. The thick 'elbow' shows that a new laying should have taken place decades ago, while the post and rail show that the hedge itself is no longer stock-proof

trees, as pollarding was neglected and imported and plantation-grown softwood timber captured parts of the market once dominated by indigenous hardwoods.

In 2000 the author proposed the following chronology in the destruction of hedgerows through the neglect of traditional maintenance (p.86):

Stage of Decline	Appearance
Well maintained	Too dense for stock to penetrate, laid within the last 20 years. No gaps or elder present
Early neglect	Still trimmed, but by machine. Laying is overdue and has been abandoned. Gaps have appeared and are clumsily blocked with fence rails etc. Elder is gaining footholds
Advanced neglect	The hedge is no longer stockproof. As the lower foliage thins, the 'elbows' of pleachers from former laying episodes are revealed. Cattle are barging through gaps and dead elder shrubs
Relict stage I	The hedge is now composed of separate shrubs punctuated by free-standing former hedgerow trees
Relict stage II	The quickthorn shrubs have died and only the old hedgerow pollards and standards remain
Relict stage III	The former hedgerow exists as an earthwork – the former hedgebank or a low ridge composed of drifting soil trapped in the rank vegetation in the foot of the hedgerow. The slight trough of a ditch may be present, as may widely spaced trees derived from the former hedge
Relict stage IV	The earthworks of the former hedge can only be recognised when intrusive archaeological methods are employed

Because of the frequent persistence of hedgerow trees long after the shrub cordon has vanished, the untutored observer will tend to mistake 'Relict stage III' survivors for field trees and specimen plantings from landscaping works. In deer parks and

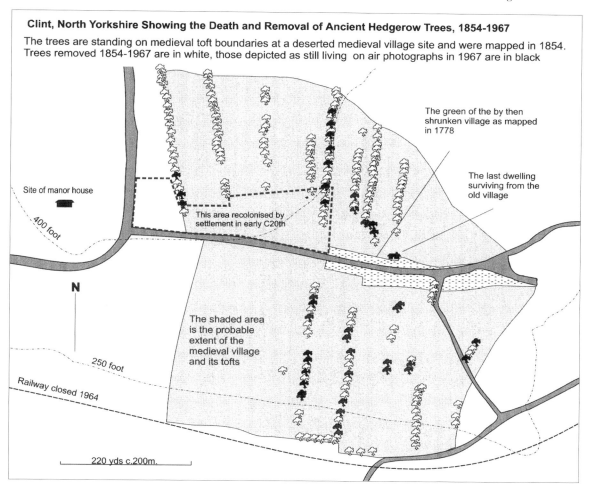

Clint, North Yorkshire Showing the Death and Removal of Ancient Hedgerow Trees, 1854-1967

The trees are standing on medieval toft boundaries at a deserted medieval village site and were mapped in 1854. Trees removed 1854-1967 are in white, those depicted as still living on air photographs in 1967 are in black

The green of the by then shrunken village as mapped in 1778

The last dwelling surviving from the old village

Site of manor house

400 foot

This area recolonised by settlement in early C20th

N

The shaded area is the probable extent of the medieval village and its tofts

250 foot

Railway closed 1964

220 yds c.200m.

landscape parks, numerous trees may often be derived from the hedgerows of working countrysides that were emparked, as described in detail in Chapter 4. Solitary field trees were sometimes planted to provide shade and rubbing 'posts' for livestock, but this class of tree should be considered very carefully. Returning recently to his native village of Birstwith, North Yorkshire, the author realised that a loose alignment of fine old oaks that he had for long regarded as field and landscaping trees were, in fact, following a faintly visible abandoned meander of the river Nidd and had probably originated as riverbank trees. The naming of components of the medieval field pattern after particular trees, like Thorn Flatt, Maple Tree Lease or Walnut Tree Close or Crab Croft show that individual field trees have long been parts of the countryside (as described in Chapter 2). However, a remarkable proportion of such trees encountered in today's countrysides are found, on close investigation, to be derived from defunct hedgerows.

A recent survey of pollarded trees in Nidderdale (mainly oaks) revealed that, of 186 trees examined, some 152, amounting to no less than 82 per cent, were

Stumps of massive felled hedgerow pollards that were probably of Tudor ages

growing on field boundaries and could therefore be considered to have originated as hedgerow trees (2000a, p.96). Of this 152, 104 were growing in extant field boundaries hedges which were still effective in partitioning the landscape, though 48 stood on relict boundaries that were often only apparent as faint earthworks. Had the survey been undertaken without a careful consideration of the archaeological context of the trees then the importance of hedgerow origins would have been overlooked.

Trees from relict hedgerows are commonly seen in most lowland locations and they sometimes exist as significant elements in the historic landscape. Rackham has described how: 'At Knapwell, Cambridgeshire, we find vast pollard elms, of surrealistic shapes, marking the deserted streets and closes of the shrunken medieval village' (1976, p.171). The author found a similar explanation for the scenery at Clint, North Yorkshire, a medieval village which decayed during the post-medieval period and was reduced to just one dwelling in the nineteenth century. In this case, we find not only the vestiges of the hedges that defined the plots or 'tofts' associated with the dwellings of the medieval village, but, most unusually, also explicit references to their layout. Quoting from the legal documents of Edward II (1325), when William, son of Adam de Clint, was arraigned at Knaresborough Castle for the death of William del Ridding ('William of the clearing') of Clint, Grainge reconstructed the proceedings from the contemporary records (1871 p.377). The two men had quarrelled in a tavern in the village of Clint during the previous year and Adam had taken refuge in the house of one Agnes Serveys, closing the door behind him. Del Ridding, armed with a bow and arrows, followed him and as he burst in through one door, so de Clint escaped through another. (Typically, the house would have been aligned along the edge of the green and divided by a passage running from its front door to its back door, perhaps with the compartment on one side of this cross passage being reserved for a few animals.) De Clint was then pursued across the space behind the village houses, where he leapt over the divers hedgerows (*sepes*) bordering the tofts towards the head of the village (probably now marked by the ruins of the seventeenth century manor house). The chase ranged over two miles, over hedgerows to a great water-filled ditch (… *usque ad magnum fossatum plenum aquæ, et quædam sepes fuit superposita ubi dictus Willemus fil*) until he could run no further and died, his breast pierced by arrows.

The relics of the hedges that Clint leapt over in his desperate efforts to escape can still be seen running down the bank below the earthworks of the medieval village. They are not rich in species in the manner of so-called 'hedgerow dating'. Instead, there are very occasional hawthorns surviving from the shrub component with just a few of the oaks standing to mark the old alignments. They no longer function as hedgerows, but rather as broken lines of old trees marking boundaries that no longer exist. The countrysides of today derive much, indeed, most, of their aesthetic and ecological interest from the presence of relics inherited from fairly distant times. In the middle of the nineteenth century, trees from the hedges marking old toft divisions from the decayed medieval village were the main factor that gave the local countryside its character. Evidence from the relevant Ordnance Survey map for 1854 shows that within a small territory of about 660 x 660 yards (*c*.604 x 604m) some 212 hedgerow trees from the toft boundaries still survived.

In common with most other parts of lowland Britain, there followed a period of accelerating destruction. While many of the oaks established in the hedgerows during the closing phases of the medieval period came to the natural end of their days, human interventions took a far greater toll. Virtually all the old hedgerow trees to the north of the deserted village site were grubbed-up in order to create an open arable expanse, a suitable playground for the juggernauts of mechanised farming. Whether arable cultivation as practised in Northern England at an altitude of more than 400ft (122m) is economically viable is something one might debate, but there is no doubting the devastating effect that farm subsidies had on old countrysides during the second half of the twentieth century. During the first half of the twentieth century settlement was attracted back to the former village site, with a string of detached dwellings being built to exploit the fine view looking southwards across the valley of the river Nidd – and these took a smaller toll of the old hedgerow trees. On the valley slope to the south, the hedge boundaries became redundant but some of their trees were tolerated with the numbers gradually declining as age claimed its victims. The evidence of maps and air photographs shows that here (as in many other places) the charms of a tree rich countryside were surrendered between 1854 and 1967.

Thorn shrubs at Wadenhow, Northamptonshire: relics of a former hedge

During this period 81 per cent of the trees disappeared in a process of removal and decay that accelerated with the passing decades.

Across the valley and about a mile upstream, ancient hedgerow trees had also graced the countryside. They were considered sufficiently remarkable to attract the region's topographers. In 1871 William Grainge wrote:

> Elton Spring and the fields adjacent present some splendid specimens of oak timber – some of them old, pollarded, knotty, 'gnarled and unwedgeable' patriachs of the old forest; others young, tall, and straight, have grown up in their shelter, and indicate a soil suitable to the sustentation of the monarch of the British woods. One oak, felled in the spring of 1867, presented a perfectly straight trunk of fifty-one feet in length – the first thirty feet without a single branch; at the ground the girth was ten feet three inches; at thirty feet it was six feet ten inches. A finer specimen of oak timber has been seldom seen of native growth; and the quality of timber grown here cannot be surpassed (pp. 431-32).

On a roadside nearby he noticed:

> Another remarkable tree of the oak species; at five feet above the ground it is

twenty feet in circumference; at nine feet it divides into three main branches, and afterwards into many more. Its trunk is gnarled and knotted in a most singular manner. It is evidently of great age – a genuine relic of the old forest day (p.432).

Like many who would follow, Grainge was confusing the old, royal hunting Forest of Knaresborough, with a forest in the later, 'woodland' sense. In fact the trees that he encountered were not 'forest' trees, and although they lay in the territory of the defunct Forest of Knaresborough, they were largely hedgerow pollards, many established in the hedges that privatised the late-medieval countryside.

The plight of the pollards

For many centuries, closely spaced ranks of trees, usually pollards, were characteristic of hedgerow country. Rather more than two centuries ago they became victims to a sustained campaign of vilification by the apostles of agricultural reform (in the second half of the twentieth century those that had survived found themselves the targets of a less erudite land lobby). Hitherto, the value of these trees had scarcely been questioned, providing, as they did, enduring boundary markers, browse, fuel and other timber and, in the case of the thorns, material for gapping up hedges.

The case that was made against the hedgerow pollard was couched in terms of economic efficiency and agricultural enlightenment, yet sometimes the veils parted and the resentment towards peasant society by the propertied classes could be glimpsed. If the pollards could be linked to the conservative yet underprivileged rural classes then they, too, could be regarded as primitive and impediments to progress and so swept away. Far more than the lord's spring woods and hags, with their conveyor-belt outputs of coppiced fuel and structural timber, the pollards represented the self-sufficiency of the yeoman, copyholder and cottager. For centuries before these classes had come into being, pollards had furnished villeins, freemen and bordars with a few armfuls of browse for the milk cow, the arching blade for a brace, a curving limb for the plough body, a bag of acorns for the pigsty or a pole for the hoe. They symbolised timeless rights, the ancient and hallowed customs of the manor, tradition and all those things that the new movers and shakers of the countryside regarded as impediments to progress.

However, as England grew to be a naval and then an imperial power, lingering anxieties about the timber supply became apparent. An Act of 1756 noted the failure of preceding Acts of Henry VIII, Charles II and William III that had been intended to encourage the production of timber. They were assumed to have been frustrated by the resistance of commoners, and so it was enacted that the owner of a common or waste could enclose land for the purpose of growing timber with the approval of the majority of commoners (in number and value). Objectors could appeal to Quarter Sessions. An expression of the continuing anxiety over timber stocks appeared in 1791, when one of the questions investigated by government concerned whether the cultivation of oak timber in hedgerows was being encouraged, or whether hedgerows were being grubbed-up to enlarge fields or for improving arable land? The commercial and maritime timber interests and judicial parties responded that hedge removal was taking place, but that its impact varied from place to place and in the South East of England it had become a frequent practice. It appears to have been most severe in places where arable farming was strongest. Even so, the hostility extended into the South West and

> By the 1840s ... the improvers' opinion had turned quite severely against the small irregular fields with their thick leafy boundaries, by then regarded as a waste of space and a danger to arable crops. ... Their exhortations to remove the old hedgebanks were clearly acted upon by many farmers (Turner, 2004, pp.29-30).

Turner then cited Long (1935), who had compared tithe map data with the 1905-6 Second Series Ordnance Survey map to show widespread destruction of field banks in the second half of the nineteenth century.

Here we have a manifestation of not only a fluctuation in market forces, but also the polemical assault on traditional rural practices. In the New Forest at least, the earlier swing away from pollarding towards the cultivation of standard trees had reflected a shift in emphasis from the provision of browse for deer to structural timbers for shipbuilding (Young, 1969, p.38), but elsewhere other factors intervened. Marshall, who had, perhaps grudgingly, recognised the value of hedgerow trees in Wensleydale, was not to be diverted: 'We declare ourselves enemies to Pollards,' he proclaimed (1796b). The modern landscape historian, Williamson, summarised the case of the reformers in the following way:

> In the later eighteenth century this irregular, pollard-ridden, 'bosky' landscape came under sustained attack. Small, oddly shaped fields were inconvenient for ploughing, tall hedges and hedgerow trees shaded out the crop and robbed soil of nutrients, while wide outgrown hedges took up large areas of potentially productive land .... Pollards were regarded with special venom: their dense, spreading heads created a particularly deep pool of shade, and they were looked on by improvers as relics of backward peasant agriculture – the larger farmers in all these districts were now increasingly using coal rather than wood for their fires (2002b, p.94).

Marshall presented his case against pollards largely in utilitarian terms and in Wensleydale (where he had noted the considerable value of the maturing hedgerow timber crop as well as the shelter that tall hedges afforded to livestock) he denounced the pollarded trees as impediments both to arable cultivation and to grazing.

… There are enclosures, every foot of the areas of which must necessarily be occupied by ash-roots; nevertheless they give ample supply of hay and pasture. One to three tons of hay per acre.

It is evident, however that oak, when suffered to thrust its slow spreading head into the inclosure, is injurious to the herbage beneath it; that the leaves of ash are very detrimental to aftergrass; and that hedges are annually receiving irreparable damage; no general plan of training up trees with tall stems having, I believe, in any instance been adopted (1976a).

Although these arguments, emotive as they often were, were generally presented in a context of improving efficiency, there are subtexts and unstated cases of political, normative and psychological characters. The same virulence displayed in the assault upon pollards was also launched against open field farming. Even the dimmest of observers should have been inclined to ask why, had it been so inefficient, was open field farming pursued for around a thousand years by communities whose lives depended upon wresting a living from the land? The same questions should have been asked about pollards by people occupying countrysides packed with ancient trees, some of which must have predated Domesday Book.

Perhaps some of the disdain directed towards the old trees derived from the guilt of the victor? For the pollard was the poor man's tree. On countless manors, peasants/tenants had the rights to lop browse and take timber for fuel, repairs, plough-making and so on, but not to fell trees. Pollards provided this periodical, renewable timber harvest, and so the rural poor were obviously tempted to convert any young tree they encountered into a pollard. In most places, pollards considerably outnumbered maiden trees, with ratios of 4:1 or 8:1 being commonplace and 20:1 being found in some places. The prosperous farmer with coal smouldering in his hearth did not gather faggots to offset the February freeze or break hedges to burn in March when all else had gone. His herd of pedigree cows found little browse and his cowmen had scant time to lop it. His apples came from the orchard beside the farmyard – scrabbling through thorns to gather crabs, sloes or damsons was not for him. When he thought of timber he thought of commercial timber – straight planks ripped from the trunk of a maiden oak or elm, not poles or curved braces from a pollard. And when he thought of where his prosperity had come from, the chances are that waves of guilt welled up inside – and so he despised the small people around him, their archaic field strips, contorted old trees and hovels littering the flanks of the common. 'Oh, to sweep them all away!'

Resources that helped to sustain the rural poor could be regarded as being responsible for the presence of kinds of people who were feared or held in contempt. Even the country-lover and critic of the town, William Cowper, (1731–1880), treated the *Gypsies on the Common* with disdain:

They pick their fuel out of every hedge,
Which, kindled with dry leaves, just saves unquench'd
The spark of life. The sportive wind blows wide
Their fluttering rags, and shows a tawny skin,
The vellum of the pedigree they claim.

There were others who pitied the poor who scavenged for survival in the countryside, like the wretched old matron in Goldsmith's *The Deserted Village* of 1770, who was forced

To pick her wintry faggot from the thorn
To seek her nightly shed and weep till morn.

The assault was not directed towards all trees, and at a time when British destiny was increasingly tied to that of the Royal Navy this could scarcely have been otherwise. In some places, oaks were planted at regular intervals in new hedgerows that were established as part of, or at the same time as, Parliamentary Enclosure. In parts of Cornwall and upland Devon, 'new' landscapes acquired a deceptively ancient appearance when beech trees were planted on newly made hedge banks. The poor man's tree, it was claimed, afflicted not only the grass or grain growing on either side but also the hedgerow itself. The ash was held to be particularly at fault, for its fallen leaves stifled pasture and its shallow roots obstructed the plough. Moreover, pollards were thought to occupy ground in the hedgerow that might otherwise have supported a tree of commercial rather than communal value. Marshall's advice to the Dalesmen of North Yorkshire was not to do away with trees and hedges, but rather to get rid of the low-spreading pollards and manage the hedgerows as nurseries for 'tall-stemmed' oaks, which seems to suggest oaks pollarded at a higher level, a later fashion in some places. These could be sold to a timber merchant when around a century old and would yield a handsome profit. Further south, his sentiments were often ignored, and the hedgerow vanished along with its pollards. This was particularly the case on East Anglian claylands, where the dominance of cereal cultivation and 'progressive' notions in the years around 1800 resulted in campaigns of defoliation that, though only at the level of the locality, matched the agri-business-led devastation of the 1960s and '70s.

It is quite ironic that the period (*c.*1750-*c.*1850) that witnessed the most concerted period of hedge planting, with new hedges being established at an average rate of about 2000 miles (3220km) each year, was also the time when old hedgerows and, particularly, their pollards, encountered unprecedented hostility. Each movement was characteristic of the age, and while some may see Parliamentary Enclosure as a conspiracy led by lawyers, surveyors and the apparatchiki of property transfer rather than by landlords, there is no doubt that the small men and commoners were its victims. With the passing of the culture of peasant self-sufficiency, so passed the age of the hedgerow pollard. Many survived, untended, to linger, hollow-trunked and burdened with heavy, sagging limbs, into the present age. However, very few young trees were pollarded to perpetuate the hedgerow tradition. They very seldom appeared amongst the geometrical networks of hawthorn hedges that criss-crossed the old upland commons, heaths, communal ploughlands and meadows. They did not punctuate the hedgerows flanking the new turnpike roads. And, because Parliamentary Enclosure and the other 'reforms' had dealt so harshly with the rural poor, there were few remaining with an interest in periodically re-pollarding the old trees that remained.

Though his advice was very seldom heeded, Marshall was in favour of including trees in the new hedgerows of former common land that had been privatised under Parliamentary Enclosure:

> Land which has lain open, and which has been kept in a state of aration during a succession of ages, is equally productive of grass and trees. And it is generally good management to let it lie to grass for some time after inclosure.
>
> In this neighbourhood [Wensleydale], it is evident to common observation, that trees flourish with unusual vigour in the newly-inclosed lands of arable fields; and that their injury to grassland is inconsiderable when compared to the value of the timber they produce. The low spreading heads of oak and the leaves of ash appear to be the chief inconveniences of these two species of trees to grassland.
>
> But an alternacy of corn and grass is generally eligible on lands which our ancestors have made their choice for common-fields; and the roots of the ash are not only obstructions to the plow, but the general nature of the plants is in a singular degree inimical to corn. It is therefore necessary to eradicate ash from the hedgerows, before the land be again broken up for arable, or to preclude this tedious operation, in the first instance, by planting oak in its stead.
>
> The head of the oak may be raised to such a height as to be no way injurious to grass; nor to the hedge, while yet in a youthful state, even though it be suffered to run up to its natural height.
>
> Whenever the inclosures are broken up for corn, the hedges ought in common good management to be headed, and kept in a dwarfish state; in which case tall-stemmed oaks would be a valuable source of timber, without being in almost any degree injurious to the hedge or the corn growing under them. But the training of young oaks, and the general management of hedgerow timber, cannot, with any degree of prudence, be left to a mere occupier. Viewing hedges as nurseries of timber, a hedgeman becomes essentially necessary to every landed estate (1796a).

In England and Wales, the planting of new, mainly single-species Parliamentary Enclosure hedges was frequently paralleled by an assault on the pollards in the old hedgerows, with the enclosing landlords often being the removers of the poor man's trees. In Scotland, however, the planting of new hedges and

A cause for caution: pollards can be created naturally when gales or lightening take the tops from trees. When in leaf this naturally pollarded tree is effectively indistinguishable from other pollards

shelter belts as part of the contemporary Improvements normally took place in countrysides that were largely bare of trees and had no old hedgerows. There, the lairds, some indigenous and some commissioners of estates forfeited after the Jacobite defeat at Culloden in 1746, took their lead from 'progressive' Scottish estates, like Cawdor and Monymusk, from the agricultural reforms in England and from examples encountered during a Grand Tour of the continent. Given the exposed northerly locations and the general absence of existing cover, the emphasis was heavily on shelter. To the native Scots pine was added the larch, soon these were joined by woods and shelter belts of spruce, Norway and Sitka, and Douglas fir, as landowners competed to reorganise their estates. Various lairds developed enthusiasms for tree planting after losing their military roles as clan chieftains. The Fourth Duke of Atholl (1755-1830) became known as 'The Planting Duke' and by the time of his death he and his forbears had embellished the Atholl estates with more than 14 million larches, the first specimens having been given to Duke James of Atholl in 1738.

Some of the alien conifers have now been around for long enough to become ancient landmark trees in their own rights. These include the Kailzie Larch growing at Kailzie Gardens near Peebles. In 1890 it was recorded that the larches had been brought north from London in 1725 by the tree enthusiast, Sir James Naesmyth, who gave one to his friend, the Laird of Kailzie. The tree presumed to have figured in the gift now stands 105ft (*c*.32m) tall. The Sitka spruce was discovered on the northern Pacific shores of the North America by

Probably the victim of an assault rather
than a deliberate act of pollarding, this
tree is still demonstrating the vigorous
recovery that was normal after pollarding

Archibald Menzies in 1792. Shortly after the species was introduced by David
Douglas in 1832, a Sitka spruce is believed to have been planted in the grounds
of Fairburn House near Contin, Highland, where a specimen reaches a height
of 147ft (*c.*49m). A much larger specimen stands in a coniferous plantation near
Fettercairn, Aberdeenshire and towers to a height of 165ft (*c.*50m). This, however,
is dwarfed by the 203ft-tall (*c.*62m) Douglas fir that was planted at Reelig Glen,
near Inverness, in 1882. Several other Douglas firs in the locality approach the
200ft mark.

Although the Scottish Improvements were generally even more sweeping
than the consequences of the Agricultural Revolution were in England, the
impact upon ancient trees in the cultural landscapes were less. Such trees tended
not to be present on estates divided into group farms and farmed on the run-
rig basis. Every morsel of dry land tended to be brought under the plough
and rural landscapes often consisted of great sweeps of unpartitioned ridged
ploughland, open upland common and waterlogged, 'moorish' grazing. When
the lairds converted the old run-rig lands into singly-tenanted farmsteads, land
drains, estate plantations and shelter belts were added, giving scenic details
where before there were very few salient features to catch the eye. The pollard-
studded hedgerow was much less commonly seen in Scotland, particularly in the
more marginal upland farming country. Thus, while in England and Wales the

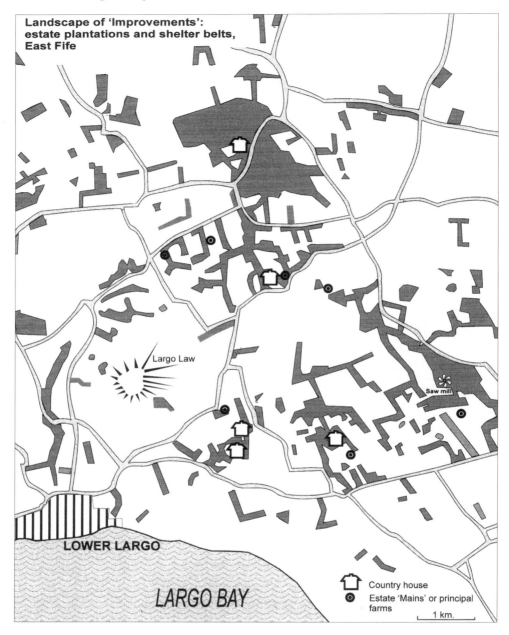

Landscape of 'Improvements': estate plantations and shelter belts, East Fife

Largo Law

Saw mill

LOWER LARGO

LARGO BAY

Country house

Estate 'Mains' or principal farms

1 km.

establishment of geometrical networks of new and largely treeless hedgerows was paralleled by the assault on ancient hedgerow pollards, in Scotland the shelter belts were extended across countrysides that often had very few trees.

Today, the battle against old pollards continued, though some of the tactics employed have damage as their by-products rather than their intents. The nature of the modern threats can be summarised as follows:

The hedgerow tradition continued until quite recent times in some places. This magnificent hedgebank planted with beeches at Callington, Cornwall, dates from the nineteenth-century enclosure of new land there. *Photograph: Sam Turner*

In parts of continental Europe roadside trees are still pollarded by farmers, as here at Versonnex in France. *Photograph: Ted Green*

- The removal of lower branches to allow tractors to pass close to the trunk of the old tree. This gives the tree a top-heavy structure and can result in the crown being blown away.
- Deep ploughing. This tears and breaks the tree's roots and allows diseases to enter the tree. The tree roots extend across an area 2.5 times the area of the canopy. Any deep ploughing less than 5 metres beyond the limit of the canopy is likely to cause damage and even ploughing beyond this zone can be destructive.
- Compaction by heavy machinery and trampling by livestock damages the soil structure and changes its drainage properties.
- Undergrazing can lead to the colonisation of the ground around the trunk by bracken or other combustible vegetation.
- Fertilisers, pesticides and veterinary residues accumulate in the soil and can eliminate the mycorrhizal fungi in the soil which gather nutrients that the tree itself cannot acquire. Constituents of chemical fertilisers facilitate attacks by micro-organisms.
- Modern stocking levels are greater than in the past and the livestock are larger. Modern farm livestock are treated with numerous chemicals which are

excreted on trees and become particularly potent if bark has been damaged by licking and nibbling.

Some of these problems can be removed if trees are cordoned off from livestock or ploughing. While such measures will protect old trees, they do not solve the problem of the shortage of new plantings. Since hedgerows have wholly or partly gone from many countrysides, the problem of the vanishing hedgerow pollard seems intractable.

REFERENCES

Beresford, M.W., 1954, *The Lost Villages of England*, Lutterworth Press, London.
Camden, 1695 edn., *Britannia*, David and Charles reprints, Newton Abbot.
Cowper, W., 'Gypsies on the Common', *Poems by William Cowper*, (N.d.)
Darbyshire, H.S. and Lumb, G.D., 1937, *The History of Methley*, Thoresby Society, 35.
Davenport, F.G., 1967, *The Economic Development of a Norfolk Manor 1086-1565*, London
Farrer, W., (ed.), 1914, *Early Yorkshire Charters*; I , privately printed.
Faull, M.L. and Moorhouse, S.A., 1981, *West Yorkshire: An Archaeological Survey to 1500*, West Yorkshire Metropolitan County Council, Wakefield.
Fisher, F.J., *Economic History Review*, **X**, p.105 quoted in Beresford, M.J., 1954, *Lost Villages of England*, Lutterworth, London.
Fitzherbert, 1534, *Boke of Husbandry*.
Fleming, L. and Gore, A., 1979, *The English Garden*, Michael Joseph, London.
Goldsmith, O., 1770, *The Deserted Village*.
Grainge, 1871, *Harrogate and the Forest of Knaresborough*, J.R. Smith, London.
Green, T., 'Pollarding – Origins and Some Practical Advice' *British Wildlife,* vol. 8, no.2, pp.100–105.
Homans, G.C., 1941, *English Villagers of the Thirteenth Century*, Norton Library edn., 1975, New York.
Jennings, B, (ed।)., 1983, *A History of Nidderdale*, Advertiser Press, Huddersfield.
Julius Caesar, 1980 edn., *The Battle for Gaul*, translated by A. & P. Wiseman, Russel Sharp, Guildford.
Long, W., 1935, 'Size of Fields in Devon', *Farm Economist*, **I.II**, 224-5.
Marshall, W., 1796a, *The Rural Economy of Yorkshire*, London.
Marshall, W., 1796b, *Planting and Rural Ornament*, London.
Millman, R.N., (1975), *The Making of the Scottish Landscape*, Batsford, London.
Muir, R., 2000, *The New Reading the Landscape*, Exeter University Press, Exeter.
Muir, R., 2000a, 'Pollards in Nidderdale: A Landscape History' *Rural History*, 11.1, 95–111.
Muir, R., 2001, *Landscape Detective*, Windgather, Macclesfield.
Muir, R. and Muir, N., 1987, *Hedgerows*, Michael Joseph, London.
Norden, J., 1607, *Surveyors Dialogue*, London.
Rackham, O., 1976, *Trees and Woodland in the British Landscape*, Dent, London.
Rackham, O, 1986, *The History of the Countryside*, Dent, London.
Tusser, T., 1573, *Five Hundred Points of Good Husbandry*.
Turner, S., 2004, 'The Changing Ancient Landscape: South-West England *c*.1700-1900', *LANDSCAPES (sic)*, **5**.1, pp.18-34.
Whyte, I., 2003, *Transforming Fell and Valley*, University of Lancaster, Lancaster.
Williamson, T., 2002(a), *Hedges and Walls*, National Trust Enterprises Ltd., London.
Williamson, T., 2002(b), *The Transformation of Rural England*, Exeter University Press, Exeter.
Young, D.W., 1969, 'The History of Forest Woodlands' in Edlin, H.L.(ed.), *New Forest*, H.M.S.O., London, pp.33-41

4

Trees in the park:
the earlier days

Parks are regarded as places where scenery has been created and maintained in an idealised form. They are seen as places for spiritual enrichment and as refuges for the temporary evasion of the ugliness and clamour associated with the world outside their gates, and their potentials for recreation and contemplation are thought to have primacy over the stresses and tedium of the workaday world. To some degree, all these perceptions are true, but they are also contradicted – for parks have almost always been multi-faceted and multi-functional. The role of the park within society shifted from one end of the spectrum to the other as the rigidly exclusive aristocratic hunting reserve evolved, by stages, into the municipal park giving free access to its crowded paths, trampled shrubberies and ice-cream stands.

Landscape archaeologists/historians have recently devoted much time to discussions about 'designed medieval landscapes'. Their perspectives would have been more refined had they partaken of the geographers' work on 'therapeutic landscapes', another topic of quite recent interest. They would have had a better understanding of why countrysides adjacent to medieval castles, abbeys or priories were frequently subject to aesthetic manipulations. Therapeutic landscapes have been created since biblical times, and aesthetic evaluation of landscape has been part of the realms of academic geography since at least the time of Vaughan Cornish (1862-1948). As well as the emerging interest in the therapeutic qualities of landscape there was a longer-standing tradition of geographical research concerning landscape taste and aesthetics. Any landscape could be therapeutic if it improved the physical health or mental well-being of those experiencing it. A designed landscape was, like any other cultural landscape, a functional landscape. Its function, however, was (largely or partly) therapeutic and recreational; it generally served the spirit more than the purse. One cannot imagine parkland without imagining trees and a park without trees

Ripley deer park: a parkland landscape composed of lawns and trees, some from earlier countrysides and some introduced as landscaping elements. The 'prospect and refuge' aspect is exemplified

would almost be unthinkable. But why should this be? Surely any consideration of the making and operation of parks should be prefaced with a discussion on *why* the tree-grove-lawn combination should be so appealing that it has been recreated in countless places over several millennia.

Trees on the brain

The case for trees in the creation of designed therapeutic landscapes (parks) comes in two main forms: the biological and the aesthetic. (The third explanation, the utilitarian, is more in the nature of a sub-case: if trees are included in the idealised landscape for psychological reasons it is only reasonable that they will then be exploited for fodder, fruits or fuel.) The two main cases concern the human mind and the psychological predisposition towards certain forms of scenery. They differ according to whether one believes that the main preferences are genetic and instinctive or whether they take shape in the conscious mind and concern aesthetic tastes such as might be cultivated and refined. On the whole, those experts based in biology will tend to favour the former interpretation and those from art history and related fields will respond to the aesthetic interpretation (to do otherwise would be to invalidate their own interpretations).

Biological explanations derive from the rich and under-exploited field of ethology, which interprets human behaviour in terms of a psychological inheritance from numberless millennia spent by human ancestors as undifferentiated members of the animal kingdom. The peoples of the temperate lands of the northern hemisphere have been the great park-makers and it might be argued that prolonged temporal isolation from the East African savannah countrysides of lawns, scattered trees and groves would have dulled any predisposition towards such scenery. However, now that the old perceptions concerning an ancient 'wildwood' are yielding, by virtue of Vera's work, to visions of woodland archipelagos broken up by natural glades, the intellectual ground has shifted. Now, landscapes with many park-like qualities seem to have been the homes and hunting ranges for our ancestors in the pre-metallurgical ages. Vera points out that interpretations of raw pollen data have created a misleading picture of prehistoric landscapes that were much more heavily wooded than they had been in reality:

> … research into the relationship between modern pollen spectra and landscapes show that pollen spectra interpreted as closed forest according to prevailing theory, were actually semi-open to very open landscapes … pollen diagrams that are traditionally interpreted as closed forest, could also have been a grazed park-like landscape (2000, p.101).

In considering how humans behave in, and towards, their setting we have to remember that the guiding influences are not just 'out there', but they also exist within our brains. The features of the world outside our bodies have no significance for us other than in terms of the meanings that we attribute to them. These interpretations are the most intricate constructions deriving from instinct and subconscious constructions, childhood experiences and conscious appraisal. Some reactions or emotions are difficult to explain in rational terms – like the drive to procreate that is said to influence those exposed to mass mortalities – while others are learned – such as not treating wasps like big, pretty flies. As Meinig pointed out, any landscape '… is composed not only of what lies before our eyes but what lies within our heads' (1979, p.34).

Some useful and thought-provoking work on the biological origins of landscape taste was undertaken as long ago as 1980, by which time the deep antiquity of human origins had been appreciated, and it had been fairly universally recognised that the sub-tropical savannahs of Africa had formed the cradle of humankind. Orians noted that these park-like environments, neither closed forests nor open plains, had provided the hominids with a wealth of useful resources that could be obtained within a couple of metres of the ground and where riversides and lake margins provided water within generally parched settings. Was it not then thoroughly natural, he asked, that experiences in the formative period of human evolution should have led, in recent times, to the creation of parks? These replicated the semi-open character of the savannahs with their stippling of trees, they almost invariably incorporated water or used landscaping tricks to exaggerate the size of water bodies.

Since this time, a reappraisal of australopithecine remains has led to changes of nuance. While earlier interpretations emphasised their human-like characteristics, particularly in relation to the upright stance and striding gait, later ones have detected attributes that fitted their owners more for arboreal life and may have made their forays into open countryside less confident. Australopithecines are still regarded as creatures of the forest and savannah margins, though they are now thought more disposed to life in and around trees than was the case before. Their lifestyles will have given them access both to fruit, nuts, eggs, hatchlings and foliage in the trees and also to roots, shoots, bulbs and carrion on the ground. The trees will have afforded some protection from large predators and terrestrial scavengers, but not from leopards, which habitually dragged their kills up to the security of treetops and which are also known to have eaten australopithecines.

A more sophisticated development of the ideas voiced by Orians was provided by the geographer Appleton (1986, 1990, 1996). Biological influences on human taste in scenery were organised into two theories: *habitat theory* and *prospect-refuge theory*. The former suggests that in psychological terms we have inherited a rather utilitarian attitude towards settings, though frequently we fail to recognise that it is operating. That people would have a positive emotional response towards a bowl of delicious fruit salad set before us is not surprising. According to Appleton a similar 'ingestive' response would be triggered by the site of a herd of cattle quietly grazing, a crystal spring or a field of barley. Thus we have, according to habitat theory, subconscious dispositions to respond favourably to those things which assist our survival. In this way our behaviour is similar to that of any other creature.

Prospect-refuge theory considered the character of settings in terms of their ability to favour the survival of countless generations of our forbears who existed as relatively weak and vulnerable hunter-gatherers in settings populated both by game and by powerful predators. He considered that the type of environment most favourable to human survival was one that gave them the ability to prospect for food and danger while remaining hidden. Survival depended upon success in the quest to see without being seen. In closed habitats, like the forest, potential food resources for an omnivorous hominid were hidden and in order to obtain them it was necessary to leave the protective shelter of the trees – thus being vulnerable to predation by others. The ideal was a partly open landscape punctuated by areas of cover – thus allowing our subjects to lurk unseen before emerging to hunt in relative safety. Such characteristics were found in the Eden-like savannahs of Africa, with their grassy plains and watering places, their scattered trees and their shady tree clusters and woodland margins. This is also the

According to Vaughan Cornish, open woodland did not feel oppressive because trees at different distances to the viewer gave a sense of depth and perspective

form of natural/semi-natural scenery that is most closely replicated by the park.

When designing landscapes under the subliminal influences of ancient survival needs, people have sought to replicate a proper balance between the needs of prospect and refuge. In the medieval garden, the prospect-refuge symbolism of the tall wall providing protection and concealment and the balancing character of the prospect mount, providing an ability to scan the refuge are fairly obvious. Orians had noted that: 'Parks and gardens in all cultures are neither closed forests nor open grasslands. In addition, great pains are taken in the creation of parks and gardens to create water or the illusion of water, or to enhance the quality and quantity of existing water resources'(1986, p.11). Appleton developed these ideas further:

> The extension of the prospect into the countryside beyond the refuge of the garden led logically to the modification of the wider landscape also for aesthetic purposes, initially by extending avenues beyond the limits of the enclosure. The technique of 'improving' parks was necessarily different from those most appropriate to the more restricted garden, but the balance of prospect and refuge was no less fundamental to landscaping on the larger scale (1996, p.172).

He added that, indeed:

> Because it was planned on a larger scale the park generally afforded greater opportunities than the more restricted garden for accentuating the prospect symbolism. Indeed the term 'prospect' permeates the literature of eighteenth century landscape gardening (*ibid.*).

Appleton believed that the landscape manipulators of the post-medieval centuries had, in seeking to turn workaday countrysides into fashionable parks, often faced a 'prospect *or* refuge' scenario. The raw materials for their creations were rigidly divided between refuge-dominant masses, like thick woods, or prospect-dominant voids, like open fields. Their task in making more idealised landscapes was one of fraying the edges and blurring the differences. Open farmland could be given a stipple of trees, while the woodland margins could be made scalloped or ragged. By creating more intermediate forms, the intuitively cherished 'edge-of-the-wood' setting could be recreated.

These ideas were given a somewhat frosty reception by some cultural geographers and art historians. This is hardly surprising. For, if the keys to human landscape taste are to be found in biology and evolutionary history, then the positions of those who have nurtured elitist views based on carefully cultivated and refined aesthetic sensibilities are undermined. If our response to landscape is fundamentally intuitive and utilitarian then intellectualisations of the more mannered and rarefied kind seem less valid. The implication is that quite ordinary people could have sentiments concerning landscape, and these sentiments would be essentially similar to those harboured by better-educated and more erudite individuals.

During the last few years of the last millennium a closely complementary interest in what came to be known as 'therapeutic landscapes' developed within the usually unrelated disciplines of medicine and geography (Gesler, 1993). The premise upon which such studies are based is quite a simple one: there are some landscapes which, as settings for human life/visits, generate therapeutic influences. The notion that some places are conducive to mental or physical well-being is scarcely a revelation. For example, it underlay the pioneering bathing activities of more adventurous members of the upper classes at Scarborough, where the efficacy of sea water was described by the local physician, Dr Witter, in 1660 and affirmed by the London doctors, Floyer and Baynard in 1702. (Why the sea water at Scarborough should have been better than at other places on the coast is not clear.) Sea water is more a chemical than a view and in considering the evidence for therapeutic landscapes, one needs to identify real *landscape* qualities. For example, the hill stations of colonial India were considered therapeutic because of their cooler climates rather than their scenic attributes, while spas like Cheltenham, Harrogate and Ilkley were mainly regarded as therapeutic because of their mineral springs and wells. (In the northern examples there seems to have been something of a sense that a measure of climatic discomfort would do one good.)

If therapeutic landscape studies amounted to no more than claiming that some places are more agreeable than others they would scarcely be worth the efforts involved. However, various subtexts, concerning topics such as childhood experiences, religious orientations, national history and identity, appear to be encoded into our therapeutic appraisals of landscape, making them psychologically complicated constructions. One can imagine that the therapeutic landscape must have its opposite in what one might term a noxious or debilitating landscape. Obviously, such a place might be blighted by pollution, poverty or lawlessness, yet someone who had undergone a terrifying experience of being cut off by the tide might respond to 'pleasant' seaside settings as though they were noxious landscapes. Therapeutic landscapes also surface in literature. For example in 'John Buchan's' *The Thirty-Nine Steps* there was no need for Hannay to hide in Galloway: he could have gone to ground in London. The invocation of Galloway has been regarded as the author's longing for Scotland at a time when he lay sick in Kent with the Great War raging just across the Channel (Daniell, 1991, pp.8-10).

Given that people have chosen to reproduce parkland landscape for century upon century, there is every reason to believe that it has therapeutic qualities. Appleton has described the park-makers' quest for balance between the secure associations of the refuge and the stimulating effects of the abilities to scan or prospect. Parkland is sufficiently diverse to avoid monotony. Unless special vantage points (mansions, mounds or mounts, towers etc.) have been deliberately provided one can seldom view the park in its entirety. Trees and groves mask more distant areas from view, so that as one proceeds around the park a succession of partly 'hidden' prospects are revealed. These constitute surprise elements, but the surprises are never so abrupt or threatening that they give rise to fear. There is nothing to compare with the terrifying (for most) exposure experienced by those who scale crags and follow arêtes. Water is provided, but not in forms that would harbour crocodiles, have toxic infestations or lap over quicksands. Diversity exists within regulated bounds; the alternation of lawn, grove, rivulet and pond is sufficient to hold and stimulate attention but not to cause alarm.

Cornish was one of the first researchers to attempt a serious appraisal of the psychological roots of landscape taste. He recalled how, on hot summer days, he would resort to the shade of local oak, beech and pine woods, some of them having a coppiced understorey. In these places he realised that he had no sense of being cramped or confined and set out to discover why this was so.

> In [a quarry] one would feel 'shut in'. How is it, then, that the wood is free from this defect? The explanation is the stereoscopic effect of trunks and boughs and slender shoots. The 'solid geometry' thus acquired greatly enhances the sense of distance (1943, pp.61-2).

The early deer parks

The manipulation of landscape by burning to open up hunting ranges and to stimulate the expansion of grazing has been proposed as beginning in Mesolithic times (e.g. Simmons, 1969, Moore, 1988). More recently, it has been argued that fire is not an effective means of reducing deciduous woodland and that Mesolithic axes were even less effective in this respect. Trees could be killed by employing smaller, sharper tools in ring-barking, while fire was effective in temporarily suppressing bracken, the coarser grasses and other plants unpalatable to herbivores within existing clearings (Simmons, 2003, p.39-42). If, as Vera suggests, the natural woodland was frequently broken by glades then it would have been converted into semi-natural woodland as Mesolithic hunters (and herders?) deliberately maintained the open character of existing glades, employed burning or other techniques to encourage better grazing and, probably, created

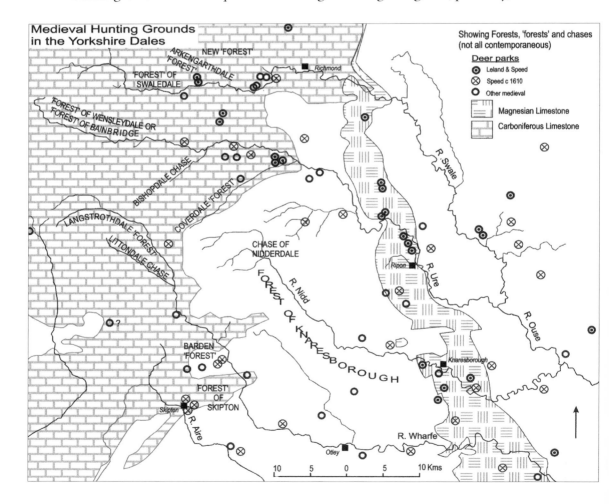

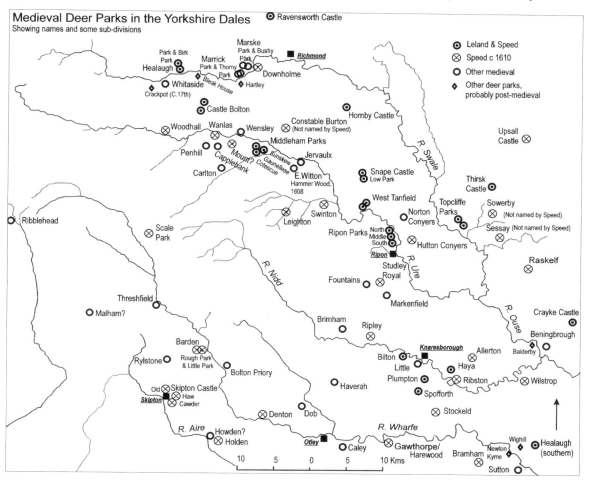

Medieval Deer Parks in the Yorkshire Dales
Showing names and some sub-divisions

new clearings. There is no suggestion that hunting was a recreation rather than a necessity at this time. (Even so, it is hard to imagine that ritual elements did not intrude and the stag frontlets found at the Star Carr settlement site in the Vale of Pickering were intended to be worn either in ceremonies or as a hunting disguise.) The creation of late-prehistoric hunting parks (perhaps in association with the sprawling Iron Age oppidum-cum-palace sites) is easily imagined and Roman hunting parks seem a still more credible possibility. Their desire for blood can only partially have been slaked by the amphitheatres built at places like St Albans and Catterick.

As long ago as 1957, Beresford remarked that: 'The *doer falds* [deer folds] of some Anglo-Saxon charters may have been parks' (p.192). It is only for the Saxon era that one can recognise the existence of deer parks, though even in this period the geographical character and institutional status of the deer park are rather blurred. One would like to know, for example, the degree to which these parks resembled the well-attested ones that post-dated the Norman Conquest — as well

Deer parks were created out of a wide variety of settings. The Tudor deer park at Ripley spanned workaday farmland and deserted settlements. The trough running diagonally across the picture is the holloway of the road to the deserted hamlet of Whipley and the flanking trees are the last remains of its roadside hedgerows

as the degree to which they lay in their lineage. In the imaginations of more enlightened times, the hunting of deer by the aristocracy has been associated with the exclusion of countryfolk from parts of their native lands, fiendish retributions against poachers, authoritarian government and institutionalised feudal inequality. Consequently, it was easy to identify the establishment of these hunting reserves with the conquest of England and Wales by the militaristic Norman elite. Feudalism was deemed a Norman imposition and the deer park epitomised the new, oppressive order. However, there are, within the Saxon records, references to things that might be likened to deer parks. The likeness is somewhat blurred by the ambiguous nature of the words employed: *haga* and *haia*, later 'hays', were terms that could also denote small woods, hedged enclosures and hedges. How the evidence is interpreted today depends, to some extent, upon whether the expert concerned adopts a traditional view of seeing the Norman Conquest as a fundamental break with the traditions, culture and institutions of Old England, or whether good measures of continuity are thought to have survived the dynastic change.

Fairly recently, evidence has come to light that suggests that no matter how vastly the conventions concerned with hunting and game conservation may have been codified and expanded under the Normans and Plantagenets, the

The roe deer: secretive and nocturnal but sometimes flushed into open countryside and coursed or else driven into concealed nets

precursors of both deer parks and Forests existed in the late-Saxon countryside. A book of Anglo-Saxon wills published by Whitelock, in 1930, mentioned, (in connection with the will of Thurstan dated to 1045) a '*derhage*' or deer hedge at Ongar in Essex. The argument that a hedge used for confining deer must be associated with a park was underlined by the fact that Ongar is known to have had a park in medieval times – one which survived until the second half of the twentieth century before falling a victim to modern agriculture. Though the northern half of Britain is a land of mystery to too many landscape historians, as long ago as the 1960s Arthur Raistrick, the great biographer of the landscape of the Dales, detected arrangements for hunting in the pre-Conquest territories of the region. The place name 'Harkerside' in Swaledale derives from Old English words meaning 'deer park', while Fleming (pp.74-75) has noted the similarities between deer parks and the 'winter parks' that existed in Swaledale around the twelfth century and perhaps earlier. Often recorded as 'parks' in the local place names, these were wolf-proof enclosures where livestock could be fed in winter on hay or leaves, while manuring the ground for future hay crops. Might not enclosures such as these, encircled by hedges or palings, have been prototypes for later deer parks?

Further south, Hook focused attention on the word '*haga*', giving it a more specific interpretation as '… some kind of strong fence, often around woodland' (1998, p.54). She noted that the term recurred in Anglo-Saxon boundary clauses and that in Berkshire and Hampshire *haga* alignments were sometimes found to coincide with parish boundaries. The *haga* features were, she thought, some kind of pale, perhaps an earthen bank topped with a timber palisade or a hedge – perhaps a dead hedge of impenetrable thorns:'The fences were almost certainly

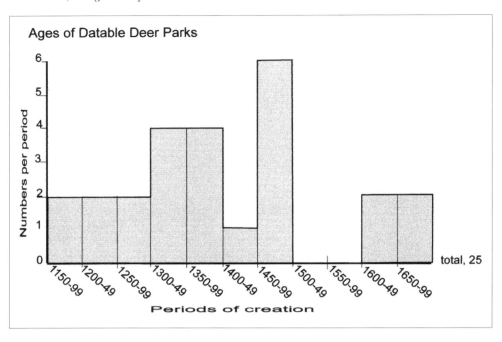

Ages of datable deer parks in the Yorkshire Dales and lands west of the R. Ouse

intended for the control of deer and the term was in fact used for a deer-park at Ongar in Essex in the eleventh century and for another deer-park at a later date in Gloucestershire' (1998, p.157). There were other pre-Conquest references that mentioned hunting, like the mention of a hunting vill or township at Bickleigh in Devon as well as the law granting every man the right to hunt on his own land. Hook quoted the late tenth-century Colloquy by a monk of Cerne Abbas, who described the use of dogs to drive boar towards an unmounted huntsman. Dogs were also used to drive deer into nets as described in a passage from the same source – and roe deer were frequently netted during the post-Conquest era.

Two decades after the Norman Conquest, Domesday Book presents the evidence of a kingdom in which the possession of one or more deer parks is a characteristic of aristocratic status. However, such is the ambiguity of '*haga*', which is applied in a range of quite different contexts from river booms to urban localities (Liddiard, 2003, p.12) that it is hard to trace the deer parks back in time. Also, there appear to have been differences in the ways that parks were (or were not) recorded in different parts of the kingdom, while, to complicate matters further, sometimes the word '*parcus*' or park is used, apparently as a substitute for *haia* and *haga* (the Old English is '*pearroc*'). The evidence for the typical topography and appearance of the Norman deer park is scarcely more revealing than that deriving from pre-Conquest England. The *haia* at Crofton in Shropshire or the four examples at Kingsley in Cheshire were said to be for the purpose of catching roe deer (Liddiard, *ibid.*). This implies a fairly dense tree cover, for roe deer are woodland animals. Some of the pre-Conquest parks that have been recorded seem to lie in woodland edge locations.

If woods and woodland edge country beyond the margins of cultivated and well-settled lands were the normal places for the establishment of pre-Conquest deer parks, this rule did not apply with any reliability as the medieval period progressed. During the three centuries after Domesday, growing populations created a tension between aristocratic recreation and the needs of mass subsistence and timber production. Downholme Park in Swaledale was established in 1377 in a setting where peasant population pressures were forcing the ploughing of former wood pasture. In the same dale and century, Healaugh Park was carved out of the wood pasture of Feetham township (Fleming, 1998, pp.91-2). Beningbrough Park, near York, was formed in 1284 from a part of the Forest of Galtres that had been abandoned by deer and comprised 56.5 acres of wood and 100 acres of adjoining demesne and Raskelf, near Easingwold, was formed from manorial woods in 1388. Often the creation of a deer park involved a ruthless disregard for the existing character of the countryside and the tenants that worked it. The establishment of a park at Hornby Castle, near Bedale, was said to have involved the casting down of 40 husbandries in the late fifteenth century. The eviction of villagers and enclosure of their fields in a deer park at Wilstrop, near Leeds, in about 1490, produced a virtual tenants' rebellion, and the New Park of the sixteenth century at Marrick in Swaledale commandeered the village ploughlands. It was commonplace for roads to be diverted to take the traffic out of a new deer park, as when Little Bolton Park in Wensleydale was created around 1314.

It may have been noted that the examples quoted in the preceding paragraph are from the North of England. Had they been from Suffolk, Bedfordshire, Kent, Hampshire and Cambridgeshire, they would have become commonplace within the academic community. This takes us to a dilemma concerning recreation and historical landscapes. In the minds of many people of influence there are places that 'matter' (i.e. the Midlands and South-East) and other places (i.e. Northern England and the Celtic lands) that 'matter' much less. Norms are set by the places that 'matter', so that situations observed in other places are 'deviations' or 'regional variations', and as such, much less important. If information from all the places that 'matter less' were incorporated into the norm then, of course, the norm would be quite different. Thus it is with deer parks, where the southern norms often seem contradicted in the North. Recent work by the author shows that the most concentrated assemblage of deer parks in the whole of England was probably to be found on the limestone lands to the west of the river Ouse. However, in terms of prevailing thinking, this heartland was a 'periphery' so the 'norm' is set by places that were more peripheral so far as hunting was concerned. These are the sort of contradictions resulting when Lewisham is judged more important than the Isle of Lewis.

It may well be that the earliest deer parks were established in the wooded or semi-wooded margins of estates, but this pattern would probably be influenced by changes in the nature of the quarry. Wild boar were creatures that rooted for food of all kinds, from newborn animals to roots, shoots, acorns and beech mast on the woodland floor. Though essentially woodland creatures, they would emerge to cause havoc among the crops and impose risks of severe punishment on feudal tenants who took reprisals. Probably already locally scarce by the Conquest, they were unable to maintain their population levels in the face of the intensity of medieval hunting and hunting grounds had to be artificially stocked – with gifts of boar, like deer, being a form of largesse. The boar may have vanished by the close of the medieval period and an attempt to restock the New Forest with boar by Charles I failed. A medieval monarch, possessing a collection of vast and widely distributed Forests, was well-positioned to provide boar or deer to favoured subjects. Boar (and their domesticated brethren) did not coexist happily with deer and would eat hinds giving birth and devour their helpless offspring. In 1269 a Forest court at Oakham heard charges against the chief forester, Peter de Neville, and his underlings, who were accused with overstocking the Forest pastures with 300 swine, to the detriment of the king's deer (Dowsett, 1942, p.180).

Before the Conquest there were two native deer: the roe and the red. The roe deer, though only the size of a largish dog, could be quite aggressive. It was very much a secretive creature of the woods, though local fen and moorland populations existed. It seems to have been present in large numbers at the time of the Conquest, declining steeply as both population and hunting expanded in the medieval period, and then increasing markedly in modern times as rural working populations have declined. It was frequently caught by netting breaks in the woodland, but its quest for deep cover made it difficult to course with dogs across open country in the preferred manner. It was also a nocturnal animal, another detraction from the perspective of the huntsman. For most of the medieval period it enjoyed the legal protection afforded to other deer, in spite of which its numbers declined, though in the fourteenth century this protection was lifted on account of its aggression towards other deer, and it became merely a 'beast of the warren', like the marten or fox.

The red deer had a less specialised choice in habitats, though its antlers would have been a handicap in denser woodland thickets. It existed in the relatively open or semi-wooded environments that existed at Hoxne in Suffolk around 250,000 years ago. In the Palaeolithic and Mesolithic periods in Britain red deer were common and very markedly larger than those seen on the Scottish hills today, the British animals having become much smaller in relatively recent times. Today, the red deer is visualised in terms of the stereotypical images painted by Landseer and other romantic painters of the Victorian era.

A lifestyle not unlike that of the Scottish survivors, that feed on high-level grazings in summer and retreat to sheltered hollows in winter, was led by some of the red deer in medieval Yorkshire. Writing of Bishopdale around 1540, the late-

Red deer in Studley Royal deer park. While the stags are impressive, they would be dwarfed by their gigantic ancestors of the prehistoric era

medieval chronicler, Leland, wrote: '… yn the Hilles about hit be Redde Deere. In fair Winters the Deere kepe there, in shrap [yes, ed.] Winters they forsake the extreme Colde and Barennes of them' (Toulmin Smith, 1907). The last wild deer in the Yorkshire Dales would disappear fairly soon after this, victims of a poaching dispute that almost amounted to a civil war between the mighty Cliffords and a collection of lesser gentry offended by their imperious attitudes to hunting rights. Efforts were made to conserve the surviving deer of the Yorkshire Dales in deer parks, but these were often broken and the deer slain or dispersed. Most of the numerous kills made by Norman hunting parties will have consisted of red deer. While some animals were kept in parks, most of the recorded material comes from Royal Forests or the chases of the greater nobles and churchmen. The Forests and chases were un-enclosed but immense, and generally spanned a range of land-use types: woodland, moorland, commons, meadows and tillage were often all represented. Consequently, one does not know which habitats the deer concerned were favouring. The red deer was relatively catholic in its tastes, tending to favour the more open uplands in the winter, while descending through wooded slopes to shelter in valleys in winter, as noted above. In medieval Yorkshire it was, like the wolf, an animal of both woodland and open fell and some of the epic hunts seem to have ranged across miles of open country. From the point of view of the huntsman and the aristocratic enthusiasm for coursing game with greyhound-like dogs it was probably most attractive as a subject for hunting in the unconfined spaces of the Forest rather than the limited confines of the deer park.

The Normans were responsible for the introduction – or, rather, reintroduction, for it had inhabited Britain during some interglacials – of the fallow deer. Though, like the wild boar, regarded as a woodland animal, the fallow deer would not only browse and eat acorns, it was also very content as a grazing animal. It was, therefore, highly suited to the deer park environment of groves and lawns. One can only wonder about the extent to which fallow deer influenced the design of such settings.

Fallow deer are not only suitable for coursing and other cruelties, they are also, even within the deer tribe, exceptionally beautiful with their palmate antlers and white-spotted skin ranging from darkish brown to gold. The merits of fallow deer as parkland animals were appreciated by the Romans, though had fallow deer been introduced to Britain by these invaders some would surely have escaped to establish wild communities. In fact there are neither archaeological nor archival evidences of the animal between the penultimate interglacial and the Norman Conquest. Rackham believed that the introduction would have occurred after the death of William the Conqueror:

> The early twelfth century would have been an appropriate time for the Normans of England to have acquired fallow deer from their colleagues, the Normans of Sicily, who had inherited Classical and Islamic traditions of keeping oriental beasts in parks. By the thirteenth century the fashion for fallow had spread to Wales, Scotland, and Ireland (1986, p.49).

Never particularly abundant in the medieval period, deer were an important form of largesse, as when in November 1414 a royal warrant granted Sir William Gascoigne of Gawthorpe Hall, Harewood, a retiring judge who had probably lent money to the king, an allowance of four bucks and four does every year from the royal Forest of Pontefract to stock his deer park (Parsons, 1834, p.259). Similarly valued gifts could be bestowed to keep a younger brother within the family fold, thus, after Richard, Earl of Cornwall emparked Bilton, near Harrogate, his brother Henry III gave him 40 Pontefract deer in 1244 to stock his park, with a further 30 from the Forest of Galtres following at the end of the decade (*Calendar of close rolls* 1227-47, p.218 and 1247-51, p.372).

Rackham regards the introduction of the fallow deer and the closely contemporaneous introduction of the rabbit as both having '… the same purpose of producing meat from poor-quality land' (1986, p.50). In fact there is considerable debate about whether the medieval deer parks should be regarded as hunting territories, venison farms or aesthetic creations. Common sense argues that most parks were probably all these things and so the issue is all a matter of emphasis.

Some old woodland names remain valid, as at Birk Crag, near Harrogate, where birch still shades the crags

The wild cherry nearest the camera), at Studley Royal, near Ripon, is thought to be the largest specimen of its kind. It is far larger than typical examples

Above Beeches, like these in the New Forest, can achieve impressive dimensions in a third of the time taken by oaks

Opposite The Major Oak in Sherwood Forest

In the quadrangle of St Mary's College, St Andrews, there are two landmark trees. Queen Mary's Thorn (*above*) is said to have been planted by Mary, Queen of Scots in 1563. The main stump is decayed, but vigorous stems have burst forth from it. Facing it across the quadrangle is the St Andrews Holm Oak (*below*) flourishing in the sheltered setting to become, with a girth of about 12ft, the largest recorded specimen of its kind in Scotland

This huge pollarded sweet chestnut crashed under the weight of its boughs in 2003. Resembling a 700-year-old oak without its tell-tale leaves in winter, it was, however, the product of post-medieval park-making at Studley Royal and perhaps only half that age

Most of the hedgerow trees in this Nidderdale locality were planted during the Tudor/Elizabethan enclosure of the common fields, but many have died to widen the gaps between the remaining hedgerow trees

Wind–blasted beech in an East Fifeshire hedge: a facet of the Improvements
and serving to reduce the effects of the frequent gales

Dense hedgerows, standard and pollarded hedgerow trees and tiny woods endow many Devon countrysides with their charms

An ancient hedgerow in deep decline: the ash pollard and thorn shrubs have become isolated and ineffectual

A magnificent ancient countryside of hedgerows and hedgerow pollards near Mortonhampstead, Devon

Wood pasture, with trees that are well-spaced, allowing grass to colonise the intervening ground, has many similarities with parkland and with 'prospect and refuge' qualities

Abbots and priors had deer parks, just like the lay nobility. In addition to its immense estates, Fountains Abbey had a home park on its doorstep and the abbot could hunt in another at Brimham, just a few miles away

Fallow deer with their antlers in velvet

'In the forests are the secret places of kings and their great delight' Richard fitz Nigel. An idyllic evening in the New Forest

A trio of beeches in the New Forest

Opposite above The medieval foresters' settlement of Bainbridge in Wensleydale as seen today

Opposite below This coppice stool is a single tree. Coppiced for as long as 1,000 years, it takes on a strange, squid-like appearance after a century or so of neglect.

Below This scene in Hayley Wood, Cambridgeshire, shows the woodland setting at its most idyllic, it being fresh and spacious, devoid of senses of monotony or oppressiveness.

Above Burnham Beeches

Opposite A woodbank at Hayley Wood, Cambridge

With an appearance that is 'smooth' rather than gnarled, this tree seems to have grown quite swiftly. It could be one of the last to be pollarded before the practice began to die out in North Yorkshire about 250 years ago

Current fashion seems to be leaning away from the hunting perspective, yet in the North of England, at least, there is abundant evidence that hunting was probably the main preoccupation of the park owners. The earthworks of hunting towers, which provided elevated platforms for shooting at deer and venues for parties after the hunt, can sometimes be detected on or near the highest ground in a medieval park (e.g. Ripley, North Yorkshire). At Healaugh in Swaledale, the park owners, either the Gants or the Bigods, had a chapel and a lead-roofed 'touresse' built to serve as a vantage point from which they could watch the deer being coursed in the park. There were also numerous written records of hunting in parks. After Edward Balliol was deposed as king of Scotland he lived at Wheatley near Doncaster. According to a record of hunting in Hatfield Chase, nearby, in the *Federa* 19 Oct 1356 (quoted in Jones, 1859, p.137), he killed 16 hinds, 6 does, 8 stags, 3 calves and 6 kids in the chase. In the park he then killed 8 damas, 1 sourum, 1 surellum (different kinds of fallow deer) before turning his gaze to the fishponds, where nothing seems to have been small to atract his attention. In the ponds 2 pikes of 3.5ft in length, 3 of 3ft, 20 of 2.5ft, 20 of 2ft, 50 pickerels of 1.5ft, 6 of 1ft; 109 perch, roach tench and 'skelys', and 6 bream and 'bremettes' were slain. The hunting of deer in parks continued through the Middle Ages and beyond it; in his almanac entry for 1 September 1665, Sir William Ingilby of Ripley Castle wrote: 'I filled a Black Bucke out of the Parke at Rypley ... another [?] before 3 fawnes this year count ten is all left ... 2 bucks killed out of the paddock this year' (Ingilby MS 3590). The royal lust for gore continued from late Tudor to Stuart times, with Henry VIII, Elizabeth and the Stuart kings setting examples for the rest to follow.

The excitement was heightened and enemies were humiliated in the most contemptuous manner when hunters broke into a park and coursed its owner's deer. In a mid-sixteenth-century court case a Lancelot Marton recalled being out with his father as a lad when he witnessed a Clifford raid on the Norton's deer at Rilston, near Skipton. He said that he saw: '... keepers of Skipton Forest hunt and chase deer out of the grounds of Rilston; and also myne old Lady Clifford mother to my lord of Cumberland that now is, hound her greyhound within the said grounds of Rilston and chase deer, and have them at her leisure, both red and fallow' (Whitaker, 1878, p.305). Lady Clifford was pursuing a feud concerning conflicting hunting rights. The actions seem amazingly stupid in the case of Sir John Robinson, the vicar of Knaresborough. Presumably in full view of members of his congregation, he broke into a royal park at Haya, Knaresborough, with a dozen companions, killing four deer and wounding several others before being apprehended (Speight, 1894, p.211).

Deer parks were hunting reserves. They confined a breeding population of deer, usually fallow deer, and protected them against unlawful predation by humans or wild animals. The owners of deer parks normally owned several manors and would progress from one to the next with a retinue of companions and servants, consuming the produce of each. On arrival at a castle or important manor house, hunting would be available in the deer park and the venison that resulted would either be salted down for future use or served to the host and his party. Who could say whether the hunting or the meat should considered the more important?

There was, however, an additional consideration: the aesthetic. So long as research into park landscapes was dominated by art historians, attention was focused on the celebrated landscape designers of the post-Renaissance period: Repton, Brown and so on. The awareness that *medieval* landscapes were very frequently transformed in the most far-reaching of manners by now-nameless designers has been the result of fairly recent work by a very different type of specialist, the landscape archaeologist. Now, in the realms of landscape history and landscape archaeology the terms 'medieval designed landscape' and 'medieval ornamental landscape' are as current as 'deserted medieval village' was a half a century ago. Perhaps a realisation of the medieval creativity should have dawned earlier, for the similarities were recognised by Beresford in 1957 when he wrote of Fountains Abbey Home Park:

> The best portions lie on the edge of the wood north-west of the great lake *which looks like the work of some ambitious landscape gardener of the eighteenth century* but is in fact the creation of the monks who dammed the valley with a great earthen bank. Just below the dam, where the stream is crossed by the monk Wall, there is the original bridge designed to let water escape while retaining the animals with which the park was stocked (p.195-7, my ital.).

There is no doubt that medieval people were at least as status-conscious as the members of any society that followed. Feudalism, a system of social organisation more rigid than almost any other, ascribed to every person in the kingdom a position in the social hierarchy, a burden of obligations to social superiors and various dues from members of lower social orders, if these existed. The existence of an institutionalised hierarchy did not remove the need for status-seeking behaviour. Rather, it increased it. While the aristocratic home had no marble statuary or hugely expensive canvases to display, its massive walls and crenellations conveyed messages that a martial society understood very well. How much more emphatic the statement would be if the guests who were the targets for the exercises in establishing status could be brought to the dynastic stronghold along a route which maximised its visual impact. Their first glimpse might see it mirrored in a lake, moat or fishpond; there might be an approach through the idyllic countryside of a deer park, or else the deer might be seen like specks of gold on a distant slope beyond the pale. The medieval designed landscapes that are being recognised at increasing numbers of palace, castle, abbey and important manor sites could never be the creations of a benighted society helplessly awaiting the birth of a Repton, Brown or Kent. Most of the telling combinations of scenic types and facets were known to the anonymous people

Framlingham in Suffolk
was an innovative castle,
with early square towers
punctuating its curtain
wall, but it was also the
hub of a carefully designed
landscape with parkland
and sheets of water

who created the settings for courtly life. Not only did the ornamental landscape display the lord's home and stronghold to maximum effect, it also provided an inviting setting for enjoying domesticated flowers and herbs and their perfumes and it served as a place for dalliance, for the enacting of roles and for the playing of games. A key feature of the carefully manipulated setting was the deer park, where the men, sometimes their ladies too, could vent their aristocratic lust for blood and practice their martial skills – all with an audience on the battlements or towers looking down to witness the display.

At Stow in Lincolnshire in the 1980s, archaeologists of the Royal Commission on the Historical Monuments of England investigated the site of a badly damaged medieval deer park. The moated site of a palace and retreat of the bishops of Lincoln was recognised, as well as the dams that had ponded back three lakes, the central dam having provided the causeway for the main approach route to the palace. An effect of the medieval landscaping was that the road leading to the palace seemed to pass over large sheets of water (Everson et al. 1991). Once the fact that medieval nobles had manipulated the settings of their domestic life in order to produce pleasing aesthetic results had been acknowledged, numerous other examples were recognised. Very frequently, the ornamental landscapes were associated with deer parks, though to avoid intrusions by deer, which are particularly partial to cultivated roses, the deer parks had to be segregated from the intimate garden beds and terraces, which were often placed beside the south walls of the palace or castle. In some cases special pavilions or 'gloriettes' were erected for spectators viewing the ornamental landscapes, while sometimes the battlements of a castle provided a viewing platform. Mention has already been made of the pavilion at Nonsuch palace, Tooting, from which Queen Elizabeth I would watch deer being coursed in the park.

Special towers might also be provided for the observation of the chase in a deer park. The lodge at Dob Park, Harrogate, a royal park that passed to the Vavasours, was a venue for the courts of the Duchy of Lancaster and before its reputed shelling by Cromwell's troops it is thought to have been a four-storey building with turrets. Harewood Castle, near Leeds had two towers reaching over 100ft and two shorter towers. Probably dating from the 1360s, the towers, the roof walkway and the upper floor chambers all enjoyed spectacular views of the park, the Wharfe valley, gardens and ponds (Jones, 1859, p.87). In some cases, the towers might have defensive as well as observational roles. The lodge of the huge royal hunting park at Haverah, near Knaresborough had a tower and in 1333-5 a substantial sum was spent on a surrounding moat some 26ft (7.9m) wide and 12ft (3.65m) deep. Was the moat ornamental like the gardens and fishpond nearby or was it prompted by the devastation of the locality by Scottish invaders in 1318-22? Further north, in Swaledale, the deer park at Healaugh had a lead-roofed touresse, serving as a vantage point from which the coursing of deer in the park could be observed. At the end of the Middle Ages, Leland mentioned another juxtaposition of a park and towers: 'From Gnarresborow [Knaresborough] over Nid ryver almost al by wood a mile to Plumpton wher is a park and a fair house with 2. Tourres longgin to the same ...'(ref. Toulmin Smith, 1907). Thus, in addition to its other roles, the deer park was a scenic attribute attached to the castle or manor and towers and vantage points were provided to exploit this function.

While the medieval deer park was a vital component of the designed scenery, it could itself also be a vantage point. Three ponds arranged in a line had dimensions increasing from east to west to offset the effects of perspective when they were viewed from rising ground inside the park at Somersham in Cambridgeshire (Taylor, 2000, p.40). While the different components of the medieval ornamental landscape could be combined and arranged in different ways, the elements of the intimate garden, the sheets of water and the enclosed, semi-wooded deer park, were included again and again in confections of contrived landscape that had the palace/castle as their foci and prime vantage point. At Framlingham in Suffolk the castle overlooked a mere; at Ravensworth, North Yorkshire, it stood in a great lake; while Leeds Castle in Kent was surrounded by water and had a detached glorictte. Each of these places had a deer park and formal gardens nearby, and at Ravensworth the landscaping priorites were plain from the way that the park and gardens flanked the approach drive (Taylor, p.41).

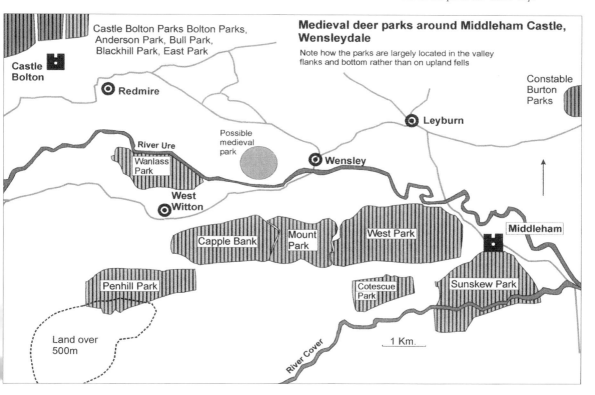

Medieval deer parks around Middleham Castle, Wensleydale

Note how the parks are largely located in the valley flanks and bottom rather than on upland fells

Castle Bolton Parks Bolton Parks, Anderson Park, Bull Park, Blackhill Park, East Park

Castle Bolton

Redmire

Constable Burton Parks

Leyburn

River Ure

Possible medieval park

Wensley

Wanlass Park

West Witton

Capple Bank

Mount Park

West Park

Middleham

Penhill Park

Cotescue Park

Sunskew Park

Land over 500m

River Cover

1 Km.

Middleham in North Yorkshire, the stronghold of the Nevilles and home of Richard III, stood at the hub of a constellation of six or seven deer parks. As the northern reaches of the Norman kingdom became more secure, William's Hill, old shell keep and bailey on the brow of the plateau overlooking Wensleydale, was abandoned in favour of a commodious hall keep in stone on the shelf below. This, in turn, gained a curtain wall in the fourteenth century and became a principal residence and stronghold of the Neville estates. East and West parks were probably created when Ralph Neville obtained a licence to empark his wood of Middleham in 1335. Landscaping operations created formal gardens and a lake – commonly mistaken for a moat – on the south-facing side of the castle, below the curtain, whose battlements and chambers will have provided idyllic views across the garden and lake to the walled park of Sunskew, on the rising slope beyond. Around 1540, Leland wrote: 'Midleham Castel ... hath a parke by hit caullid Sonskue, and a nother caullid Westpark and the third caullid Gaunelesse half a mile of Westparke and Gaunelesse be wel woddid' (Toulmin Smith, p.26).

It is clear that the medieval determinants of landscape taste were not greatly different from those of the 'great masters' of post-medieval landscape design. Indeed, were we to arrange the deer park to envelop the setting of the dynastic home the effect would be not too different from the first generations of post-medieval park – and were we to get rid of the formal gardens and let the lawns

At Bodiam Castle the context was designed to maximise the impact on the visitor, with the castle emerging from its manicured setting as though floating like a great warship on the sea of its moat

of the park lap up to the castle walls then the result might be passed off as a creation of Lancelot 'Capability' Brown. Leland travelled the length and breadth of the kingdom as the medieval period ended and would usually remark on any deer park that he passed. Two adjectives in particular were used to describe these parks, one was 'praty' or 'pretty', the other is 'wel woddid' (sometimes 'meatly wel woddid'). The almost invariable inclusion of parkland in ornamental landscapes leaves little doubt that then, as now (but perhaps not for identical reasons), it was regarded as pleasing to the eye, or 'pretty'. Also, when Leland praises parks in terms of their pretty and well-wooded characters it is the case, as it were, that he combines the two qualities in the same breath. And so it seems highly likely that the two qualities were considered closely related. Sometimes the timber resource itself was described as 'pretty', as at Thirsk, North Yorkshire: 'At Tresk was a great castel; of the Lord Mowbray. And there is a park with praty wood about it' (Toulmin Smith p.67). Lawns, water, shade and perfumed flowers and herbs were organised and inter-meshed to produce the desired responses to the senses, but there seems to have been an additional ingredient in the medieval landscape taste.

This was the utilitarian notion of landscape beauty, embodying the idea that there was a link between beauty, wholesomeness and productivity. The animosity

Castle Bolton in Wensleydale: a great palace masquerading as a castle, with an array of deer parks tiered behind it and spreading to either side

towards open uplands, including mountains and moorland country, that persisted until the rise of Romanticism at least in part reflected the lack of economic fruitfulness associated with such landscapes. To Thomas Tusser (1524–80) there was a close connection between enclosed countrysides (as opposed to those where much was held in common) and agreeable and fruitful countryside. He wrote in this *Five Hundred Points of Good Husbandry* of 1573:

> More plenty of Mutton and Beef
> Corn, butter, and cheese of the best,
> More wealth anywhere (to be brief),
> More people, more handsome and prest,
> Where find ye? Go search any coast
> Than there where inclosure is most.

Almost two centuries earlier Geoffrey Chaucer made a similar association between pleasantness and productivity in *The Oxford Scholar's Tale* (translated by David Wright):

> Not far from the magnificent palace

Deer parks were normally hosts to agisted livestock but were closed to swine during the month when vulnerable fawns were being born or were hiding in the grass

In which the marquis made his plans for marriage
Stood situate in a most pleasant place
A hamlet, where the poor folk of the village
Would keep their livestock, and where they would lodge,
And where they'd make a living from their toil,
Depending on the richness of the soil.

Leland frequently linked the fairness of a deer park to the abundance of its timber resources, as noted above, and he also associated 'fairness' with the venison and hunting resources. Of Bishop Aukland he recorded: 'There is a fair park by the castelle having falow dere, wild bulles and kin [cattle]' (Toulmin Smith, p.70). Permeating the medieval view of what constituted aesthetically pleasing landscape was the utilitarian perspective which saw beauty in the economic resources that sustained human well-being. This equation of beauty and productivity is not surprising if we remember that the Industrial Revolution, which impacted so violently on the sensibilities of those who witnessed its effect on countryside, did not begin until a good two centuries after the end of the medieval period. Much medieval manufacturing took place in woods and by streams that were well removed from the sites of most habitations. Agriculture was, of necessity, organic and untainted by scandals associated with agri-business

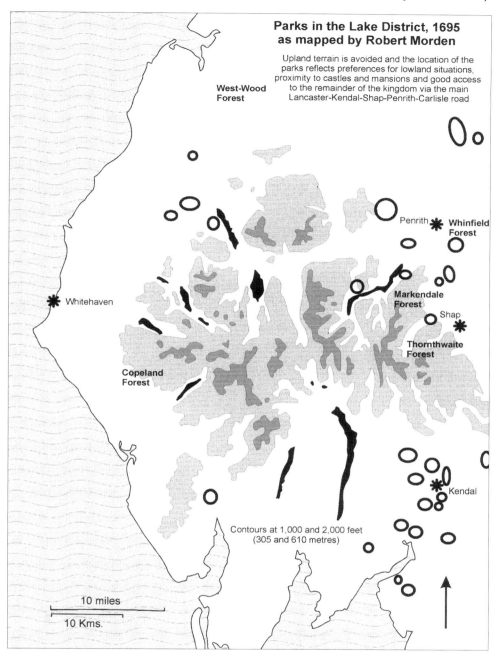

**Parks in the Lake District, 1695
as mapped by Robert Morden**

Upland terrain is avoided and the location of the
parks reflects preferences for lowland situations,
proximity to castles and mansions and good access
to the remainder of the kingdom via the main
Lancaster-Kendal-Shap-Penrith-Carlisle road

West-Wood
Forest

Penrith ✳ Whinfield
Forest

Markendale
Forest

Shap ✳

Thornthwaite
Forest

Whitehaven ✳

Copeland
Forest

Kendal

Contours at 1,000 and 2,000 feet
(305 and 610 metres)

10 miles

10 Kms.

or fears concerning chemicals or genetic manipulation. If forge hammers or
the paddles of a fulling mill were heard, they would probably be the only loud
sounds heard in that day – they did not assault ears already plagued by factory
clamour, traffic noise or electronic gibbering. Not surprisingly then, it must have
seemed quite normal and natural to find beauty in those things that sustained

human life and there were fewer contradictions in blurring the boundaries between the economic and the aesthetic.

These lines of thinking take us straight back to Appleton and his habitat theory. The medieval references to the aesthetic aspects of landscape are shot through with (partly subconscious) ingestive associations. Woods were pretty and they were important components of ornamental landscapes. But part of their prettiness derived from the fact that they provided timber, fuel and browse. Perhaps the differences between the medieval ornamental landscapes and those produced by the celebrated landscapers and arbiters of taste of the centuries that followed concerned the fact that the anonymous medieval landscapers did not see the same separation between the realms of the aesthetic and the workaday world. Woods were pretty and woods were wattle and faggots; deer were pretty and deer were also venison; smooth, emerald launds complemented the darker, bobbled texture of the grove – but launds could also be attractive because they produced revenue from agisted cattle. And the cattle were pretty because they were meat, hides and milk. Throughout the whole era of the aristocratic park, the noble in occupation generally liked little better than to gaze across the grove-fringed lawns and watch a flock, a herd of white cattle or a group of deer feeding and getting fatter all the while.

By the time that the celebrated 'creators' of landscape parks began their work, the repertoire of eye-gladdening topographical associations was more or less complete, while the concept of what constituted parkland scenery was well established. In 1624 Sir William Wentworth wrote that Gawthorpe Park, Leeds, had been an extensive park in former times that was well-stocked with deer: '… a parklike place it is, and a brook running through the middle of it, wch turnes 4 payer of millstones at 2 miles' (Parsons, 1834, p.259). Everyone knew very well what parkland scenery was like before the famous landscapers arrived.

Trees and woodland in parks

Rackham, (1986, p.125) wrote that: 'The real purpose of a park was the prosaic supply of venison, other meat, wood, and timber.' However, the records relating to the North of England, where the deer parks were most numerous, leaves one with no doubt that hunting was a frequent activity and that the deer parks were located around castles to provide 'sport' rather than to stock their already well-filled larders. Had venison been the sole concern, the parks could have been sited in remote wildernesses where the land was cheap and the venison cull left to their parkers. The conflict between the Cliffords of Skipton Castle and the lesser nobles, that disrupted life for decades around and after the close of the Middle Ages and virtually reached civil war proportions, was not fought for meat and timber. It was a conflict about hunting rights. This is not to suggest

The deer park earthworks and boundary wall in the form of a deer leap at Chatsworth, Derbyshire

that the deer parks did not offer economic opportunities: the very nature of the favoured scenery ensured that they did. Most medieval deer parks contained a wooded component.

This was not absolutely a prerequisite and a deer park could, for example, comprise open moorland. When Scale Park was enclosed under licence by the Earl of Westmorland in 1409, this area of steep fell side above Kettlewell was probably largely unwooded. In 1608 Edward, Lord Bruce was allowed to enclose the open common and stinted pastures by Witton Fell, in Wensleydale, as well as 300 acres (121ha) of moorland to make a deer park. Other parks began by being almost entirely wooded, as seems to have been the case with the parks at Tanfield in the same Dale; more than two centuries after their creation, Leland wrote; 'There be 2. Fair parkes at Tanfield and meatley plenty of wood' (Toulmin Smith p.83). Parks appear frequently to have been created from wood pasture, as noted earlier. In 1540, for example, the property of Fountains Abbey in Masham parish mentioned '... a close of pasture callid Littell Nether Wood inclosed within Lighton Park, which the said Sir Crisatofer Danby kny occupieth' (Fisher, 1865, p.511): the great advantage of wood pasture was that it needed very little manipulation in order to obtain a 'parklike' character. Fragments of wood pasture from this lofty park, with stunted oaks, still survive.

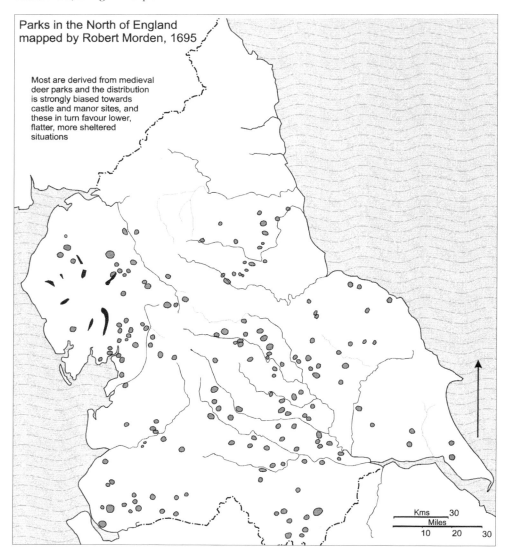

Parks in the North of England
mapped by Robert Morden, 1695

Most are derived from medieval
deer parks and the distribution
is strongly biased towards
castle and manor sites, and
these in turn favour lower,
flatter, more sheltered
situations

Kms 30
Miles
10 20 30

Some later deer parks occupied the margins of the settled area, but a study of deer park distributions during the medieval period in the most favoured hunting territory of the Yorkshire Dales shows that the parks were not situated in remote and wooded outposts. Instead, they were closely tied to the abodes of their feudal owners. These abodes were located in attractive situations, on routeways, frequently in the floors of valleys, just above the floodplain, or overlooking their territories from shelves on the valley sides. Less easily explained is the well-marked association between these castles and fortified manor houses and limestone, Magnesian or Carboniferous. Turning to the Lake District, where there was an abundance of woodland carpeting the sides of glaciated valleys and expanses of wild upland fell country, we find a similar pattern. The deer parks were not relegated to wildernesses but were concentrated on low and valley bottom ground, close to the homes of their noble owners.

Woodland was not essential as a source of food for deer, and fallow deer would graze and forage in open country. It was, however, a valuable source of browse, which could be lopped and fed to supplement the diets of deer and domestic animals. The cultivation of browse in places that were amongst yet above the deer was an encouragement to the practice of pollarding. There are records to show that the lopping of browse ('brusynge' in some documents and 'greenhews' or 'water boughs' in the north) took place in parks. The accounts for Middleham Castle for 1466-7 show expenditure of 18s 8d for the cutting of 'deer fall' as winter fodder in the parks of Sunscogh (Sunskew) and Wanlace (Wanlas) (*Gen. Min. Acct.* 1085/20). The value of browse resources should not be neglected and rights to lop branches of soft leaf fodder or holly could be crucial as winter put pressure on hay stocks. Hollins (see Chapter 1) were frequently found in deer parks. In the early thirteenth century, for example, Gilbert de Grant (d.1241) granted extensive grazing rights in upper Swaledale to Rievaulx Abbey. The grant included the right to kill wolves and to cut evergreen branches for winter feed and to exclude the cattle of local laymen from the lands concerned (*Cart. Rieve.* Surtees, vol.83, pp.304-5). Deer, like cattle, could be supported by holly fodder, sometimes grown in parks like the one associated with the still-standing hunting lodge of the Cliffords in Barden, Wharfedale. In the Clifford's Household Book for 1510 is the entry: 'Itm. Payd the xiiij th day of May by the hands of Mr Stewart for hollen fall the last wynter in Barden, vs [25p]' (quoted in Speight, 1900, p.168). Similarly, when Abbot Marmaduke leased a holding on the Fountains Abbey estates at Pott to Margaret and Richard Atkinson in 1518, they were … not to fell, or cause to be felled any of the abbots and convent's 'wood of warraunt' within the lordship of Pott without their license except for:

> Lefull fellynge of hollynge bowes and othre brushewode at seasonable tyme of yere callide brusynge for pastour of cattell and also oke bowez, not tymber, for ther fewell and makynge of ther fenciez (quoted in Michelmore (ed.), 1981 p.147).

Hollins (from the Old English *holegn*) were frequently included amongst the small woods inside medieval deer parks, as at Ripley, North Yorkshire, where the old hollin is indicated by the names Holly Bank Wood and Holly Bank Lane. Some holly trees still grow around there.

As well as their aesthetic value in deer parks, trees and woods also provided cover and gave the deer a (false) sense of security, encouraging them to breed and feel less stressed. Sometimes, deer were stalked by archers wearing elaborate stalking frames and disguised as livestock or deer, and the presence of trees and thickets gave cover to the stalker. There were also compelling economic uses for woodland in parks, and these gave the parks significant commercial viability beyond the considerable value of the venison produced, so that the 'luxury'

Middleham Castle in Wensleydale was at the centre of a constellation of deer parks and administered their maintenance and the exploitation of their grazing and woodland resources

aspect of recreational landscape was much diminished or removed. Woodland was vital in some forms of hunting (in addition to the netting of the secretive roe deer). Woodcock were netted as they passed through breaks or glades, often when moving from woodland to water. This practice seems to be very long established, for the term *cocc-(ge)scete* or 'cock-shoot' occurs in Old English. The evidence of place names shows that these cock-shoots were frequently located in medieval deer parks (Faull and Moorhouse, 1981, p.837).

Woods, inside parks or outside, could be useful feeding grounds for swine, which relished the pannage or acorn crop or the mast found on the floor below beech trees. A swineherd needed to be in close attendance, for pigs competed with deer in some of their feeding activities, could cause immense damage to recently coppiced enclosures and, as mentioned, would devour newborn deer and hinds that were giving birth. In 1269, Peter de Neville, the chief forester of Rutland Forest, was charged that he had not only taken nuts, mast and windfall, misappropriated poaching fines, had his own private prison and kept hounds for illicit hunting, but had also kept 300 swine in the forest pastures, to the detriment of the king's deer (Dowsett, pp.179–81). When kept in parks, swine were evicted for the month when fawns were born. While the feudal community used the manorial resources of the deer park extensively, they did so under conditions of close regulation. The lord could derive substantial revenues from pannage and agistment, but he would also suffer if the animals were not properly supervised.

Agistment or the letting-out of land as cattle grazing, mainly in the summer, was a very significant source of revenue in deer parks. It did not just concern the open lawns, for many parks retained or had acquired wood pasture components, while forage could be found in the woods and groves as well. Cattle could feed in quite densely covered country; after Haya park, near Knaresborough, was disparked in the seventeenth century the cattle grazing its woods had small bells fastened around their necks so that they could be found amongst the trees (Sheahan, 1871, p.83). Looking at the little constellation of parks associated with the royal castle at Knaresborough, in 1358–9, Haya Park had 126 beasts agisted for the summer season running from the Finding of the Holy Cross (3 May) to Michaelmas at a rate for most of them of 1s (5p) for the season, while in the winter season there were 30 beasts agisted at 6d (2½p). Five years earlier, the four parks had produced a revenue of £41 7s 10d from hay and agistment (about £41 38p) (*Exchq. K.R. Accts* 154/12). In the 1358–9 season the enormous park of Haverah had supported some 357 cattle and 18 horses, while in Haverah and Haya, hay crops were sold at 2s 6d (22½p). Even the very small park facing the castle from across the river Nidd produced herbage that was sold for 14s (70p). Large vaccaries or cattle farms developed in various parks, like Erringden Park in the manor of Wakefield.

As well as its deer and cattle, the park was likely to contain a good number of horses. Some would graze there freely as privileges enjoyed by manorial officials such as the parker, but there would be a fluctuating proportion of mounts and baggage animals that rose and fell with the arrival and departure of the lord, his guests and retinues. In some cases, the deer park served as a horse stud, with high-quality animals being bred in the royal park at Haverah. The presence of sheep in deer parks probably increased in the course of the medieval period, despite the damage that these animals could cause if they escaped into the wooded sectors. Around 1610, the Earl of Cumberland's shepherds were sent to Appletreewick fair to buy lean sheep for fattening in the deer parks around Skipton castle. There they were set upon by the bailiff and servants of Sir John Yorke, and became victims in a poaching feud that would culminate in the extermination of wild deer in the Dales (Whitaker, p.513).

Mining for iron ore existed in several medieval deer parks, like Haverah and Haya. In some cases, the forges were also sited within parks, where they would consume reserves of park woodland. Forges were leased by Richard de Goldsborough in his park of Creskeld, near Wakefield. There was also an iron-working site in Rothwell park, also in the Wakefield area. In 1322 the parker there recorded that herons and sparrow hawks had been frightened away, and, more surprisingly, there was a shortage of honey and beeswax. One imagines that the wildlife of today would have become more immured to such relatively small-scale disturbances. The three forges that existed then were burning both the stumps and timber of trees. In 1341, the iron mine was recorded but was said to be producing no income, though its presence created a potential market for the oaks and underwood in the surrounding country (Faull and Moorhouse, eds, 1981, p.780). Forges could be remunerative to the park owner, and in 1342 two forges in the Outwood of Wakefield were leased at a rent of 15s (75p) per forge per week (*op. cit.,* p.781). The existence of commercial demesne woodland in a park was bound to attract members of a variety of specialist occupations. Charcoal burning produced fire, smoke, sawing noise and other disturbances to trouble game and it devoured masses of timber. However, the burners would swiftly move through a coppice and be gone within a few weeks of paying the lord for the licence to practise their craft. Metallurgical industries can scarcely have been complementary to the aesthetic charms of the park, even when practised on modest medieval scales. The inefficient forges will have required enormous amounts of fuel and their appetites must have extended cutting beyond the coppiced areas of most parks. In addition, the mining of ore left the land surface scarred and pitted with potentially dangerous shafts and the slag produced by the furnaces led to many industrial sites being marked by the name 'Cinder Hills'. Coal mining and quarrying were also quite frequently present in parks, but as merely extractive industries they had little impact on the neighbouring woods.

Trees and woodland were crucial components in the landscape of the deer park, while commercial grazing and foraging of various kinds were extremely profitable. However, the two aspects of land-use were not essentially compatible and the old wood pastures had needed careful regulation. In the reign of Henry

VII, Henry, Lord of Northumberland wrote to his cousin Sir Robert Plumpton, commanding him to go to his park at Spofforth, near Wetherby, in order to discover what horses and cattle had got into his spring (coppices) there and to drive out any that were trespassing (Stapleton, 1990, letter XLV). Wherever there were spring woods they had to be given peripheral defences against both domestic livestock and deer. When these woods were located in deer parks then the greatest of vigilance was needed. For several years after the last cycle of coppicing, a spring wood had to be fenced against incursions by all forms of deer and domestic livestock. Thus, when William Scaife and his wife, Sarah, took over the lease of a holding at Braisty Woods on the Fountains Abbey estates they were allowed 'lawful brusynge' except in 'sprynges' and they were required to undertake that they would not keep or suffer any cattle within the springs

> … durynge the years of fence tyme of the same, that shulde in eny wyse be hurtfull to them or eny of them and all the heigies of the said sprynge maide and to be maide thei and iche of theme for their parties shall at ther chairgies ande cost repareth and upholde… (Michelmore (ed.), p.192).

The particular vulnerability of the spring wood and the hedges and/or banks employed for its protection meant that when found in a deer park context it was within yet not really a part of the park. Rackham has made a distinction (1986, pp.125-6) between *compartmental* parks and *non-compartmental* parks. In the former, the territory was divided between the woodlands and the launds, and the woods were subdivided into a series of coppices. The coppices might be cut on staggered rotations, so that there was a fairly continuous production of light timber, and the coppices would be made deer- and stock-proof during the years following felling, when soft, leafy growth was springing from the coppice stools. In 1483, an Act made it lawful in the Royal Forests, where all enclosures that restricted the movement of deer had been illegal, for a newly-cut coppice to be surrounded by a ditch and a bank that was planted with thorns. The conventional time taken for young coppice timber to become safe from herbivores was seven years.

As well as having pollards and, possibly, some spring woods, a park would also have some reserves of structural timber for heavy engineering works. In the medieval period, houses and other substantial works were commonly pre-fabricated at the felling sites, so that construction works will have been associated with park woodlands. In 1383-4 a complete waterwheel was constructed in Rothwell Park from large timbers felled and shaped nearby. It was then transported in assembled form to a mill site 3 miles (4.8km) away. Feudal tenants would normally have rights in and access to other woods lying outside the park, but it was normal for the woods of the deer park to provide the timber needed for work on the demesne. 'Vast quantities of timber were felled in parkland, as the accounts for Leeds show during the fourteenth century, the repairs to manorial buildings there drawing heavily on the resources of Leeds Park, Rothwell Park and Roundhay Park' (Faull and Moorhouse (eds), 1981, p.688). Park oak timber could also be used as a source of bark for use in the tanning industry. Other barks could be used, but that of the oak, which was peeled from the living tree, was considered superior and the only kind that could legally be sold. Once peeled, the bark would be stored nearby in a shed of some kind, and in 1523 the rector of Ripley leased a little pasture called 'Barkhouse Garth', which lay on the margins of Sir William Ingilby's deer park, close to the beck that powered a mill (Ingilby MS 1064). Oak provided tannin and also the best and most weatherproof of timber, but all forms of timber had their uses. Alder, useful as fuel and for clog-making, was favoured on wet land, and hazel was a very useful coppiced underwood crop that produced pliable wands of use in thatching and hedging.

In some cases, a wood seems to have been regarded as a part of a park, yet lay outside it, as evidenced by the 'Outwood' place names. The connection to the park may just be a tenurial one and the outwood might lie some distance from its park. In the non-compartmented parks, the deer and lifestock could roam at will, and it followed that established trees would normally be pollards. Newly planted trees would need to be fenced and would then either be pollarded or grow with a browse line marking the level into the canopy that browsers could reach. Though browsing was a threat to young trees, the pollarding of trees that were scattered across the lawns of a park frequently had the provision of lopped foliage for browse as its main function. In the New Forest, some of the most celebrated ancient trees, like the Knightwood Oak and the beeches in Mark Ash, were pollarded and in the Forest pollarding was undertaken to provide browse for deer. However, there was a conflict between the interests of shipwrights and housewrights, who wanted straight lengths of timber for heavy construction work and favoured standard or maiden trees, and the pollarders. Old pollards could provide curved timbers for braces and some maritime uses, but they were not favoured by timber merchants. In 1698 an Act allowed 6,000 acres (2,428ha) of the New Forest to be enclosed, with pollarding for browse being banned, new trees planted and restrictions being placed on the burning of charcoal (Rodgers, 1941, p.53).

Wherever the original park-maker had incorporated existing trees in a park that was not compartmented, the replacement of trees that died must have been a considerable problem. Whether in woods or wood pastures, trees were most unlikely to reproduce without considerable efforts being made to protect their seedlings. One might expect, therefore, that there must have been numerous parks that began as woodland or wood pasture and gradually became lawns with only fragmented islands of woodland as trees died and could not be replaced. There is, however, evidence that numerous parks were still considered to be 'well wooded' several centuries after their creation. Leland found that the park by the side of Pickering castle '... is not welle wooddid' (Toulmin Smith, p.64) yet a few miles away: 'The park of Hinderskel by my estimation is 4. Miles in cumpace, and hath much young wood yn it' (*op. cit.* p.65). In the south of Yorkshire, at Helaugh: '… here I saw great ruines of an auncient manor place of stone that longgid with the fair woddid park thereby to the Earl of Northumberland' (*op. cit.,* p.44). I have noted how Haya park was so heavily wooded at the time of its disparking that cattle in it were fitted with bells. The Nortons, who had been heavily involved with the hunting feud with the Cliffords, had some 120 fallow deer in their 80-acre park at Threshfield in Wharfedale in 1603. It must also have been packed with valuable timber, for this was estimated to be worth no less than £400 in the same year (Speight, 1900, p.425).

Considerable planting of a functional nature could accompany park-making. We know that in 1497-8, when the local mob attacked the new park created by the singularly unpleasant Wistrop family from the place of the same name near York, the 200-strong crowd pulled down the boards of the paling and tore up its associated quickethorn hedge, also uprooting 100 walnuts and appletrees. The nature of recording is that we know more about the extraction of resources – deer, hay, cart-loads of bark, bundles of faggots, etc. – from the medieval parks than we do about investment, in the form of new plantings. It is plain from the records of the medieval manor courts that measures were usually in place that would protect woodland in parks and penalise those who damaged it. As a result, numerous parks were still recorded as being well wooded when the medieval period came to a close. Many of them evolved to become landscape parks, displaying the various tricks of topographical juxtaposition that had been developed centuries before. Each park had its own landscape but, as places in which the archaeologically destructive practice of ploughing was largely or wholly excluded, each also existed, to a greater or lesser degree, as an open air museum of preceding manners of rural life.

REFERENCES

Appleton, J., 1986 'The Role of the Arts in Landscape Research' in Penning-Rowsell, E.C. and Lowenthal, D. (eds) *Landscape Meanings and Values*, Allen & Unwin, London, pp.26-47.
Appleton, J., 1990, *The Symbolism of Habitat*, University of Washington Press, Washington, DC.
Appleton, J., 1996, *The Experience of Landscape*, John Wiley, Chichester.
Chaucer, Geoffrey, 1985 edn., *The Canterbury Tales*, trans. David Wright, Oxford University Press, Oxford.
Cornish, V., 1943, *The Beauties of Scenery*, Frederick Muller, London.
Daniell, D., 1991, 'The Scottishness of *The Thirty-Nine Steps*' in Herbert, W.N. and Price, R. (eds) *Gairfish: Discovery*, Gairfish, Bridge of Weir, pp.4-15.
Dowsett, J.M., 1942, *The Romance of England's Forests*, John Gifford, London.
Everson, P.L., Taylor, C.C. and Dunn C.J., 1991, *Change and Continuity*, HMSO, London
Faull, M.L. and Moorhouse, S.A., (eds), 1981, *West Yorkshire: An Archaeological Survey to 1500*, West Yorkshire Metropolitan County Council, Wakefield.

Fisher, J., 1865, *The History and Antiquities of Masham and Mashamshire*, Simpkin Marshall & Co., London.

Fleming, A, *Swaledale, Valley of the Wild River*, Edinburgh University Press, Edinburgh.

Gesler, W., 'Therapeutic Landscapes: Theory and a Case Study of Epidauros, Greece', *Environment and Planning D: Society and Space*, **vol.** 11, pp.171-190.

Hook, D., 1998, *The Landscape of Anglo-Saxon England*, Leicester University Press, London.

Jones, J., 1859, *The History and Antiquities of Harewood*, Simpkin, Marshall & Co., Leeds.

Meinig, D.W.,1979, 'The Beholding Eye' in D.W. Meinig (ed.), *The Interpretation of Ordinary Landscapes*, Oxford University Press, New York.

Moore, P.D., 1988, 'The Development of Moorlands and Upland Mires' in M. Jones (ed.) *Archaeology and the Flora of the British Isles*, Oxford University Committee for Archaeology, Oxford, pp.116-122

Orians, G.H., 1980, 'Habitat Selection: General Theory and Applications to Human Behaviour' in J.Lockard (ed.), *Evolution of Human Social Behaviour*, Elsevier, New York, pp.49-66.

Orians, G.H., 1988, 'An Ecological and Evolutionary Approach to Landscape Aesthetics' in Penning-Rowsell, E.C. and Lowenthal, D. (eds) *Landscape Meanings and Values*, Allen & Unwin, London, pp.3-25.

Parsons, E., 1834, *Miscellaneous History* [of West Riding], F. Hobson, Leeds.

Rackham, O., 1986, *The History of the Countryside*, Dent, London.

Rodgers, J., 1941, *The English Woodland*, Batsford, London.

Sheahan, J.J., 1871, *The Wapentake of Claro*, vol III, John Green, Beverley.

Simmons, I.G., 1969, 'Evidence for vegetation Changes Associated With Mesolithic Man in Britain' in P.J. Ucko and G.W. Dimbleby (eds), *The Domestication and Exploitation of Plants and Animals*, Duckworth, London, pp.111-119.

Simmons, I.G., 2003, *The Moorlands of England and Wales*, Edinburgh University Press, Edinburgh.

Speight, H., 1894, *Nidderdale and the Garden of the Nidd*, Elliot Stock, London.

Speight, H., 1900, *Upper Whardedale*, Elliot Stock, London.

Stapleton, T.,1990, (ed.), *The Plumpton Correspondence* , Alan Sutton, Gloucester.

Tatlor, C., 2000, 'Medieval Ornamental Landscapes' *LANDSCAPES* I, I, pp.38-55.

Toulmin Smith (ed.), 1907, *Leland's Itinerary in England and Wales In Or About the Years 1534-43*, George Bell & Sons, London.

Vera, F.W.M., 2000, *Grazing Ecology and Forest History*, CABI Publishing, Wallingford.

Whitaker, T.D., 1878, *The History and Antiquities of the Deanery of Craven*, 3rd edn., Leeds.

5

Later parkland trees
and forests

Parks are the subjects of many misunderstandings. The original word, from the Old French, could relate both to a place set aside for hunting the main beasts of the chase and a prosaic enclosure, such as a paddock. In medieval documents the appearance of the words *parcus*, *parcum* or *parke* were not in themselves sufficient evidence for the existence of a park in the sense that is conventional today. To complicate matters further, recent scholarly interpretations of medieval and later parks have evolved in contrasting directions. At first it was assumed that parks were hunting reserves for the feudal aristocracy – though the evidence quoted in the preceding chapter reveals a multiplicity of uses with hunting often paramount. Next, it became fashionable to assume that while deer parks *began* as confined hunting territories, hunting petered out in the course of the Middle Ages and they became cattle farms or vaccaries and horse studs. Then the fashion was to play down the hunting role altogether and regard the medieval park as a venison farm. The deficiencies of all these views must result in considerable measure from extracting evidence from very circumscribed regions within the home counties/East Anglian area and assuming that it applies in other places. In the main, northern, areas of the deer parks there is abundant evidence of their use for hunting (as shown in Chapter 4), even though parks inevitably had other uses. Northern parks were being established long after the assumed heyday of the park as evidenced by the southern norms, and hunting in parks was actively pursued throughout the medieval period and into the centuries that followed. Even in the south, more ritualised forms of hunting were practised in deer parks up to and after the Civil War.

As has been seen, the medieval park landscape developed in accordance with certain standards and expectations. The repertoire of features needed to create harmonious, dramatic or intimate associations was well known, while lakes, causeways, lawns, groves, gardens, even trees that blossomed in the spring were set out in carefully considered positions. Their extents and juxtapositions were designed with the house/palace/castle as the hub of the arrangements and with the provision of pleasing prospects, particularly from elevated apartments, walkways, pavilions or towers, being crucial. A pleasantly landscaped 'home park' could provide a link between the house and its deer park and would accommodate all the horses brought by visiting retinues. The park itself did not necessarily play a passive part within the ornamental landscape; it could contain nurseries where trees and shrubs were raised for ornamental plantings associated with the house, its gardens and immediate setting. Meanwhile, outwoods could carry the parkland ethos beyond the confines of the park itself, and this is another motif that the famous landscapers would sometimes adopt.

Whatever the precise character of the park, whatever its age, and however it may have inclined towards one function or another, it invariably resulted from a change of function in the countryside and was established in a place that had experienced a different tradition of scenic evolution. The makers of parks did not obliterate the pre-existing scenery. Rather, they worked with what was there, adding and subtracting, encouraging one aspect of ecology and discouraging another. A good number of parks appear to have been created from woodland, as we have seen, and while the woods will have sheltered deer and contained valuable mast and pannage, continuous tree cover will have impeded both the horseman and the archer. It seems likely, then, that any existing clearings might have been enlarged to become lawns – *laund*, Old French *launde,* is a useful place name clue to the former existence of a park. Parkland was not an alien landscape, but rather one in which some elements from workaday countrysides (small woods, pastures, ponds) were encouraged, and other elements (ploughland, field boundaries) were normally evicted. Rather than being agents for destruction within the historic landscape, the park tended to play the role of the deep freeze or the ring fence. Ploughing is the main agent for the fairly rapid removal of the evidence for human activities. Where it is excluded, as in most parks, quite slight earthwork features from a wide spectrum of ages and functions can survive as archaeological features across many centuries. (During the World Wars it was commonplace for blocks of surviving parkland to be ploughed up in a drive to bolster home front food production.) Where it has happened, the earthworks from activities that pre-dated the medieval park (e.g. ridged ploughland), or coexisted with it (e.g. carriageways), may be abruptly curtailed. Every park will contain some archaeological legacy from the period before its establishment. Trees may well form a very significant part of this legacy and old parks may be the best sources of information about ancient tree patterns.

The Barden Tower, Wharfedale, was built as a hunting lodge by Henry, Lord Clifford in 1485. Though then the property of the Countess of Cork, in the 1650s Lady Ann Clifford took it upon herself to renovate the tower at a time when the open chases were unviable and deer were being herded into parks for protection against poachers and the raging game wars

The park evolves

Hunting in deer parks continued through the medieval period, while at and after its close most Tudor and Stuart monarchs were bloodsports enthusiasts. Deer parks were still being enclosed and used as deer parks in the North of England during the fifteenth century (e.g. Scale Park and Ripley Park). In 1608, East Witton Fell and Hammer Wood in Wensleydale were emparked and fenced for deer (Fisher, 1865). At Crackpot Hall, overlooking the gorge of the river Swale, the Out Pasture was enclosed for deer in 1636 (Hartley and Ingilby, 1956, p.266). Parks there were still being managed as deer parks in the traditional way in the seventeenth century. For example, in 1612 Francis, Earl of Cumberland, attempted a valuation of the Skipton lands, comparing their current value to that given in the reign of Edward II (1307-27). It showed that the feeding of browse to deer had continued: 'The parke, adjoining ye castle rated then, besydes the fedyng of the deare, to LX s (£3) ys now w'rth besyde the same feiding 10 l (£10)' (quoted in Whitaker, 1878, p.296). Lord Latimer, whose widow, Catherine Parr, married Henry VIII and managed to survive him, is recorded as having hunted in disputed lands in Litbank and Howden, Wharfedale (Whitaker, p.306). In the 1540s and 1550s disputed rights to hunt deer in the Yorkshire Dales resulted in cases being brought to the President and Council at York. About this time, the Nortons built a lookout tower to watch for Clifford men coming to attack their park and walled their grounds. In 1654, with the feud with local families of the lesser gentry still rumbling on, Lady Clifford allowed the Countess of York to keep her deer in the relative security of the recently walled park of Barden until a walled park could be made for them at Bolton in Wharfedale. Lady Clifford would keep one half of the deer in return (*op. cit.*, p.302). The Bolton Priory park was walled in the 1680s and a tenant was evicted for poaching at that time. As Catholics involved in the abortive northern uprising, the Nortons forfeit their lands in 1569, though in the first quarter of the seventeenth century the feud over hunting rights was perpetuated by Sir John Yorke. All this points to the existence of Tudor and Stuart realms in which hunting for deer was only too actively pursued.

The situation seems to have been similar, if less unruly, in the South. An enthusiasm for the killing of deer had revived in the reign of Henry VIII, the king having increased his holding of deer parks by appropriating those of his ecclesiastical and political victims. He also created several new parks, including the gigantic 'Chase' at Hampton Court. The royal taste for bloodsports was inherited by his daughter, Elizabeth, who, as mentioned above, delighted in watching the coursing of deer. The desire to hunt deer fluctuated thereafter, though at the age of 52, James II was still an obsessive hunter of deer. In a letter of 2 May 1686 Sir John Reresby recorded:

> I went to New Hall in Essex, the Duke of Albermarle's house, the king having promised that duke to go and stay two days there to hunt, which he coming the day after performed accordingly. These two days his Majesty killed two stags he was indefatigable at that sport, loving to ride so hard that he usually lost his company (Cartwright (ed.), 1875, p.362).

The Civil War was thought to have caused a crisis in the recreational landscapes, and park pales were vandalised while organised gangs of poachers and disorderly soldiery took heavy tolls of the deer stocks. As symbols of aristocratic/Royalist status, deer parks seemed to contradict the ethos of the Parliamentarian cause (though Cromwell is said to have been an enthusiastic hunter). They were costly to operate and might be considered dispensable luxuries in times of uncertainty – though their resources of timber, rented grazing and so on could equally be thought to be assets. In addition, parks confiscated from the bishops, as took place in 1646, and from the Crown (no stranger to the confiscation of parks) three years later put parkland on the market that was frequently bought as farmland, often for fragmentation among numerous landlords or owner occupiers. Queen Anne (1702-14) banned deer hunting from Windsor Great Park and the long era of the deer park might have seemed to be ending. In fact, it remained customary for the great mansions of the seventeenth century to have a deer park in attendance and the ownership of deer continued to signify aristocratic status. When a new mansion was built, the provision of an associated park was almost inevitable, while the modernisation and rebuilding of an older aristocratic residence was paralleled by the preservation and enhancement of the park.

About 1700, Timothy Nourse outlined his plans for a formal garden. He wrote of the Pleasure-Garden that it should be divided into three equal 'Parteries or Gardens'. The first would be divided by a grand Alley running down the middle, at the mid-point of which there would be a fountain, while the borders should be made with equally spaced small evergreen bushes. The second Garden would be of the same size with the '… same Order of Walks, Alleys, Borders, Grass Plots and Fountains' and there would be '… Two Terras Walks overlooking the Country on either side. … The Third or Last Region of our Pleasure-Garden I would have wholly to be designed for Boscage. …. And at the upper end of this Wilderness, let there be a Grate Gate … beyond which and without the Territory of our Garden, let there be planted Walks of Trees to adorn the Landskip; likewise Bowling-Green and Paddock' (quoted in Sheeran, 1990, p.11).

This description signals a new twist in the evolution of recreational landscapes but, before exploring the directions in which it led, it may be useful to consider the changing role of the Forest.

Forests and landscape

In his *Dialogus*, written in the reign of Henry II (1154-89), Richard fitz Nigel wrote:

> In the forests are the secret places of kings and their great delight. To them they go for hunting, having put off their cares, so that they may enjoy a little quiet. There, away from the continuous business and incessant toil of the court, they can for a little time breathe in the grace of natural liberty, wherefore it is that those who commit offences there lie under the royal displeasure alone …. The king's forest is the safe dwelling place of wild beasts, not of every sort, but of the sort of place, but in certain places suitable for the purpose [which lie] in wooded counties where the lairs of the wild beasts are, and very rich feedings (translated in Stenton, 1951, p.101).

This description is echoed in the passage from Manwood, quoted in Chapter 1, who added:

… a Forest must be stored with great woods or coverts for the secret abode of wild beasts and also with fruitful pastures for their continual feed … for that the nature of the wild beasts of the Forest is, to flee into the thick coverts for places of secrecy to rest in, whereof if there be none within the Forest, then they leave the Forest, and wander up and down until they find coverts elsewhere … then they are hunted and killed to the utter destruction of the Forest … (quoted in Grainge, 1871, p.50).

Forests appeared in England as an element in the institutionalisation of feudalism and authority in post-Conquest England. The Norman monarchs were avid huntsmen and seem to have been more concerned with their game than with their subjects – though the imposition of anti-poaching measures seems generally to have been less draconian than is sometimes suggested. In accordance with the pressing need to placate the barons, the composing of *Magna Carta* was followed, in 1217, by the issuing of the *Charter of the Forest* as its supplement in the name of the child king, Henry III. It marked a watershed in the development of Forests and their institutions, which would never be as strong again. It was promised that:

In the first place, all the Forests which Henry, our grandfather, afforested shall be visited by good and lawful men; and if new afforested any woodland other than that of his own demesne to the damage of him to whom woodland belonged, let it be disafforested. And if he afforested his own proper woodland, let it remain forest, saving common of herbage and other things in the same forest to those who were accustomed to have them before.

The third clause added that:

All Forests, however, which were afforested by King Richard, our uncle, our father, down to the time of our first coronation, shall at once be disafforested, excepting our own demesne woodland.

In the popular imagination the term 'Forest' has become associated with woodland of the denser and more extensive kind. In fact, in the medieval context, the word signified a large territory that was subjected to Forest Law, concerning the imposition of constraints deemed necessary for the preservation of deer stocks (see Chapter 1). The inhabitants of a Forest, who could be quite numerous, were prevented from injuring or even disturbing deer and their dogs were 'lawed' or partly crippled by removing a forefoot claw, to prevent them from chasing game. Feudal tenants within a Forest might have quite onerous duties concerning, say, the care of hounds, but the Forest also gave employment to a number of officials – regarders, foresters, verderers and so on – and so Forests contributed considerably to local economies, as described in the chapter that follows. Some of the considerable costs of the administrative infrastructure were recouped from fines levelled against those who had offended against the game or the woodland. Areas of woodland were present in almost all Forests, although some could be predominately moorland. In some cases the woodland was extensive, Galtres in the Vale of York would be an example. In many cases, an expanse of woodland provided a sheltered haven for deer within a Forest that extended beyond this core to cover surrounding areas of working farmland.

In Scotland the situation was rather different, for the kingdom, independent throughout most of the medieval period, contained extensive areas that were composed of lightly-settled and rugged terrain, with little permanent farmland and abundant resources of wild game. David I (1124-53) has generally been regarded as the monarch responsible for introducing Forests to Scotland and he granted the monks of Melrose Abbey the rights of pannage in what later became known as Ettrick Forest in 1136. The hunting lands of Scotland were topographically more exciting and challenging than those of England, but since they lay largely in areas where traditional clan loyalties rather than feudal traditions persisted, they were also dangers to kings who might be regarded as interlopers by the clan chieftains. Both James II and James III were kidnapped while hunting in their own kingdoms. Referring to the popular perception of Forests in association with the Robin Hood legends in England, Crone and Watson wrote:

> That image may or may not be true for England, where central authority was one of the strongest in Europe. In Scotland, exclusion from the forests seems to have been less stringently applied (certainly owners allowed use, including grazing, for a fee). However, this should not lead us to conclude that legal ownership was in any sense less well established in law in Scotland: it merely means that the exercise of ownership might be different (p.69).

Scottish Forests were organised to harmonise the conservation of game, the use of timber and the grazing of domestic livestock. The 'Tinchel' or hunt was as popular in seventeenth-century Scotland as it had been in England, and when the English travel writer John Taylor attended such a hunt in the Braemar locality of Deeside he described a hunt that lasted for 12 days, employed 1,500 beaters and caused the death of 80 red deer within two hours. All this would shortly change, for on the death of James VI (James I of England) in 1625, the Scottish holding of Forests was largely dispersed into private ownership.

Forests were a hallmark of kingship (though nobles and leading churchmen had their chases). They provided a far-flung system of facilities for royal hunting – a system that was far more extensive and comprehensive than a king would ever need. Although medieval monarchs led rather peripatetic existences, being forever on the move to consume the produce of their own manors, sit in judgement and enjoy the hospitality of their leading subjects, neither the most energetic nor the most gluttonous of them could ever hunt in all their Forests. Several will have died without ever hunting in more than a small fraction of them. The Forests did, however, serve an additional purpose, for, as noted, they contained the wherewithal for the largesse that was so crucial in establishing a bond between the monarch and his subjects. Galtres was one of the favoured sources of largesse; in 1250, 30 deer were consigned to stock the Earl of Cornwall's parks at Haya and Bilton (*Calendar of close rolls*, 1247-51, p.218) and in 1308 Edward II awarded a tithe of the Forest's venison to be given to the abbot and convent of St Mary's York (Dowsett, 1942, p.160). The Forest of Galtres was well placed to provide largesse to northern subjects and its resources were not confined to game; in 1280 Edward I gave the prioress and nuns of St Clement's, York, six oaks fit for structural timbers and the Franciscans of Scarborough also received timber (*ibid.*). In 1227 Henry III provided timber from the Forest to warm the palace of the archbishop in York, and in the same year, ten oaks left Galtres for the prior of Marton's church. The same king donated 71 oaks from the Forest of Dean between 1241 and 1265 for the construction of the Dominican friary at Gloucester '... where they remain to this day' (Rackham, 1976 p.65). In ways such as these, the Forests provided the gifts that nurtured loyalty and gave influential subjects a dependency upon their monarch.

Forests differed from deer parks in the nature of their ownership: the Forests were owned directly by the king, while the parks were licensed by him/her, perhaps mainly as a means of raising revenue. Deer parks were modest in size – a few hundred acres or less – while Forests were very extensive, with dimensions that could normally be measured in miles. Deer parks were very rigorously bounded, with banks, hedges, palings of oak boards and walls, and generally with specially constructed deer leaps to facilitate the entry of, and prevent the departure of, wild deer. Forests were not physically bounded, though their bounds were strictly enforced in judicial matters. Woods within the royal Forest would normally exist with lay ownership, but the regarders of the Forest would inspect these woods, and if they were being badly maintained then they could be expropriated by justices sitting at the Forest court or 'eyre'– church woods were not exempt. Many Forests seem to have adopted pre-existing boundaries of one kind or another (generally parish and township boundaries), so that the position of a key boundary in the landscape, separating land subject to conventional law and courts from that under Forest Law and courts, will have been well known. However, if local people disputed the disposition of Forest land then those who felt aggrieved could apply to the Forest court for a perambulation of the boundaries concerned. Such discontent could arise when foresters behaved in tyrannical ways and bullied or extorted goods from adjacent communities.

The conservation of hunting resources and the presence of commercially valuable timber and other resources linked parks and Forests, but as well as the differences noted above, Forests were managed for the benefit of the Crown rather than that of a local potentate and they all included substantial

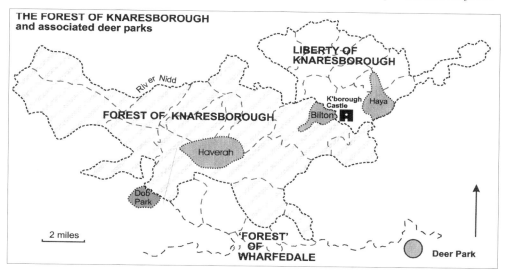

THE FOREST OF KNARESBOROUGH
and associated deer parks

LIBERTY OF KNARESBOROUGH

River Nidd

FOREST OF KNARESBOROUGH

K'borough
Castle

Haya

Bilton

Haverah

Dob
Park

2 miles

'FOREST'
OF
WHARFEDALE

Deer Park

rural populations. In some cases, like the 100,000-acre (40,470ha) Forest of Knaresborough, the increase and dispersion of impoverished squatters became a major problem, causing the woodland area to diminish markedly. Galtres, running northwards for 20 miles from the walls of York, also covered about 100,000 acres and it embraced 60 townships (Dowsett, p.160). Like the royal deer, trees were a valuable Forest resource that could, as described, be employed as largesse. As the centuries passed, royal control of vital and diminishing timber reserves came to the fore, providing the commercial *raison d'être* for some Forests. Much has been made of the demands for timber during the post-medieval centuries, and it is sometimes mentioned that 1,000 oaks were needed to build a man o'war like Nelson's *Victory,* while a 64-gun vessel like the *Agamemnon* consumed twice this number. Something of the glamour of this heroic era has captured the popular imagination: one does not hear of the destruction or depletion of woods by the merchant navy, though it had many more ships than the military branch. Moreover, the realm had far more houses and churches than ships and Rackham (1976, p.74–5) calculated that:

> Grundle House, Stanton, a timber-framed house typical of hundreds built in W. Suffolk around 1500, contains some 330 trees, a tenth of which are elm …. Half of these were less than 9 inches in diameter at the base; 32 trees were as small as 6 inches; while only 3 exceeded 18 inches, a usual size for a 'mature' oak nowadays. The roofs, floors and internal walls of the mid-fourteenth-century Old Court of Corpus Christi College, Cambridge, contained about 1,400 oaks, most of them less than 9 inches in diameter. Turning to grander buildings, the fifteenth-century main roofs of Norwich Cathedral contained some 680 oaks, mostly around 15 inches in basal diameter.

Since distant prehistoric times, woods had been managed to allow the production of masses of timber for purposes such as the construction of homes. Carefully managed medieval woods provided timber for the homes of nobles and yeomen and served the demands of *husbote* for the dwellings of their tenants. Far more voracious than the naval requirements were those of the tanners, who required a constant supply of bark — preferably from the oak, the favoured tree of the shipwright and housewright. Glassmaking was also a source of enormous consumption by inefficient and wasteful technology, as was the iron/armaments industry. Particular industries were likely to produce local shortages of timber because they required a special facet of woodland production. Hop growing had a special greed for poles from ash coppices; fencing, the demands of which could be immense when the circuit of a park required a paling, could consume huge amounts of oak boards or chestnut posts; the great ships of the line and devoured huge amounts of heavy timber, some of it from centuries-old trees that took a similar time to replace. Most requirements could have been satisfied from well-managed coppices of forms that had existed in prehistoric times and Roman times.

The pressure on these reserves mounted during the sixteenth century. The modestly sized Forest of Duffield Frith, to the north of Derby, appears to have been almost entirely woodland when the territory was confiscated by Henry III in 1266. Initially, it functioned primarily as hunting territory and was favoured by Edward I at a period near the close of the thirteenth century when wolves were still present there. At Belper there was a larder used for the salting and storage of venison. As the medieval period progressed, timber rose in relative importance and in the decades around 1400, groups of friars, the Dominicans of Derby and the Carmelites of Nottingham, received oak structural timbers from the royal Forest; the church at Duffield also received oak timbers and other trees were donated for bridge building over the Derwent. A survey of the Forest in the first half of the sixteenth century revealed 11,968 trees which included 59,412 large oaks, 32,820 small ones and some 19,736 'dottard oaks', which could have been old wood pasture pollards and which were considered to be fit only for fuel. The underwood included hawthorn, blackthorn, hazel, holly, field maple, crab apple and alder and there were birch woods near Belper. Another survey towards the end of the century, revealed a drastic depletion of timber stocks and showed that the number of large oaks had fallen to 2,764 and that of small ones had dropped to 3,032 (Dowsett, p.161). With the timber reserves greatly depleted and popular sentiment moving against him, Charles I attempted to assert his hunting rights in Duffield Frith. This served as a provocation and in 1643, commoners opened all the enclosures in the Forest, while in 1786 the 1500 acres of common were enclosed and divided amongst all those able to establish rights to the land. The situation was rather similar at the much larger Midlands Forest of Sherwood. When surveyed in 1609, the wards of Bilhaugh and Birkland contained 49,909 oaks, but by 1686 there were 37,316 left, many having been consumed in shipbuilding.

This motte mound near Laxton in Nottinghamshire was the castle of the de Caux dynasty, who held the hereditary stewardship of Sherwood Forest in Norman times, and so it became the administrative centre for Sherwood Forest

A Forest could be a Forest, if not a forest, with no trees whatsoever (a survey of Exmoor Forest by Richard Hawkins at the start of the nineteenth century revealed only 37 trees of a size that might interest the Navy, and seven of these were pollarded limes). It was because the Forests were subject to direct royal control that they were of special value as places for the production of timber. However, the degradation of the woodland character would generally have more to do with social and political factors than with profligate management and over-exploitation. As unfarmed areas, the wooded components of Forests were bound to be targeted by members of the landless mass of rural poor who would exploit periods of political instability. The distinction between Forest and common was not as clear-cut as might be imagined. Forests had populations and these populations could not survive without access to the common resources of the Forest. It was when the royal concern with the conservation of hunting and timber clashed with the subsistence interests of the tenants that trouble was likely to occur. Generally, systems of checks and balances were in place to avoid such conflicts. Thus, as mentioned in Chapter 4, while the woods and wood pastures might be opened so the swineherd and his pigs could exploit the pannage and mast and other resources of the woodland floor, the swine and other livestock were removed during the 'fence month', a fortnight on either side of midsummer, when deer were fawning. Similarly, timber for basic domestic and practical needs, and sometimes leaf fodder as well, might be taken providing that no serious injury was done to the trees and no substantial trees were felled.

The conventional image of heartless monarchs and a harsh and oppressive Forest apparatus is rather out of tune with the evidence. Poaching was most likely to incur a severe penalty when it was practised by organised gangs linked to butchers or merchants who were involved in the disposal of illicit venison. Such gangs might be sufficiently numerous and well armed to engage with forces of foresters, so then poaching became more than a felony and challenged the authority of the state. At the Forest courts more generally, fining seems often to have been treated as a means of raising revenue. Rather than being exemplary, penalties were generally set at levels that seemed to compensate for the harm that had been done to the environment or the losses and injuries caused to deer or other game. Problems caused by ill-tended animals or injuries to the 'vert' were much more commonly heard than were those concerning outlaws-cum-poachers. In some cases it is not clear whether a 'fine' was of the nature of a local tax for an accepted practice rather than a penalty.

In fact, the survival of a Forest as a partly wooded area that was capable of harbouring wildlife in accordance with the definition recorded by Richard fitz Nigel depended on a series of delicate controls and relationships. Under the Norman autocracy the necessary balances could be maintained by terror, might and decree, but with the passage of time more and more interests gained the capacity to influence a Forest's destiny and more and more incompatible demands were brought to bear on it. The incompatibility between unrestricted public usage and landscape conservation was epitomised in the case of Epping Forest. This was, with Hainault Forest, a component of the Forest of Waltham, which provided the Plantagenet monarchs with hunting territory on the margins of their capital and on lands probably hunted by late-Saxon monarchs. Subsequently, royal indebtedness and boundary disputes reduced the area of the Forest, while at some uncertain stage in the Middle Ages, the citizenry of London gained a right to stage an Easter hunt in Epping, and the city corporation also gained hunting rights.

The hounds were a motley pack; the huntsman and his whipper-in wore uniforms that must have been comic in the extreme. The chase in and out of the trees must have been a matter of some difficulty to the hounds, which were in constant danger of being trampled underfoot by excited riders and pedestrians so that they could devote but little attention to their quarry. But that did not matter in the least, for they were not expected to pursue the chase to any serious end, since the carted stag was a tame animal which went through the same procedure year after year and generally made for his paddock at Woodford as soon as he had enjoyed enough exercise for his simple needs (Dowsett, p.263).

The Epping Hunt became an occasion for great drunkenness and rowdyism as well as massive disturbance of wildlife until it dwindled away in the mid-eighteenth century.

In 1641, Epping and Hainault contained 43,000 acres of Forest land (17,402ha), but in the years that followed effective Forest land contracted as enclosure, felling, the grubbing-up of roots and conversion to farmland proceeded. The Lord Warden of the Forest, rather than enforcing his powers to protect the Forest, was active in enclosure on four of its manors and employed the Forest's own Steward to exploit legal loopholes for its destruction. Boundary stones were removed, while the experiences of the Easter hunt had spawned a tradition for popular recreational land uses. By 1793, Epping Forest had dwindled to just 900 unenclosed acres (364ha) while a survey by the Lord Warden in 1813 revealed a proliferation of unsanctioned sand and gravel pits, unsustainable cutting of underwood and digging of turf, a mismanagement of oak trees and pollards and a profusion of deer stealers. All this underlined the fact that elitism and autocracy had been instrumental in establishing and preserving the Forests; when they weakened, the preservation of woodland on the doorstep of Europe's most populous area was a nightmarish task. In 1851, Hainault Forest was disafforested. The trees on the Crown's allotments were stubbed up, the timber sold and the cleared lands divided into farm holdings. Epping Forest survived in a fashion, but the enclosures continued into the second half of the nineteenth century, when public concerns with amenity and conservation began to stir. Eventually, and following a tortuous series of legal hearings concerning the rights of commoners versus the actions of enclosers, 6000 acres (2428ha) of Epping Forest were secured for the public.

Ironically, commoners, whose depredations had so often disrupted the delicate ecology of the kingdom's Forests, had been instrumental in Epping's salvation. In Loughton, the Lord of the manor, the Rev. Maitland, was also its rector. Inhabitants on this manor enjoyed rights to lop firewood from pollards between St Martin's Day (11 November) and St George's Day (23 April). Folklore maintained that the rights had been granted by Elizabeth, with the provision that to establish these rights, the commoners should be ready to commence lopping at midnight on 10 November. The branches then had to be piled-up at the roadside and drawn away on sledges, the first of which was to be drawn by a white horse. Whether this was really a much more ancient right that had been revamped to provide the opportunity for a late night drinking session, one cannot tell. In any event, the commoners would meet at Staples Hill for a bonfire and copious intake of ale before lopping began. On the night concerned in 1863, John Willingale and his two sons broke through the rector's fences and commenced the custom. He and his boys were arrested and

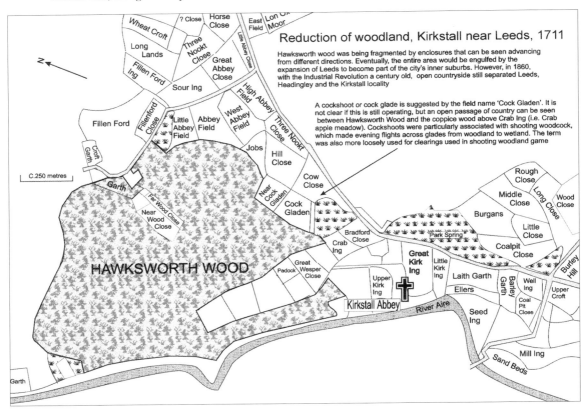

Reduction of woodland, Kirkstall near Leeds, 1711

Hawksworth wood was being fragmented by enclosures that can be seen advancing from different directions. Eventually, the entire area would be engulfed by the expansion of Leeds to become part of the city's inner suburbs. However, in 1860, with the Industrial Revolution a century old, open countryside still separated Leeds, Headingley and the Kirkstall locality

A cockshoot or cock glade is suggested by the field name 'Cock Gladen'. It is not clear if this is still operating, but an open passage of country can be seen between Hawksworth Wood and the coppice wood above Crab Ing (i.e. Crab apple meadow). Cockshoots were particularly associated with shooting woodcock, which made evening flights across glades from woodland to wetland. The term was also more loosely used for clearings used in shooting woodland game

HAWKSWORTH WOOD

Willingale was tried for trespass by magistrates who were also Maitland's tenants and one of Willingale's sons died of pneumonia, contracted in a damp prison cell. This captured the public's support. Meanwhile, the persistence of Maitland in pursuing his cause in the face of attempts to evict him and thus deprive him of the residential basis for his commoner's rights, combined with the support of the *Commons Society* proved the dynamic force for the salvation of at least the surviving portion of the Forest.

If uncontrolled foraging by domestic livestock was inimical to the survival of woodland, so too were badly regulated coppicing and also the beasts of the forests themselves. An unfenced coppice would, as noted above, soon be transformed into a permanent clearing if animals were able to feed on the shoots springing from the coppice stools. One suspects that coppices of an environmentally unfriendly character existed for a long time; in 1334 an eyre for Pickering Forest reacted firmly on learning that the prior of Malton had taken a large quantity of green thorn and hazels from a place called Allantofts ('Allan's holding') to use for kippering his herrings. In 1483, an Act required that coppices in Forest land should be ditched and hedged; a statute of 1543 required that all woods should be enclosed for four years after coppicing, with a minimum of 12 trees being left to grow as standards, and a century later, in the reign of Elizabeth I, a census recorded 5800 acres (2347ha) of such encoppicements in the New Forest (though, as usual with such surveys, many will have been overlooked). However, systems of regulation that may have been effective in a feudal realm became ineffective with the drift towards democracy.

This Elizabethan figure for New Forest coppices seems to have been taken into account in an Act of 1696, which sought to restore 6000 acres (2428ha) of Forest by planting 2000 acres (809ha) directly and then replanting at a rate of 200 acres (81 ha.) per annum for the next 2 years (Edlin (ed.), 1969, p.35). Events did not proceed so smoothly and there were conflicts of interest between the royal Forest, the numerous and vociferous commoners and the strategic demands for timber for the Royal Navy. It took 15 years for 1022 acres (414ha) to be replanted, though in 1776, with the outbreak of the American War of Independence, 2044 acres (827ha) were planted. The generalised popular assumptions about the depletion of woodland by a Royal Navy with an insatiable appetite for oak has more relevant focus when applied to the New Forest. It lay virtually on the doorstep of the royal dockyards at Portsmouth and its woods produced great oaks with spreading tops that created the curves of trunk and bough needed to give a range of different structural components. In the period 1745–1818 some 54 warships with oak hulls, elm and beech planking and pine masts were built there. If one allows a range of 500 to 2,000 oaks being used per vessel then the impression of a genuinely substantial demand is gained. However, this demand will have diminished with distance from shipyards and the Elizabethan statute of 1559, which forbade the use of heavy timber (i.e. not pollard or coppiced underwood timber) for charcoal-making, applied to timber growing within 14 miles of the coast or of navigable rivers. This would seem to have been the threshold for serious maritime involvement in woodland affairs.

The fact that many regulations for the protection of game remained extant in Forests remaining with the Crown gave the authorities a certain leverage during the two post-medieval centuries. A flavour of the game conservation legislation as it existed in the Forest of Knaresborough just after the close of the Middle Ages can be found in the following extract of 1576, when a court set out a number of 'pains' concerning the hunting of Forest game:

[No person should 'cocke']… that is, go abrode in wynter season, in, and throughe the woodes and other places within the precyncte of the said Forest with his bowe, his boltes or arrowes, pretendynge to kill the woodcock, onless he or they have speciall lycense by writinge of the quenes majesties head steward ther, or under the handes of the deputie stewardes and learned steward jointlie, upon pane to forfeit to the quenes majestie xxs [£1]. And the partie so lycensed not to take, kill, or distroie anie haire, conye, ffesaunt, or partridge, or anie beaste or fowle of warraunt, upon paine likewise to forfeit xs [50p]. [Gamebirds killed under licence were to be offered to the officials mentioned before being sold to others.]
    A paine laide that no person or persons inhabitinge within the said forest nor

any person dwellinge without the same, not beinge the quenes majesties copyholder or freholder ther, shall take or kill anie partridge within the said forest with settinge spanyell or nett, or by dryvinge the same with horse or paynted clothe, or by anie other policie, practice ort devise, except he or they be speciallie licensed by writinge…upon paine to forfeit (to) the quenes majestie XXs [£1] ….

A paine sett that no stranger or forener dwellinge without the said forest, nor any person inhabitinge within the same, shall follow the trace of any haire in the snowe, havenge with him any dogge or bytche, or carienge with him or about him any bow, bolte, or arrowe, or any other engyne, or devise to kill the same hayre, upon paine to forfeit to the quenes majestie xs [50p] ….

A paine sett that no person or persons dwellinge within the same forest shall kepe or have in his house, or otherwise any fyrrett, cony, haire, or other nett or netts, except he…be warrenner or conykeper to suche person as haithe suche lawfull graunt, warraunte or license, upon payne to forfeyt to the quenes majestie xxs (quoted in Grainge, 1871, pp.94-6).

When poaching was a serious matter – as it remained throughout the eighteenth century, perpetrators in the Robin Hood mould are seldom easy to identify in the records. More frequently, we encounter people of some standing in local society who were engaged in feuds with each other or with the authorities. In all such confrontations, Forests often featured prominently; they harboured royal game; they had preserved expanses of woodland; they were guarded by officials who were ready targets for resentment; they were associated with legends of defiance and derring-do, and their wooded cores provided cover and control over routeways passing through the Forest. In 1334 a gang, which had several members of the local gentry in its ranks, flaunted their defiance of the royal foresters of Pickering by meeting with their greyhounds and bows and organising a drive that resulted in the slaughter of 43 red deer. The heads of nine deer were then impaled on stakes and displayed in the Forest (Dowsett, p.176). Epping Forest covered important approaches to London – and also provided cover for unsavoury elements. In the eighteenth century it was regarded as a venue for rowdyism and a dangerous place haunted by highwaymen like Dick Turpin. Turpin himself had come to highway robbery via a butcher's business and the poaching of venison with the 'Gregory Gang'. Prominent amongst the Forest's rogues were the Waltham Blacks, named after a seminal gang of deer poachers from Waltham in Hampshire. The Waltham Blacks consisted of 'gay, young blades' and revellers who built their reputation upon poaching royal deer, some evolving from this into highway robbery and even a plot to kidnap William III when he passed through Epping Forest on his way to Newmarket.

Because the rights of commoners were so well established and so comprehensive, with squatting increasing and entrenched rights being expanded as royal control and resolve wavered, the transition from the Forest to the common was much easier and more simple than one might imagine. There was

A timeless scene of grazing in the New Forest

a long history of commoning rights that had been regulated by codes of checks and balances. These, for example, were committed to writing in the Forest of Knaresborough in 1563, at the close of the medieval period:

> … if any tenant seized of any customary land whereupon any great trees of the age of twenty four years or above, be, or shall be growing, shall cut them down and sell them, or any of them, he shall be grievously amerced; but yet nevertheless, it shall be lawful to and for the said customary tenants to take fire-wood meet for fuel, growing upon his or their customary lands, to burn in their houses, upon the same lands and holds, and to take trees growing upon the same, meet for repair, or to build his or their messuages or ancient buildings there (*Enquiry into the customs of the Forest* 24.5.1563).

It seems that pressure on the Forests rose to intolerable levels in the years between the sixteenth century and the Civil War. During the Elizabethan era, timber in Forests, such as Knaresborough, was consumed in great quantities for the smelting of iron ore. Apparently, one speculator there obtained the rights to all leafless (i.e. dead) timber and proceeded to create havoc in its woods by felling

Legends claim that the stocks for Cromwell's muskets were made from pollarding trees at Burnham Beeches. This Burnham Beeches pollard is old, though probably not ancient enough to fit the bill

in winter, when all trees were leafless. If the legend is untrue, it does seem to encapsulate memories of a time of great losses. The Civil War itself was a time of great disruption when the breakdown of civil power and traditional rights of ownership could affect the woodland. According to local tradition, the old beech trees on the common at Burnham Beeches were pollarded to produce timber for the stocks of Cromwell's muskets — though if pollard timber was sought there would have been a wait of a few years for the poles to grow and thicken. Perhaps burr timber from old pollards was sought? Pollarding at Burnham Beeches around 450 years ago could have affected trees that are still standing, but it was primarily concerned with the need for fuel.

Though the hunting and coursing of deer had gained in popularity under Henry VIII and his daughter, and this bloodlust infected the Stuart monarchs, the conservation of deer stocks in the Forests and chases was proving increasingly difficult. In the Forest of Pickering the woods and moors were under pressure

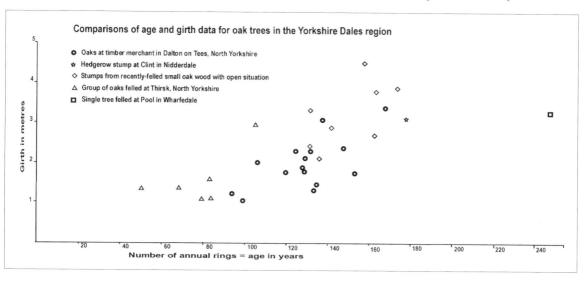

Comparisons of age and girth data for oak trees in the Yorkshire Dales region

○ Oaks at timber merchant in Dalton on Tees, North Yorkshire
★ Hedgerow stump at Clint in Nidderdale
◇ Stumps from recently-felled small oak wood with open situation
△ Group of oaks felled at Thirsk, North Yorkshire
□ Single tree felled at Pool in Wharfedale

Girth in metres

Number of annual rings = age in years

from a rising population of tenants and commoners. In 1503 there were 200 to 300 red deer there, though in 1608 only 15–16 stags could be counted. Fallow deer were kept in Blansby Park, just to the north of the king's castle of Pickering. But though these had numbered 600 in the mid-sixteenth century, the park wall had been breached and just 100 fallow deer remained in 1608 (Rutter, p.94). The disruption and local anarchy caused by the Civil War had detrimental effects on both Forests and parks. From the Clifford's park at Brougham in the north to the estates around London, destruction by troops or vandalism by 'mischievous persons' was likely. In the Yorkshire Dales, the uncertainties encouraged the aristocracy to convert their chases into protective parks and to strengthen the perimiters of existing parks. The Earl of Burlington walled his Bolton Park in Wharfedale in the 1680s and Lady Anne Clifford had made parks in her hunting ranges, nearby. Bilton park, Knaresborough, was recorded as being well stocked with fallow deer in 1626, but after the Civil War they had all gone (Sheahan, 1871, p.165). Though some deer parks were vandalised and had their deer stocks slaughtered by dissidents, others suffered from neglect, with deer escaping through gaps in their pales. Soldiers and civilians killed all the deer in the huge royal park complex at Eltham, near London, but the trees survived, and of the 4,005 trees in the Great and Middle Parks, 2,200 were designated for naval use, and though the 2,620 trees in the home park were considered to be too old and decayed, the demesne contained a further 3,700 trees suitable for shipbuilding. It was during the years of the Commonwealth that followed that the Eltham estates were granted to Sir Thomas Walsingham and were ruthlessly stripped of timber, to the value of £5,000 (Dowsett, pp.237–8).

It has been noted that much of what has been written of the Forests of the Elizabethan and Jacobean periods has concerned debates about the availability or otherwise of sufficient quantities of structural timber for the expanding shipyards. This can distract one from the larger transformation that had affected woodland in the course of the Middle Ages and its aftermath. Our understanding of the nature of woodland at the start of this period is clouded by a variety of factors. The evidence contained in Domesday Book of 1086 seems sometimes to be at variance with place name evidence and we are not told whether many wastes or commons were wooded, supported wood pasture or were largely treeless. What is clear is that in the course of the medieval period the extent of coppiced woodland increased enormously. It is commemorated in names like 'hagg', 'spring' and 'fall' and might be raised with or without an upper storey of standard trees. The widespread conversion of land to coppice may have occurred in different parts of England and Wales at different times. In the North it could have occurred later than in the South and it appears to have been a feature of the century-and-a-half preceding the Dissolution, with much of the land subject to this conversion having previously existed as wood pasture. In the south of Yorkshire one appears to have gone from a situation in which coppiced woods fenced against livestock were singularly rare to one in which almost every wood consisted of coppice with standards (M. Jones, pers. comm.). Here the woods most typically ran down to boundary streams from the crests of steep sandstone escarpments. Typically, too, the Elizabethan coppices were being cut on 20-25 year cycles for the production of charcoal.

While the shipyards were consuming growing amounts of heavy timber, one should not forget the demands of metallurgical industries for charcoal, the other fire-dependent forms of manufacturing with their hunger for 'white coal' or kiln-dried wood, as well as the fuel needs of a growing population that was now exceeding the pre-Black Death levels. Household and farming demands for iron were greatly augmented in times of uncertainty by the calls of the armaments industry. The inefficiency of the smelting and forging techniques heightened the demand for charcoal fuel, and signs of poor resource management and depletion were apparent in the Weald and neighbouring areas. An Act of 1585 recognised the wastefulness of the charcoal-using industry for the '... great Plenty of Timber which hath grown in [the Weald and Surrey] hath been utterly decayed and spoilt, and will in short be utterly consumed, and wasted'.

Royal Forests that had begun as the exclusive hunting territories of autocratic medieval kings experienced a revival of the hunting role under the Stuart kings. However, this served to provoke popular resentment against what had become an outmoded form of monarchy. In the decades and centuries that followed, Forests met different but generally ignominious ends. Some were completely eroded by piecemeal enclosures, some were informally dismembered by their surrounding communities, and some were formally dismantled. The great Forest of Knaresborough survived various attempts at its enclosure and, though much affected by squatters and their enclosures, it lasted until an Act of enclosure was obtained in 1770. The legislation was of a ponderous nature as the administration struggled with the division and disposal of an entity that had greatly affected the region since at least the building of Knaresborough castle in 1130. The king retained ownership of mines and mineral rights, but woods, underwoods and stone quarries were vested in the owners of the soil. All the king's foresterial rights were abolished and the rectors and vicars received lands in lieu of tithes. Commoners who had enjoyed their rights to the Forest commons for 40 years or more retained them. Another three Acts were needed to complete the legislative process. The Forest that was described in 1775 was very different from the great swathe of land with its attendant castle and deer parks that occupied the south side of the Nidd valley. There were eleven 'constableries', hamlets or townships and more than 30,000 acres of common (*c*.12,141ha) between the Nidd and the Wharfe. This common was open and comprised peat diggings and greazings for sheep, horses and young cattle. The author of this *General View of the Agriculture of the West Riding* for 1794 praised the 'opulent yeomanry', while characteristically directing derision, against the 'necessitous cottager' who was not content with a little milk but also attempted to keep a horse and a flock on the common (Grainge p.82 *et seq.*).

At the time when the Forest of Knaresborough was being dismantled, a Royal Commission investigating the condition of the Crown woods and forests recommended the reorganisation of the New Forest and the development of timber production. In the first half of the next century great planting programmes were instituted, with oak for the Navy and pine, which sheltered the oak and was cut mainly for pit props, being planted in rows. The original *raison d'être* of the Forest as a hunting reserve was set on its head in 1851 with the Deer Removal Act, which ordered the destruction of the very animals that had brought about the creation of the Forest, but which were now regarded as pests by commoners and foresters. Then, with great stands of a pine monoculture being established and the dramatic ancient oak pollards being cleared away, public amenity sentiments began to be expressed. In 1871, an early victory for conservation over narrowly targeted forestry was won and the House of Commons passed a resolution that the cutting of old trees and the making of new enclosures would end (Young, 1969, p.39).

Exploring the 'parkive'

Parks can be magnificent archives for landscape research, for the features derived from earlier cultural landscapes generally have much better chances for survival than they do in other settings. There are various reasons for this, of which two seem particularly important. Firstly, while parks contain a spectrum of land-use types (wood pasture, launds, groves, plantations, coppices, water features and so on) ploughing is but infrequently encountered. It is not necessarily entirely absent; crofts with some arable land might be tenanted within parks, while

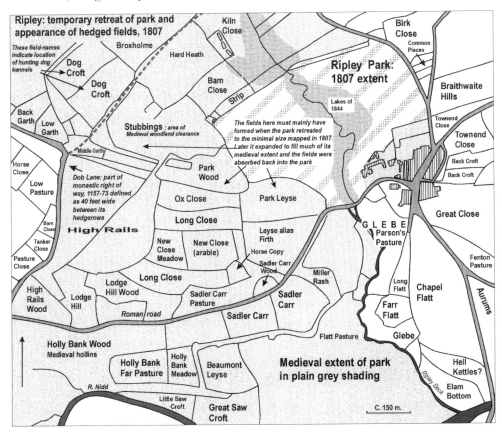

Ripley: temporary retreat of park and appearance of hedged fields, 1807

These field-names indicate location of hunting dog kennels

Broxholme

Hard Heath

Kiln Close

Birk Close

Common Pieces

Dog Croft

Dog Croft

Barn Close

Strip

Ripley Park: 1807 extent

Braithwaite Hills

Lakes of 1844

Back Garth

Low Garth

Middle Garth

Stubbings : *area of Medieval woodland clearance*

The fields here must mainly have formed when the park retreated to the minimal size mapped in 1807. Later it expanded to fill much of its medieval extent and the fields were absorbed back into the park

Townend Close

Townend Close

Back Croft

Back Croft

Horse Close

Low Pasture

Dob Lane: part of monastic right of way, 1157-73 defined as 40 feet wide between its hedgerows

Park Wood

Park Leyse

Great Close

Barn Close

High Rails

Ox Close

Long Close

Leyse alias Firth

G L E B E

Parson's Pasture

Tanker Close

New Close Meadow

New Close (arable)

Horse Copy

Fenton Pasture

Pasture Close

Sadler Carr Wood

Miller Rash

Long Close

Lodge Hill Wood

Sadler Carr Pasture

Sadler Carr

Long Flatt

Chapel Flatt

Aurums

High Rails Wood

Lodge Hill

Roman road

Sadler Carr

Farr Flatt

Flatt Pasture

Glebe

Holly Bank Wood

Medieval hollins

Holly Bank Far Pasture

Holly Bank Meadow

Beaumont Leyse

Medieval extent of park in plain grey shading

Hell Kettles?

Ripley Beck

Elam Bottom

R. Nidd

Little Saw Croft

Great Saw Croft

C. 150 m.

work at Ripley (Muir, 2001) revealed the intrusion of nineteenth-century steam ploughing in a then-reduced park and later, the insertion of ploughed blocks during twentieth-century wartime self-sufficiency drives. One such block completely levelled the ridge and furrow that had been enclosed within the Tudor deer park. Ploughing is the great leveller and eradicator of earthwork evidence and its general absence from parks may allow the survival both of features of the park and features that predate it. Secondly, parks were, at least to some degree, exclusive. There was a general recognition of the basic incompatibility of game and timber interests and peasant cultivation, though again, some parks – Ripley at an early stage in its development and Haverah at a late one – did contain holdings. Normally, the parker and his servant(s) were the only permanent human occupants of the park, so that the disturbances associated with villages and village life were excluded. For these and other reasons, conditions tended to be evolutionary rather than revolutionary and earthworks derived from earlier periods of life, even if they were quite slight, could endure for centuries without being ploughed out or settled upon.

Parks, as we have seen, commandeered a broad spectrum of different countryside types, and while wood pasture contexts may have been popular at

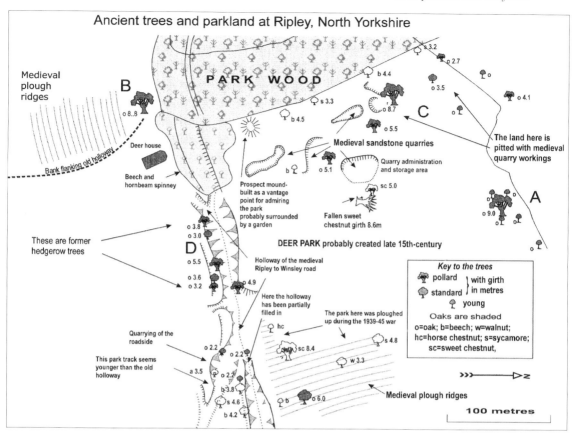

Ancient trees and parkland at Ripley, North Yorkshire

Medieval plough ridges

B

PARK WOOD

o 8..8

Deer house

Bank flanking old holloway

Beech and hornbeam spinney

These are former hedgerow trees

o 3.8
o 3.0

o 5.5

o 3.6
o 3.2

o 4.9

Prospect mound- built as a vantage point for admiring the park probably surrounded by a garden

Quarrying of the roadside

This park track seems younger than the old holloway

Holloway of the medieval Ripley to Winsley road

Here the holloway has been partially filled in

o 2.2
o 2.2

a 3.5

o 2.2

b 3.8

s 4.6

b 4.2

D

s 3.2

p 2.7

b 4.4
o 3.5

o
o 4.1

s 3.3

o 8.7

t

o 5.5

b 4.5

C

Medieval sandstone quarries

b
o 5.1

Quarry administration and storage area

sc 5.0

Fallen sweet chestnut girth 8.6m

o 9.0

o
o

The land here is pitted with medieval quarry workings

A

o

DEER PARK probably created late 15th-century

The park here was ploughed up during the 1939-45 war

hc

sc 8.4

s 4.8

w 3.3

b
o 6.0

Medieval plough ridges

Key to the trees

pollard \ with girth
standard / in metres
young

Oaks are shaded
o=oak; b=beech; w=walnut;
hc=horse chestnut; s=sycamore;
sc=sweet chestnut,

100 metres

earlier stages, parks could encompass near-continuous woodland; the homes of an evicted community; former ploughland, pastures or waste. Most new parks inherited an endowment of trees from the preceding, working countryside. Since trees were things that most park-makers would have sought to encourage, it would have been folly to fell this endowment and then be obliged to wait many decades for new seedlings to mature. This common sense based interpretation is supported by evidence from the field. In order to test the hypothesis that a park provided a safe haven for trees inherited from an earlier phase in the evolution of the cultural landscape we need but two sources of information. Firstly, we need a date for the emparking of the land (and for any subsequent enlargements). For medieval parks, the date may be found in a royal license to empark, though these are sometimes lacking and the change in land-use may be hidden in a grant of free warren. Post-medieval parks are generally datable from archival material. Secondly, we need a reliable curve that relates the girth of a tree to its age, and this will allow us to compare the ages of the trees to that of the park they stand in. However, rather than co-operating with our work, trees develop in a contrary fashion and, while their sizes do relate to their ages, slight genetical differences, soil chemistry and structure, climate and micro-climate, proximity to the sea, altitude and various other factors prevent the tree researcher from developing a single, reliable growth curve. In addition to this, trees come in different species, and while the commoner species, like oak and ash, have yielded many measurements to researchers, others have provided much less reference material. To the outsider it might seem that the answer is simple: either count tree rings or take samples for radio-carbon dating from the oldest timber at the heart of the tree. Sadly, in the fields of landscape history research that concern us here, we tend to be dealing with old and ancient trees – and these virtually always prove to be hollow (a condition which may assist the survival of the tree by giving it the structural strength of a cylindrical tube). In any event, the taking of a core from the heart of a tree is thought to induce rotting, which could have severe consequences for the health of the tree.

The researcher must review the different dating systems that are available, choosing that which seems most closely to mesh with any datable trees in the particular locality within which he/she is working. When the comparisons are made, any tree that yields a date earlier than that of the park *must* have been inherited from an earlier landscape. Sometimes it can be associated to other trees and earthwork features to provide insights into the organisation of that older countryside. The written evidence shows that many Georgian parks had elderly tree populations. In some cases these populations could have originated in a medieval deer park, while in others they must have been features of an emparked countryside.

Sheriff Hutton, near York, provides an example. In 1335, the Nevilles created a park here from wet woodland or 'carr' and from the lands of the deserted village of East Lilling that lay to the south of Hutton village (Beresford and St Joseph, p.155). A market charter was granted to Hutton in 1378 and in 1382 an imposing seat of the 'quadrangular palace castle' type was built, making the place a centre for recreation and prestige. The Earl of Warwick died in 1471 and the park reverted to the Crown and was favoured during royal hunts in the Forest of Galtres nearby. James I sold the park in 1622, though Charles I leased the castle back two years later. A survey by Norton in 1624 mentioned certain decayed fishponds and said that '... the bowells of this worthy pile and defensive howse are rente and torne ... to this Castle garthe adioyneth Sheriff Hutton parke well stored with fallow deere and sett with neer 4000 decayed and decaying okes' (Leeds City Archives TN/B/41). In 1824, Todd recorded that the king had leased the park with a covenant to maintain 300 deer and paraphrased Norton's survey: 'To this Castle Garth adjoineth Sheriff Hutton Park, well stocked with fallow deer, and set with neer 4000 decayed and decaying oaks, the most of them [stag] headed' (p.38).

The significant facts here are the date of the park, 1335, and the fact that within less than three centuries the almost 4,000 oaks in the park were in decline or decay. Stag-headedness can begin at various stages in the life of a mature oak, but it is very hard to imagine that, had the trees been planted after the park's creation, the assemblage of 100-, 200- or almost 300-year-old trees would have assumed the appearance associated with oaks of 500-800+ years of age. Infinitely more credible is the notion that trees from woods and carr and hedgerow trees from the lands of the lost East Lilling were incorporated into the Nevill's new park.

Any documentary evidence apart, there are two quite different techniques that can be applied to provide a date for a tree relative to that of a datable cultural landscape in which it is standing. The *first* of these involves measuring the girth of the tree at chest height and then relating the value obtained to a curve or scale that suggests ages for such values. An early attempt is represented by Mitchell's claim that 1in/25mm of girth represents one year of growth for a free-standing tree and that this rate is halved for a tree growing in a woodland context (1966, 1974). This scale is crude and unrepresentative because it assumes that trees grow at steady rates and it fails to take account of the marked slowing down of growth after trees have reached their maximum canopy size. Having said this, the woodland scale was found to provide a useful approximation for former hedgerow oaks of late medieval to Jacobean ages in northern England (Muir, 2000 and see Fleming, 1998).

In 1994, White proposed a new growth curve that took account of the patterns of growth displayed by real trees, which tend to grow quite rapidly to attain their maximum canopy and then enter a decline phase, during which the increase in girth and width of annual rings are markedly reduced. Though being linked to the growth characteristics of trees, this is not an objective technique and various subjective inputs are required. It is proposed for oaks that each decline year involves the production of rings of only 0.6mm width compared to the 3.5mm width associated with trees growing at the maximum rate. He explained that:

> Once optimum crown size is reached (at about one tenth of the potential natural lifespan of many oaks), the pattern of growth changes .…Whereas the core of the tree is characterised by wide even ring widths … the subsequent rings tend to reduce in width although the annual production of new wood now becomes less constant. This is because the foliage area is no longer spreading but also remains more or less constant' (1995, pp.10-11).

He clarified this elsewhere:

> The second phase of tree growth is a stable one. It may last 400 years in open-grown oak; only 30 years in birch; and sometimes almost nothing at all in cultivated poplar. In the cut stump, this period is represented by slowly-decreasing annual ring width. What is actually happening is that wood production is remaining constant except for the occasional effect of weather or caterpillars … so the area of each ring is more or less the same. This is regulated by crown size and leaf area,

which remain more or less static. The annual increment graph is no longer an upward curve but becomes a horizontal line (1997, pp.224-5).

(It should be noted that in a tree producing annual growth of equal area, the rings will progressively narrow because their circumference is increasing.) However, the observer may have to decide (guess?) when the decline arrived and adjust his/her calculations accordingly. All manner of climatic and soil-related factors could affect the growth pattern of an individual tree. Each species has its own size range and data for each of them based on measured and ring-counted trunks is not available. Also, one need only measure trees in an avenue that were all planted at the same time and which share similar environmental settings to realise that variations occur even in such relatively controlled situations. Furthermore, the history of tree management can be very important. Pollarding appears to prolong the life of trees and this is not only because the lack of potential for commercial planks deters timber merchants. It may

> ...be partly because restriction of their crown development delays the stage at which the demand for water and minerals begins to outstrip the tree's ability to increase its absorptive root area. Also, since more branches join the bole than in a maiden tree, there is a correspondingly larger number of vascular connections within the bole (Lonsdale, 1996, p.100).

The true picture is likely to be highly complex, for, while pollarding is thought to have a rejuvenating effect, it must also cause stresses, like the sudden reduction in the energy-producing canopy and the exposure of the bark to sunlight after each pollarding event, the opening of wounds that might be exploited by parasites or fungi, and so on. The White method of dating trees does seem to require subjective recalibrations by the researcher, and when applied by this writer to northern English pollards in its 'raw' form it yielded dates that were impossibly young (Muir, 2000). The predicted rate of growth was 3.5mm annual ring width, but young oaks in the 50-200 years old age range that were ring-counted at saw mills in the region were found to have been producing rings of width around 2.5mm.

The *second* group of approaches is related to techniques and concepts current in field sciences like geology, archaeology and geography. They concern the relative positions of phenomena. Thus, in geology, a band of rock in an undisturbed sequence of strata must be younger than the rock that lies beneath it. In physical geography, a river that runs against the grain of a passage of topography is likely to have been superimposed upon it by the erosion of overlying rocks, while in archaeology, if the ruts and ditches of a trackway cut a series of field boundary banks, then the track should be younger than the field system. Travelling by train, one will often see how the Victorian engineer's track has sliced across older field networks, cutting off corners and creating access problems for the farmer. With such principles in mind, one can imagine exploring the medieval earthworks entombed in a park (as they so often are). Reasonably well-developed ridge and furrow earthworks can be recognised fairly well, even when the grass in the pasture is almost knee-high. If one finds trees growing on plough ridges or in furrows (or anywhere except at the old field margins) then it is safe to assume that the trees are younger than the last ploughing event. The logic is plain, for nobody would have wanted to plough around them.

However, the fact that trees are found growing in such relationships does not demonstrate that they are 'young'. At Cadzow in Lanarkshire the former hunting park contains about 300 magnificent sessile oak pollards that probably date from the second part of the medieval period, though they are reputed to have been planted by David I (1124-53). Though some sources identify them as wood pasture trees, they are described as standing on the ridged ploughland that must have been abandoned when the land was emparked for hunting. The parkland/wood pasture will in this case have been established on the former arable fields (Crone and Watson, 2003, p.74).

The historical relationship between trees and their cultural and historical setting may not be as simple as that of trees growing on older plough ridges. If we turn to Ripley, North Yorkshire, then the deer park provides different examples of the complexity that may be associated with the relationship. Here, the oldest of the oaks in terms of its girth measurement of 9m (over 29ft) has an age of 891 plus a decline phase according to the White system or one of about 700 according to the Mitchell woodland system). Whether it dates from the Norman era or from the thirteenth century it has certainly been inherited from a countryside that predated the deer park. The earliest occasion upon which the park could have been created was around 1400, as part of the creation of a new village and church and a reorganisation of the township by the Ingilby family. However, there is no hint of the existence of a deer park in the relevant documents until 1488 when a debatable 'Pacrofte', possibly 'Park Croft' is mentioned (Ingilby MS 227) and the most likely time of origin lies in the decades bracketing 1500. This oak pollard (now) stands in a rather solitary position close to a sike or stream and might have originated in wood pasture or at the margins of agricultural land.

The best contemporary account of the countryside in which the sapling or acorn of such a tree developed is found in a charter of around 1200, in which Nicholas de Cayton granted to the monks of Fountains various lands: '… meadow in the Vale of Ripley and his land down from the said meadow between the wood of "Rippeleia" and up from the wood as far as the road which goes from the said wood as far as the road and the spinney north of the house of Ralph Blaber' (Chartul. of. Fount., f.98b). We cannot know where Ralph Blaber lived and the 'Ripley' referred to cannot be the village but the vill or township. However, we do get a picture of meadowland in the valley bottom around Ripley Beck with the wood, soon to be reduced by assarting, covering the higher ground in the general area of the modern Park Wood.

Trees growing on the ramparts of hillforts, like the small example from Epping Forest (*right*) or Cholesbury, Berkshire (*left*) do not tell us much about the forts, but they do suggest that woodland has colonised the setting since the Iron Age. Tree-covered earthworks like ridge and furrow, field boundaries and so on also show that woodland can advance as well as retreat. The willows fringing the flanks of the medieval fishpond at Landbeach in Cambridgeshire (*below*) could have overlapped with the last phases in the pond's use and would thus be contemporary with the pond. The contorted ash tree growing through the rubble of a former house at a deserted clachan site in Glengairn (*below right*) is at the limit of its range and must be at least 200 years old. This could take the age of the clachan back to the shameful Highland Clearances in the decades around 1800

The next oldest oak pollard is almost as old according to the girth data and has a more distinctive position for it stands at the terminus of a low bank that followed and flanked a lost medieval routeway that linked the Ilkley–Aldborough Roman road to the (deserted) medieval village of Owlcotes. To one side of the bank was the holloway of the road and to the other was, or developed, ridged ploughland. The old pollard might have originated in a hedgerow growing upon the roadside or it might have been a solitary boundary marker.

On the brow of the hill and just below the hilltop, Park Wood is an area of medieval quarrying. Hammers and wedges must have been used to split off slabs of a coarse, purplish sandstone, which could then be shaped and stored before being sledged downslope to building sites. (The township contained a belt of Magnesian Limestone, normally a much sought after building stone, but this was quarried for marl and the sandstone was used for local building.) Some workings are still open, some probably infilled with rubble, while accumulations of chippings produce a very hummocky land surface. Associated with this quarrying area are several ancient oaks, though their archaeological relationship(s) with it is/are not clear. The stone concerned appears to have been used to build a church at a holy springs site in the township. This church could well have been recently rebuilt when it was dismantled and its materials, stone and timber, transported and incorporated in a new church built in the new village around the end of the fourteenth century. This stone also appears to have been used in the Ingilby's gatehouse of 1434-57 and tower of 1555. If one guesses that the quarries were in use from around 1300 to 1550 one may not be too far wrong. The oldest of the oak trees here, a giant pollard with a girth of 8.7m would seem, therefore, to have preceded the quarrying activities and might possibly have stood in a zone of wood pasture lying between the meadows, below, and the manorial wood, above. The other oak pollards in this locality are smaller/younger and one can imagine that the dross from quarrying would have provided protection from grazing animals, allowing acorns to germinate in pockets among the waste and trees to grow to a height where they could be pollarded and included within the timber and browse resources of the township or park. The last association is particularly revealing. It comprises a group of rather small pollards that are the last remnants of hedges that flanked a routeway leading from probable old manor and mill site to the (deserted) hamlet of Whipley. This track, deeply hollowed into the brow of the slope, must have been in use for a long time until the enclosure of the deer park in Tudor times put it out of use. There could have been no use for hedgerows inside the new deer park, though plainly the hedgerow pollards were preserved. The sizes of these trees are modest in comparison to the giants with girths of over 8m described above. However, they can only have existed as trees before the creation of the park and their forms and conditions suggest great ages and stunted growth. Perhaps the proximity of the sandstone bedrock to the surface here slowed their growth, but their sizes do show that there is no simple correlation between age and girth.

In parts of the park, medieval plough ridges can be seen, though this is not the highly developed ridge and furrow such as can be seen on deep soils in the Midlands subjected to up to a millennium of arable cultivation. The rather shallow and somewhat narrow ridge and furrow at Ripley is complicated by the effects of twentieth-century wartime ploughing of blocks within the park, which has erased the medieval corrugations in the area affected. Where there was medieval ploughland, as one would expect, there are no medieval trees. The trees seen growing on plough ridges have been deliberately planted, mainly as landscaping involving species like beech, horse chestnut, walnut and so on. The landscape in this sector of the deer park at Ripley does demonstrate the complexities in the relationship between ancient trees and parkland and the importance of considering documentary, archaeological and environmental evidence. One final warning concerns the widespread planting of sweet chestnuts in northern parks. These replicate the forms and sizes of ancient oaks, though most/all are the result of deliberate landscaping (there is some debate about whether the sweet chestnut ever spreads in Britain, some believing that it is capable of setting seed in hot years (Ted Green, pers. comm.)). Any field surveys undertaken in winter, when the distinctive foliage of the sweet chestnut is not displayed, should take account of the ease with which pollarded sweet chestnuts seen in the middle distance can be mistaken as old oak pollards. They are sometimes planted amongst them (e.g. Ripley, Studley Royal, etc), perhaps as efforts to fill-out a pattern of ancient oak pollards. Being much more quickly growing, they are well suited to this task (they also produce an excellent timber that faintly resembles oak and is much more easily worked). The most popular 'eye-catcher' in Ripley park is a fallen sweet chestnut that had achieved a girth of 8.6m before it toppled over in 1962-3.

The preceding discussion shows that the detection of ancient hedgerow trees within a park can be difficult. It is very easy to assume that any hedge alignments found within parks must be older than the park concerned and must represent hedgerows whose trees have been incorporated into the parkland. Things in landscape history are seldom as simple as this. At Ripley, a few enclosed holdings appear to have survived the emparking, at least for a while, for in 1523 Sir William Ingilby engaged in an exchange of leases with his rector, allowing Sir William to lease an enclosure called 'Tyndall Close' which lay in his own park. Many parks ended their existences by being converted into working farmland, either part of their owner's home farm or land partitioned and divided between various tenants or freeholders. The gigantic Haverah park became 13 farms.

More complicated than this arrangement for the disposal of parkland was one that is exemplified at Ripley in the general vicinity of the former hunting tower and kennels. Here the launds, where fallow deer still graze, are traversed by alignments of trees. At first, one might imagine that these are hedgerows that were incorporated in the late medieval park when it was founded. However, the trees that are present are much too young for this. The clues may be found in

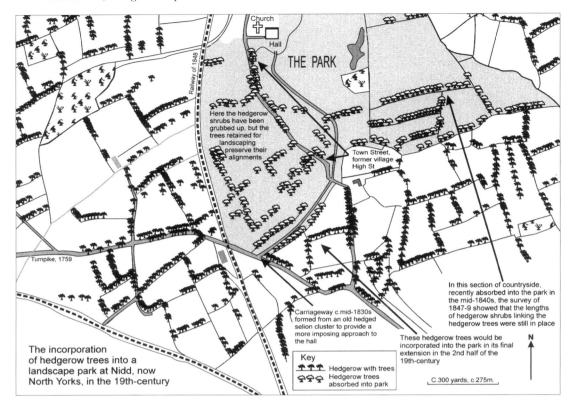

Church
Hall
THE PARK

Railway of 1848

Here the hedgerow shrubs have been grubbed up, but the trees retained for landscaping preserve their alignments

Town Street, former village High St

Turnpike, 1759

In this section of countryside, recently absorbed into the park in the mid-1840s, the survey of 1847-9 showed that the lengths of hedgerow shrubs linking the hedgerow trees were still in place

Carriageway c.mid-1830s formed from an old hedged selion cluster to provide a more imposing approach to the hall

These hedgerow trees would be incorporated into the park in its final extension in the 2nd half of the 19th-century

N

The incorporation of hedgerow trees into a landscape park at Nidd, now North Yorks, in the 19th-century

Key
Hedgerow with trees
Hedgerow trees absorbed into park

C.300 yards, c.275m.

the fact that the boundaries of deer parks were not necessarily permanent and immovable, as commonly imagined. It was quite possible for a park, normally in times of economic stringency, to contract and be partitioned into hedged fields. Later, a revival in the fortunes of the family concerned could allow a re-advance of the park over ground that had been lost. Thus, at Ripley, the tree alignments seem to reflect a contraction of the park, its division into fields bounded by hedges and hedgerow trees, followed by an advance across the ground converted to farmland and an incorporation of the hedgerow trees into the park landscape. There is evidence that deer were hunted in the park in the 1660s, but in 1684 a farm in the park called The Lodge and parcels of ground called Low Forth, Stelling, High Forth, Old Park and Park Lees were rented-out to John Hare and Nicholas Bradley for 11 years at a rent of £5 (Ingilby MS 2125). Presumably, the park lodge had been converted into a farmstead. It lay not far from the tree alignments described above, so they could quite easily derive from hedgerow trees planted after this agricultural intrusion. However, the park did not come to rest at this point. A survey by a relative of the furniture designer, Chippendale, in 1752 showed the park had expanded again and almost filled its medieval limits, though by 1807 a decline in family fortunes reduced it to a quarter of its medieval extent, though later in that century it expanded again and in 1892 it covered 300 acres (121ha) and supported about 80 fallow deer (Whittaker, 1892, pp.182-3).

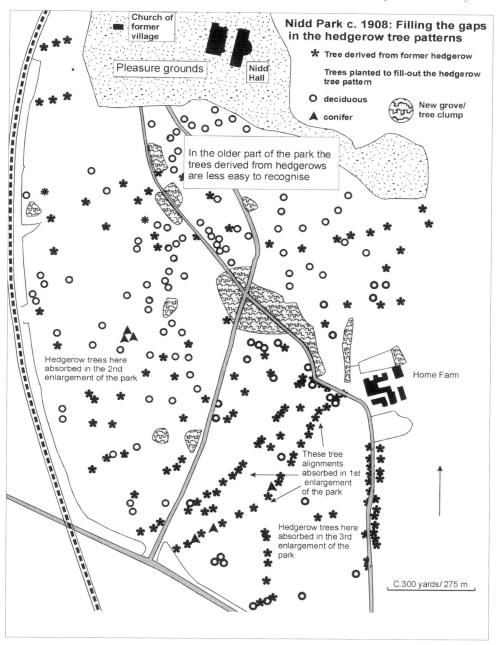

Nidd Park c. 1908: Filling the gaps in the hedgerow tree patterns

* Tree derived from former hedgerow

Trees planted to fill-out the hedgerow tree pattern

O deciduous

▲ conifer

New grove/ tree clump

Church of former village

Pleasure grounds

Nidd Hall

In the older part of the park the trees derived from hedgerows are less easy to recognise

Hedgerow trees here absorbed in the 2nd enlargement of the park

Home Farm

These tree alignments absorbed in 1st enlargement of the park

Hedgerow trees here absorbed in the 3rd enlargement of the park

C. 300 yards/ 275 m.

Leaving Ripley just about a mile behind and heading in the direction of Knaresborough, one comes to quite a different park at Nidd. The mansion is now a country hotel, but the surrounding parkland is the result of a very late sequence of emparking episodes (Muir and Amos, 1998). Nidd had existed as an unspectacular village and township; it bordered upon Ripley but had not been remodelled under ambitious patronage in the way that had happened there. The removal of villages by imperious lords is regarded as being feudal in character, or at its latest, an occasional feature of seventeenth- or eighteenth-century overlordship. In the 1760s-70s, Harewood House appeared on a village site and at Castle Howard the village of Hinderskelfe was evicted and its site was drowned by an ornamental lake. Sometime before 1818, the creation of a park at Nidd destroyed a part of the old village on the eastern side of Town Street. The floor of the village street was greatly over deepened and the spoil heaped to one side of the 'trench', with the objective of making travellers using it invisible from the mansion. In 1825 the Trappes sold their estate to Benjamin Rawson, a prosperous Bradford merchant. He extended the park and built a curving carriageway leading to his mansion, thus avoiding the common highway. The village was now riven by gaps caused by emparking and in the 1840s, enlargements to east and west that tripled the size of the park brought its final destruction. A smaller extension to the south completed the park.

The Trappes, Benjamin Rawson and his daughter Mary, who died in 1863, had completely transformed the locality from an agricultural landscape, well populated with village tenants, to an empty expanse of parkland. In the course of this transformation, they grubbed-up hedgerows, but retained hedgerow trees in order to accelerate the development of 'mature' park landscape. The trees, of course, formed alignments. In order for the 'random stipple' associated with typical parkland scenery to be obtained, the patterns inherited from the agricultural context had to be complemented by new plantings, with the trees carefully positioned to fill any 'unattractive' voids in the scene – notably the scene as viewed from the mansion.

Nidd is an outstanding example of the way in which trees from the hedgerows of working countrysides were employed to provide the mature tree component so valued in parkland. It is remarkable because it is relatively recent, so that the whole progression of emparking and the enlargement of the park can be followed through a sequence of accurate maps. Any who deny the significance of this oft-occurring process could do no better than to examine the maps of the locality that were drawn in the middle of the nineteenth century. There one can see the working hedgerows, dotted with hedgerow trees running up to the perimeter of the park. Having reached it, the hedgerow itself vanishes, but its line is traced by the former hedgerow trees. The wonderful thing about Nidd is that the cartography of the late 1840s captured park-creation as it was happening. In some parts of the park the hedge shrubs have gone, leaving just the trees, while in others, hedgerows and trees are both captured within the new park boundary. In the early days of emparking, the park can mirror the countryside that preceded it. The hedgerow shrubs may have been grubbed up, but one needs only to 'join up the dots', as represented by the hedgerow trees which are now stranded in parkland, to recreate the lost fieldscape. Having recognised the initial arboreal layout as composed by former hedgerow trees, one can then identify the supplementary plantings designed to 'fill out' the pattern.

Trees from a hedgerow that must have been planted during a temporary retreat of Ripley deer park boundary

Research student Lee Hunwick measuring the girth of a medieval oak pollard in Ripley deer park

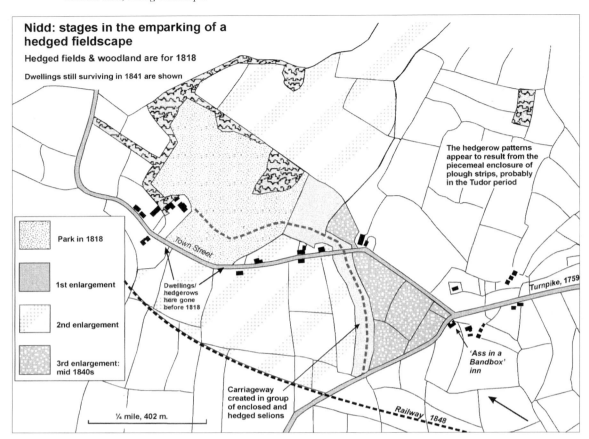

Nidd: stages in the emparking of a hedged fieldscape

Hedged fields & woodland are for 1818

Dwellings still surviving in 1841 are shown

The hedgerow patterns appear to result from the piecemeal enclosure of plough strips, probably in the Tudor period

Town Street

Dwellings/ hedgerows here gone before 1818

Park in 1818

1st enlargement

2nd enlargement

3rd enlargement: mid 1840s

Turnpike, 1759

'Ass in a Bandbox' inn

Carriageway created in group of enclosed and hedged selions

Railway, 1848

¼ mile, 402 m.

Nidd is now the recreation ground attached to a country hotel, but not far away there is a much more famous passage of parkland: the park attached to Fountains Abbey and Studley Royal. Here, the history is less certain, for though a licence of free warren at Studley was granted to Thomas de Bourne in 1343, such grants were normally associated with hunting small game on the demesne and, as at Ripley, there is no trace of a licence to empark. On Sexton's map of Yorkshire of 1577, the territory is shown to be bounded by a park paling, so the lord probably designated part of his demesne as a hunting reserve. Meanwhile at neighbouring Fountains, the monastic deer park was taken over by the Greshams at the Dissolution. In the post-medieval era, some form of association between hunting and farming may have existed at Studley. Then, between 1670 and 1675, George Aislabie initiated a formal designed landscape and his ambition was pursued by his son. From the early 1680s, tree planting work was undertaken, with the creation of some avenues (M. Newman, pers. comm.). The park and gardens do not seem to have extended beyond the valley slopes until the eighteenth century, and in the early or mid-1740s, a park wall was built across the agricultural territory of Mackershaw, lying to the south of the Studley Lake and to the east of the water gardens at Fountains. Fieldwork in the Mackershaw locality

A beech that was planted and pollarded to fill a gap in the commandeered hedgerow tree pattern at Nidd. Note how it fits into the scene as viewed from the hall, behind

demonstrates the alignment of parkland trees that must predate the eighteenth-century extension of the park, showing that here, too, hedgerow trees formed the framework for the new park. Elsewhere in Studley Royal one can recognise very few surviving medieval hedgerow pollards from the centuries preceding the sixteenth-century park, with girths of 6.0m and 7.9m, while girth measurements in the 5.0m region seem to identify the seventeenth-century oak alignments.

This historical background can be used to illuminate the ancient tree patterns, just as the patterns can be used to enhance historical understanding. The value of the hedgerow as an archive has seldom been recognised (the confusion associated with so-called 'hedgerow dating' probably has much to do with this). Hedgerows preserve former countryside layouts and property divisions in other manners than that of commandeered landscaping material. For example, the author's former Ph.D. research student Ian Dormor showed that as the Healey Spring Wood in Colsterdale contracted from the east and had around two thirds of its area converted to farmland, so hedgelines, some now studded with ancient oak pollards, remain and preserve the outlines of the old coppice compartments. The ancient woodbank on the eastern side, now far removed from the surviving wood, is revetted with drystone walling and punctuated with numerous oak

These trees derive from a hedgerow at Mackershaw that preceded the advance by Studley Royal park

pollards. Finally, the incorporation of hedgerow trees in parks is certainly not just a northern phenomenon. Wainwright has shown that at Powderham Park in Devon, around 1785, numerous alignments of hedgerows trees were standing. Their lines could be shown to correspond to field boundaries as plotted on an earlier map. He found that one alignment still survived, running alongside a public footpath (2005, pp.10-11).

The park moves on

Our understanding of parkland landscapes has suffered from the perspectives adopted by scholars in art history, who have elevated the landscape park of the eighteenth century as a work of genius and have failed to appreciate both the long history and the workaday aspects of the park. Landscape parks were not born anew in the minds of a Repton or a Brown. Rather, the park-makers tweaked and tinkered with the products of a near-ageless and, perhaps, innate enthusiasm for associations of trees and grassy spaces. Mansions did not suddenly acquire parks in accordance with eighteenth-century fashion. Most of them had

Stumps, tree holes and ancient pollards mark former hedgerow alignments at Studley Royal

them already: they had begun as medieval deer parks and many of them still contained deer. The civilising influences of the Renaissance did not cause an abandonment of the cruel and gory ritual of the deer hunt; rather the ritual grew significantly in strength under Henry VIII and Elizabeth I. The newest weapons were employed in what became a yet more uneven contest and these devices were also taken up by the poachers. The butcher and two labourers who killed a doe with a young fawn in the king's chase of Bishopdale in 1621 employed a crossbow, perhaps its silence suited their purpose, but 10 years earlier a John Bentham of Horton in Ribblesdale killed two of the Earl of Cumberland's does illegally on Pen-y-Ghent with '... a certain gun and pellets, anglice gun and pellets' (Speight, 1892, p.397). There is no doubt that the well-armed soldiery and local insurgents were able to inflict considerable damage on the deer parks they encountered or camped beside. The parks were both symbols of a generally loyalist aristocracy and, in more prosaic terms, of sources of food that could not escape.

This disruption was not sufficient to prevent the deer park remaining a familiar facet of the scene. Many will have needed to be restocked and to have their pales repaired, while many of those sequestered from bishops in 1646, and from the king in 1649, were converted into agricultural land. Some families, penalised for their actions or loyalties, were obliged to turn their parks to more economic uses. Parks of the traditional type continued to be created and enlarged in the seventeenth century, like the out-pasture of Crackpot Hall in Swaledale, enlarged for deer in 1636 (Hartley and Ingilby, 1956, p.266). Under Charles II (1660-85) forfeit deer parks were recovered and damaged ones were restored and sometimes, enlarged. It was probably in the immediate aftermath of the medieval period that ornamental plantings became more elaborate, while another important aspect of landscaping concerned the selective preservation of trees from the working countryside that were assimilated in the process of park creation of enlargement, as described in the previous section.

By the time, in the late seventeenth century, that oak avenues were being extended across former farmland at Studley Royal, the profile of deer hunting, so prominent in Stuart and Tudor times, had been lowered, though hunting deer had certainly not vanished. The deer, along with flocks of sheep or white park cattle, where they could be found, were now valued for their aesthetic qualities. Many owners faced difficulties in maintaining stocks in the face of organised poaching and in obtaining replacements from elsewhere. Even so, more than 330 deer parks still existed in the 1860s. (Their number did not include the park at Caley, near Leeds, which was stocked in the 1820s with zebra, wild pigs and goats, which must have contrasted with the conventional red and fallow deer. All were destroyed when the park was divided by a road in 1840 (Speight, 1900, p.131).) Most of the fashionable landscape parks were organised or expanded from a deer park, and in most cases the landscaping involved a judicious trimming or 'enhancement' of what was there already. The parks were closely attached to their mansions – but in the northern dales and fells, and probably elsewhere too, they always had been so. Charles II was responsible for an almost obsessive enthusiasm for tree planting in his Forests, and this enthusiasm spilled over into his parks. This trend was adopted by many of his park-owning subjects, though since deer parks had traditionally been associated in some way with woodland production, this was no innovation.

Trees found in the landscape parks of the Georgian–Victorian eras can be grouped in the following classes:

• Trees incorporated into the landscaping from former, working countrysides.
• Woodland incorporated from a preceding deer park, or working countryside.
• Trees planted for structured landscaping purposes in an existing park (e.g. avenues, groves around a temple, etc.).
• Trees randomly planted to provide a transition from wood to laund or to fill out a pattern of incorporated trees.
• Timber plantations within a park, planted primarily for economic gain but with secondary landscaping uses.
• Collections and assemblages of exotic trees forming an arboretum.

To these classes a possible seventh may be added, consisting of trees/shrubs

At Studley Royal isolated hedge species like field maple and hawthorn suggest possible hedgerow origins. This hawthorn is part of a broken alignment of parkland trees that mark a medieval hedge line

derived not from the hedgerow *tree* contents of an incorporated hedgerow, but from the hedgerow *shrubs*. At Studley Royal there are several free-standing examples of hawthorn and field maple, typical hedgerow shrubs of the locality, and they may have originated in medieval hedgerows bounding 'cultures' or furlongs or lanes. Some on field boundary earthworks certainly did. Any researcher studying the landscape historical evidence associated with parkland trees is likely to encounter a challenging and potentially confusing picture of a complex intermixing of trees of different ages, species and origins. In Studley, and many other places, the oldest trees from the pre-park phase are pollarded – but pollarding was frequently applied to trees planted in parks. Species types may give some assistance, for exotic trees and debatable cases like the sweet chestnut can be assumed to have been introduced as landscaping materials, though the oak figured in both working and landscaped countrysides.

Ages are difficult to calculate owing to factors like hollow cores, conflicting dating systems, a lack of proposed growth curves for many species, and so on. But in the cases of trees that are plainly older than the park in which they stand, insights to the nature of the preceding countryside are provided. These insights are much more valuable if the evidence of the tree patterns can be linked to associated earthworks which help to trace out the alignments of track-side hedgebanks, headlands, settlements and so on.

Despite the emphasis on enlightened patronage and sensibility that the

Parkland can survive long after the extinction of the formal park, as here at Feolallt near Llanddewi Brefi

art historians have placed on the commissioners of landscaping schemes, the evidence of the present day aristocracy suggests that much of the landscaping represented attempts to enhance status and follow fashion. The niceties of the symmetry of patterns traced by low box hedges or the curves in a serpentine lake may have been somewhat lost on owners who viewed their parks as places to race thoroughbred stallions or lose fortunes around the cock pit. There were also those who, deprived of the stimulation of following an occupation, loved to potter and meddle. The park provided them with ample opportunities. With Charles II, George III (1760-1820) and several other tree-planting and estate-organising leaders as examples, many of these park owners found fulfilment in improving their estate woods in the park and the out-woods beyond its pale.

Some of their interest was cosmetic: with the employment of trees from preceding landscapes as featured items of the contrived scene. This included the retention of clusters of mature elms at Wimpole, Cambridgeshire, the Hanoverian adoption of ancient oaks from Windsor Forest in Windsor Great Park and the incorporation of the great pollard beeches of Aylmerton Common in the park at Felbrigg, Norfolk (Rackham, 2004). The ancient trees may have been thought to symbolise an antiquity and continuity that might, rightly or wrongly, reflect upon the park-owning dynasty. In many other cases it was the working wood that captured the imagination and zeal of the owner.

Some of the journals and diaries that record this infatuation survive. In 1668, Sir Wiliam Ingilby of Ripley (1620-82) was still engaged in the traditional pursuit of hunting the deer in his park (August 24, 1668: 'I killed a fat Buck out of the paddock ... 7 faunes'). A century later, Sir John Ingilby kept a studious record of the trees that he had planted in the park and on the former common. He began his record in October 1782 but included a retrospective entry:

... before book begun − 19 Sept 1781 − upon Scara Moor [the old common] in the banks opposite Cayton to 13500 oaks ... about 800 oaks ... A great many oaks at the top of the closes near Thornton fence −1500 Scotch firs on [?] This year And

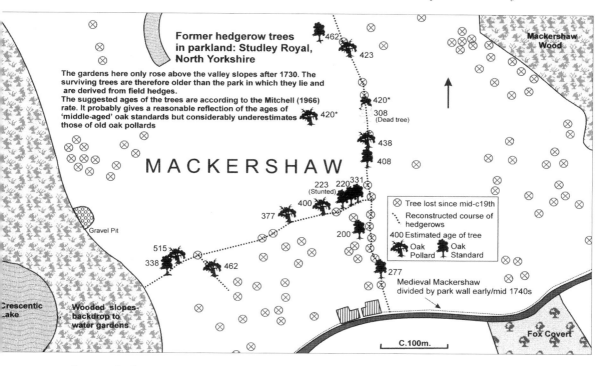

Former hedgerow trees in parkland: Studley Royal, North Yorkshire

The gardens here only rose above the valley slopes after 1730. The surviving trees are therefore older than the park in which they lie and are derived from field hedges.
The suggested ages of the trees are according to the Mitchell (1966) rate. It probably gives a reasonable reflection of the ages of 'middle-aged' oak standards but considerably underestimates those of old oak pollards

MACKERSHAW

Mackershaw Wood

Gravel Pit

⊗ Tree lost since mid-c19th
⋰ Reconstructed course of hedgerows
400 Estimated age of tree
Oak Pollard
Oak Standard

Medieval Mackershaw divided by park wall early/mid 1740s

Crescentic Lake

Wooded slopes-backdrop to water gardens

Fox Covert

C.100m.

the year before 700 oaks on sawcroft brow and Acombe in Holling Bank [the old hollins in the park]

1781 I continued the line of Silver Firs in little sorrowsikes [part of the park beside the Castle] against the road taking away the old fences and continuing the pale at the same time

Planted a Holly and Yew hedge at the High End of the Park and behind it

Ash and a few sycamore

Planted Scotch firs weymouth pines and silver firs in the little [?] offsett in Martin pasture

A small orchard of apples in Mary Parlour Garth

Planted upon Tom Hill (upon Scara Moor) oaks, ash, Beech, birch, Holley a great quantity and 2000 Scotch firs 700 Spruce and 600 Larches and 1000 Sycamores In Scara Bottoms [the north-western margins of the park].

Nov. 1781 Made the shrubbery behind it planted a duble row of quick [hawthorn] – upon the square piece on Scara Moor – several Turin Poplars and about 500 Willow

Oaks at the Corner and 600 alder from Harwell

Not all this planting succeeded: '… the poplars did not thrive and very few of the willows – this piece was over-drained against my opinion'. Nevertheless, the planting continued at an even more frenetic rate in 1782. From the massive numbers of trees involved and the great range of varieties, one might imagine that a vast estate was being afforested, yet the total area available to Sir John was probably only about one square mile. It is not clear quite what his motives were, for he began the planting season by replacing dead trees in a shrubbery with ornamental trees, like jasmine, laburnum, weeping birch, sea buckthorn, laurel and broom and then proceeded to plant commercial softwoods, large landscaping trees, hardwoods and holly.

Oct 28 1782 A Spruce fir on the terrace opposite and gate into sorrow sykes ...
Nov 13 1782 Planted three hundred and twenty birches upon the square piece upon Scara Moor [?] holly berrys Horse chestnuts...about 2 bushels
Dec 6 1782 On the square piece on Scara Moor 430 birches from Harewell [were the birches being used to shelter young conifers?]
46 Sycamore in James Islands at Scara and 290 in the Old Clint Lane
Dec 1782 Fenced new [?] from the walks with a ditch under the Holleyes [?] and planted Hollins [holly] against the walks firs in the stubbings with pailes and planted Holly drives and then laid the whole with a good fence...
Dec 1782 Planted Sycamores in W. Old whipley Lane [Whipley was a deserted hamlet on the western margin of the park]
Dec 1782 Planted upon Tom Hill on Scara Moor 300 Beech 900 Dutch Elm 1000 Scotch Firs 500 Spruce...500 Larches 100 Hornbeams 200 Lymes 200 wild black cherries and in the little piece in the Ings 2 pinetrees 2 [?] 4 Firs 5 Larch 2 scotch firs and 2 stone pines
At the same time 3 Gales or Dutch myrtyles at the fish pond

And so the work continued in 1783, undeterred by failures on a fairly massive scale: '1783 Planted 140 large oaks in broxholm behind the wall [in the western end of the park] ... [all died] ... March 15 1783 Planted 140 large oaks in broxholm as before' [all died]. The source for the journal is Ingilby MS 2838, while a more concise account of the activities is found in the Gardener's List of plantings in 1783 (Ingilby MS 2839):

Account of trees planted Nove and Dec 1783

800 oaks 2 feet
800 Scotch Firs 1 ft { all Planted in Low Piece in the High Rales [at the top of the park]
103 Scotch Firs 1 ft
3 Pine 2 feet
3 Chester Pines 2ft {all in the Low Piece in the High Rales
3097 Scotch firs 1ft
400 Larches 1 ft
90 Chester Pines 1ft
200 oaks {all planted on Kettle Spring Banks[in the west of the township outside the park]

100 Horse Chestnuts 12ft { planted in the park
34 Larches 12ft
10 Spruce firs 12ft { planted against park wall
15 Horse Chestnuts 12ft
10 Larches 12ft { ?Milner?
700 Hazel Nut Trees planted on Tom Hill
10 Spruce Firs 3ft
10 Larches 3ft{ planted in the Near Clump in the High Stubbins
6 Larches 12ft
5 Horse Chestnuts 12ft
5 Weymouth Pines 3ft
6 Chester pines 2ft
6 Pines Asters 2ft
1 English Elm{ high orchard
1 Chester pine 2ft
1 pine aster 2ft { planted in little nursery in the Ings [old meadow land]
1 stone pine 2ft
1 Chester pine 2ft
1 Weymouth pine 3ft
1 pine aster 2ft { Terris [terrace]

Total of every sort
4000 scotch firs 1ft
1000 oaks 2ft
150 Horse chestnuts 12 ft
700 Hazels 12 ft
50 larches 2ft
100 pine asters 2ft
100 chester pines 2ft
400 larches 1ft
10 spruce firs 8ft
10 spruce firs 3ft
10 larches 3ft
<u>6 Weymouth pines 3ft</u>

6538 in all [according to the gardener!]

All this frenetic planting might seem to be a manifestation of English aristocratic eccentricity. Another eccentricity for those times was to take a bride, Elizabeth Amcotts, who came without a properly secured dowry. This did not prevent Sir John from becoming the High Sheriff of Yorkshire in 1782/3 and the MP for East Retford in 1790, though the issue of the marriage settlement remained unresolved. With his tree planting operations in full force and with ambitious

63 Sweet chestnut was very popular as a landscaping tree. Seen from a distance, especially when leafless, it resembles gnarled oaks and so it could combine with oaks derived from former hedgerows. An enormous fallen specimen is seen on the left in this scene from Ripley deer park

plans for rebuilding the family seat at Ripley in hand, he borrowed the huge sum of £12,000. In 1794, now with six children to support, the dowry from Sir Wharton Amcotts had still not materialised and the financiers were increasingly restless. Sir John and his wife left their children scattered around England and fled to Switzerland and the time that followed was spent in keeping ahead of French armies. Until 1803 the Ripley estate was managed through a process of correspondence between Sir John and John Hewitt, his agent. This was done with more perspicacity than previous undertakings and, though Elizabeth fled to stay with an aunt in 1801 and refused to return to the estate that had caused so much consternation, Sir John was able to return to Ripley, free of debts, in 1804. The planting of timber resources, which might have seemed an obsessive diversion, actually played a very significant role in producing the income to finance the homecoming. Revenues from timber sales continued to flow in into the 1830s.

The following extract from a letter of 1800 (Ingilby MS 2835 additional letter 37 Accession 2662) demonstrated that Sir John was conscious of amenity and environmental aspects, despite the pressing need for income:

You will be satisfied I was in the right about the Wood and I am resolved to cut down as much [trees] as possible, without much defacing Ripley, that I may get my affirs as clear as I can and as firm as I can – Let High Rails and the Lodge Wood [at the top of the park] be both sold, these are already fenced off with a little care the moor will thrive again, and High Rails perhaps must be new planted ... some surface drainage – a very trifle.... I think if it was plowed and sown with mast [beech], acorns ... it wd come quicker and better however the walk from gate to gate must be left, there are a great many trees in Hollin bank [the old Hollins in the park beside a Roman road] from the lane gate to the End of Dearloves Pasture that may come down – I leave all this to your judgement ....

The greatest problem regarding ancient trees in parks concerns their very antiquity, and of the old parkland trees plotted on maps of the mid-nineteenth century, now just a fraction – often just a small fraction – remains. Rackham (2004) has noted an unwelcome 'tidying-up' of ancient trees in parks in the second half of the twentieth century. He noted the disappearance, after 1973, of the ancient hawthorns that Lancelot Brown had deliberately retained at Heveningham Hall and the burning of 'unsightly' trees in Hatfield Forest, as well as the earlier removal of many late Tudor oaks and elms from the Regent's, St James's and Hyde Parks. Wherever parks are subject to public access, as most are, ancient trees are likely to become victims of the modern litigation culture. There are plenty of owners, municipal authorities in particular, who would far rather fell every parkland tree in sight than risk a legal action by some litigious member of the public who has had a twig fall on his/her head. The community pays the damages and this is a culture that is costing society dear in terms of the cancellation of activities and access and the erasure of character from our scenes. Some spectacular trees remain, and may best be viewed from afar, or at least from beyond their spreading roots. A large proportion of the grand old trees, mostly pollards, come down from Tudor and Elizabethan times. As members of these generations come, ever more rapidly, to their demise, the question of what can replace them is a troublesome thought.

REFERENCES

Beresford, M.W. and St. Joseph, J.K., 1978, *Medieval England, An Aerial Survey*, 2nd edn., C.U.P., Cambridge.
Cartwright, J.J. (ed.), 1875, *The Memoirs of Sir John Reresby*, Longmans, Green & Co, London
Crone, A. and Watson, F., 2003, 'Sufficiency to Scarcity, Medieval Scotland, 500-1600' in Smout, C. (ed.), *People and Woods in Scotland*, Edinburgh University Press, Edinburgh.
Dowsett, J.M., 1942, *The Romance of England's Forests*, John Gifford, London.
Edlin, H.L.(ed.), 1969, *New Forest*, H.M.S.O., London.

Fisher, 1867, *The History and Antiquities of Masham and Mashamshire*, Simpkin, Marshall & Co, London.

Fleming, A., 1998, *Swaledale, Valley of the Wild River'*, Edinburgh University Press, Edinburgh.

Grainge, W., 1871, *Harrogate and the Forest of Knaresborough*, John Russell Smith, London.

Hartley, M. and Ingilby, J., 1956, *The Yorkshire Dales*, Dent, London.

Lonsdale, D., 1996, 'Pollarding Success or Failure: Some Principles to Consider' in Read, H.J. (ed.), *Pollard and Veteran Tree Management*, Corporation of London, pp.100-104.

Muir, R., 2000, 'Pollards in Nidderdale: a Landscape History', *Rural History*, 11, 1, pp.95-111.

Muir, R., 2001, *Landscape Detective*, Windgather, Macclesfield.

Muir, R. and Amos, J., 1998, 'Nidd, the Death of a Village'. *The Local Historian*, 28, 4, pp.208-216.

Mitchell, A.F., 1966, 'Dating the Ancient Oaks', *Quarterly Journal of Forestry*, 60, pp.271-6.

Mitchell, A.F., 1974, *A Field Guide to the Trees of Britain and Northern Europe*, Collins, London.

Rackham, O., 1976, *Trees and Woodland in the British Landscape*, Dent, London.

Rackham, O., 2004, 'Pre-existing Trees and Woods in Country-House Parks'. *LANDSCAPES*, 5.2.

Rutter, J.G., 1972, 'History and Antiquities', in H.L. Edlin (ed.) *North Yorkshire Forests*, H.M.S.O., London, pp.85-97.

Sheahan, J.J., 1871, *The Wapentake of Claro*, vol. III, John Green, Beverley.

Sheeran, G, 1990, *Landscape Gardens in West Yorkshire, 1680-1800*, Wakefield Historical Publications, Wakefield.

Speight, H., 1892, *The Craven and North-West Yorkshire Highlands*, Elliot Stock, London.

Speight, H., 1900, *Upper Wharfedale*, Elliot Stock, London.

Stenton, D.M., 1951, *English Society in the Early Middle Ages*, Pelican, Harmondsworth.

Todd, G., 1824, *Some Account of Sheriff Hutton Castle*, J.&G. Todd, York.

Wainwright, A., 2005, Focus: New Doctoral Landscape Research, *Society For Landscape Studies Newsletter*, **Autumn/Winter** 2005, pp.10-11.

Whitaker, T.D., 1878, *The History of the Deanery of Craven*, 3rd edn., Leeds.

Whittaker, J., 1892, *Deer Parks and Paddocks of England*, Ballantyne, Hanson & Co., London.

White, J., 1994, 'Estimating the Age of Large Trees in Britain' *Research Information Note 250*, Forest Authority Research Division.

White, J., 1995, 'Dating the Veterans', *Tree News*, Spring/Summer 1995, pp.10-11.

White, J., 1997, 'What is a veteran and where are they all?, *Quarterly Journal of Forestry*, **vol. 91, no 3**, pp.222-226.

Young, D.W., 1969, 'The History of the Forest Woodlands' in H.L Edlin (ed.), *New Forest*, H.M.S.O., London, pp.33-40.

6

The Men of the Forest

All men in yon forest they asked of me,
'How many strawberries grow in the salt sea?'
And I answered them with a tear in my e'e,
'How many ships sail in the forest?'

This verse from the traditional ballad *The False Bride* or *The Week Before Easter*, a song about the impossibility of regaining a lost sweetheart, reflects the 'otherness' of the forest community. One of the main themes in the understanding of landscapes in England and Wales concerns the difference between the countrysides of fielden, champion or field country on the one hand and those of the arden or woodland settings on the other. These differences are by no means mere differences of scenery, for they are bound up with shaping *by* cultures and the shaping *of* cultures. The men of the forest inhabited settings that looked different, they had different customs and traditions of land organisation, they lived in different sorts of settlement, and though most of them were tenant farmers or freeholders, some had full-time or part-time occupations that concerned timber, its production and uses.

Woodland settlements

The concept of an England composed of countrysides of two contrasting personality types was explored by Homans (1941) Rackham (1986, pp.4-5), Williamson and Bellamy (1987, p.10 *et seq.*) and is inherent in the more recent well-publicised work by Roberts and Wrathmell (e.g. 1998, pp.95-116). Essentially, the contrast is between countysides that have developed gradually, over thousands of years, by evolutionary processes and those that have been transformed in the course of far-reaching local rural revolutions. The ancient or woodland countrysides retain features that one would find in prehistoric

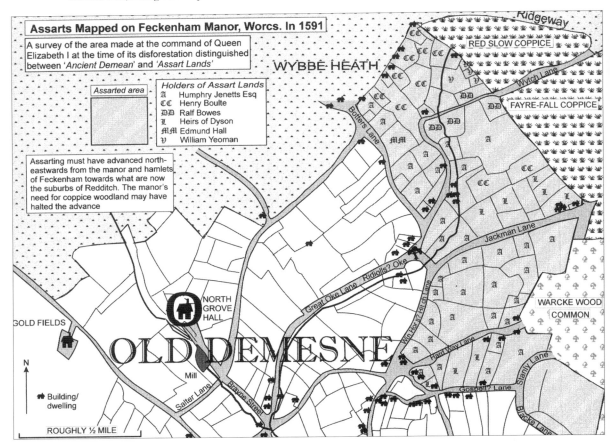

Assarts Mapped on Feckenham Manor, Worcs. In 1591

A survey of the area made at the command of Queen Elizabeth I at the time of its disforestation distinguished between '*Ancient Demean*' and '*Assart Lands*'

Assarted area

Holders of Assart Lands
𝔞 Humphry Jenetts Esq
ℭℭ Henry Boulte
𝔇𝔇 Ralf Bowes
𝔩 Heirs of Dyson
𝔐𝔐 Edmund Hall
𝔶 William Yeoman

Assarting must have advanced north-eastwards from the manor and hamlets of Feckenham towards what are now the suburbs of Redditch. The manor's need for coppice woodland may have halted the advance

WYBBE HEATH

RED SLOW COPPICE
Ridgeway
Wytch Lane
FAYRE-FALL COPPICE
Botters Lane
Jackman Lane
Great Oke Lane · Ridiolls? Oke
Win Hors? Hit Ch Lane
WARCKE WOOD COMMON
NORTH GROVE HALL
GOLD FIELDS
OLD DEMESNE
Mill
Hard Way Lane
Stanly Lane
Gospell? Lane
Blacke Lane
Salter Lane
Brayne Street

N

Building/ dwelling

ROUGHLY ½ MILE

Assarts mapped on Feckenham Manor. The main holder of assarted lands is Humphry Jenetts esq, suggesting that the leader of the local gentry may not only have been the main beneficiary of assarting, but also its instigator (another beneficiary is shown by his surname to be a yeoman). The lands that were cleared lay on the margins of the old demesne but the advance into the wooded area halted (perhaps by design or by the intervention of the Pestilence) in time to leave a reserve of wooded common and manorial coppices. The assarters must have come from the villages and hamlets comprising the old, generally nucleated settlement pattern but in the assarted area a looser, more dispersed pattern of small hamlets and scattered homesteads developed. A string of dwellings formed along the margins of a common, Wybbe Heath, all apparently in the holdings of one Henry Boulte. Some of the place names reflect the wooded or formerly wooded character of the locality. Wytch Lane must refer to the wych elm in the flanking woods rather than to witches. Red Slow Coppice is probably named from the sloe or blackthorn, while Warcke Wood might contain 'works' or earthworks. Blacke Lane might have black soil or be heavily wooded, though it could also have crossed black, burnt-over ground, while Stanly Lane could be stony or might lead to a quarry. The 'Hitch' in the puzzling Win Hors? Hitch Lane might refer to hurdles set around newly cleared land and the 'Rid' in the equally strange Ridiolls Lane might be a reference to land rid of trees. Great Oke Lane leads to the large oak indicated at the convergence of the roads. Gospell Lane is probably a place where readings were made from the gospels during the perambulation of bounds. Salter Lane is a fragment of a long-distance salt trading routeway, perhaps a branch from the Ridgeway, top right.

countrysides. Their wooded or 'bosky' character is not imparted by vast, continuous expanses of woodland, but rather by the presence of numerous, small woods and by ancient, dense hedgerows punctuated with mature hedgerow trees. Settlement patterns are largely composed of dispersed hamlets and farmsteads, roads are mainly ancient, winding and deeply incised into the landscape and although some common fields might be found, the number of tenants and the extent of the shared arable and meadowland were much less. The people of these countrysides tended to be more independent and less involved in communal arrangements. The planned or champion countrysides had much less intimate, more open aspects and had been produced by the revolutions that accompanied the adoption of open field farming from the eighth century onwards and its dismantling by Tudor piecemeal enclosures and the great privatisation of parishes under Parliamentary Enclosure in the eighteenth and nineteenth centuries. These countrysides have woods, both the remains of medieval manorial woods and later estate plantations, but woodedness is much less a part of their ethos, which tends to be coloured by broad vistas across the former communal ploughland with its now declining and poorly tended hedgerows.

The differences between the two countrysides were recognised by their inhabitants. Williamson quotes William Harrison (1534-93), a topographer, clergyman and writer, who described a land divided into '... champaine [champion] ground and woodland [where in the latter the houses] stand scattered abroad, each one dwelling in the midst of his owne occupieng'(originally quoted in Homans, 1941, p.21). Thomas Tusser (1524-80) wrote in 1557 of the prosperous and prudent character of the enclosed woodland countrysides, in contrast with the deprivation and profligacy he associated with the champion lands, which were permeated by common rights. Champion Leicestershire and (partly) woodland Suffolk and Essex provided examples.

> Example by Leicestershire,
> What soil can be better than that?
> For anything heart can desire,
> And yet doth it want ye see what
> Mast, covert, close, pasture and wood,
>
> And other things needful as good.
> All those do inclosure bringe,
> Experience teacheth no less,
> I speak not to boast of the thing'
> But only a truth to express.
> Example (if doubt ye do make),
> By Suffolk and Essex go take.

Superb 'ancient' or 'woodland' countryside exemplified near Luppitt in Devon

More plenty of Mutton and Beef,
Corn butter, and cheese of the best,
More wealth anywhere (to be brief),
More people, more handsome and prest,
Where find ye? Go search any coast,
Than there where inclosure is most.

These characteristics, so vividly described by contemporaries, found expression in the character of the 'pays' or localities. Having, for whatever reasons, escaped

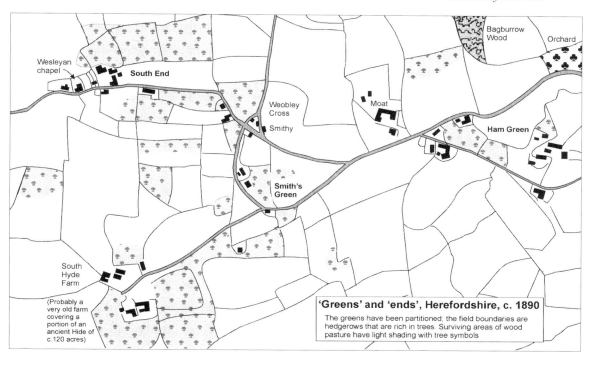

'Greens' and 'ends', Herefordshire, c. 1890

The greens have been partitioned; the field boundaries are hedgerows that are rich in trees. Surviving areas of wood pasture have light shading with tree symbols

becoming too tightly enmeshed in the nets of feudal obligation and communal interdependence associated with fully-developed open field farming, the members of the woodland societies retained more independence and control. Where they were found working in association with other manorial tenants, these tenants were far fewer and the links between them less constraining. By living in isolated farmsteads or small farmstead clusters they were less ordered and scrutinised by both their lord and their church than were their counterparts in the bloated dormitories for agricultural bondsmen that were the big villages of the champion lands. When they spoke their minds, there were fewer ears to hear them, when they worked there might be none watching and they could more easily slip away on small, illicit escapades. Not surprisingly, the people of the woodland countrysides became known for their more individualistic attitudes.

The people of woodland countrysides tended to live in seclusion or in hamlets of farmstead clusters that were frequently designated 'Green' or 'End'. The ends could be free-standing or they might exist as satellites of a larger, village-sized settlement. Often, they took the form of a single row of farmsteads and their outbuildings that straggled along one side of a track or lane, and sometimes the dwellings faced each other across a track. Where the rural settlement pattern comprised both hamlets and one or more villages, and, if the experience at Ripley (Muir, 2001) is typical, then during the great fouteenth-century retreat and decay of settlement it was the hamlets that experienced the most desertion. In the greens, the farmsteads and their outbuildings were organised around one

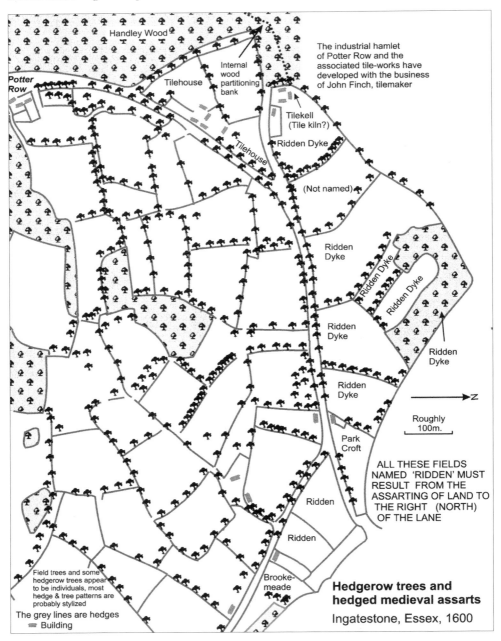

Handley Wood

The industrial hamlet of Potter Row and the associated tile-works have developed with the business of John Finch, tilemaker

Potter Row

Internal wood partitioning bank

Tilehouse

Tilekell (Tile kiln?)

Tilehouse

Ridden Dyke

(Not named)

Ridden Dyke

Ridden Dyke

Ridden Dyke

Ridden Dyke

Ridden Dyke

Ridden Dyke

Ridden Dyke

Roughly 100m.

Park Croft

ALL THESE FIELDS NAMED 'RIDDEN' MUST RESULT FROM THE ASSARTING OF LAND TO THE RIGHT (NORTH) OF THE LANE

Ridden

Ridden

Field trees and some hedgerow trees appear to be individuals, most hedge & tree patterns are probably stylized

The grey lines are hedges

Building

Brooke-meade

Hedgerow trees and hedged medieval assarts

Ingatestone, Essex, 1600

or more small greens. Such greens would tend to be strung along little routeways like beads on strings, and the presence of a patch of common grazing may have been the bait that had attracted settlement. There may have been a measure of social distinction between the populations of the two hamlet types. Dyer (1991, p.41) writes:

The messuages [roughly, 'peasant farmsteads'] in the ends are not distributed at random, but form an orderly pattern along the roads. A tempting argument might be to link this with their customary status, and to think that as the *villani* [villeins] of the eleventh century probably lived here, they had begun as the houses of *buri* or *geburs* (boors) settled on the demesne by pre-Conquest lords …. However the ends were not peopled entirely by tenants of servile origin – the de Hanburys lived in Moreweysend, for example. The greens also, which were mainly free settlements in which the lord had less influence, were not entirely anarchic in their plan …. The grouping of customary tenants in the ends, and the tendency of high-status settlements and the messuages of freeholders to lie on the margins, together with the proliferation of freeholdings on the outer fringes when new lands were being developed, made for a striking social segregation ….

Tenants in woodland country had parts of their holdings in selions or strips of ploughland that were, at least to some extent, scattered across the territory of the manor, though the freeholders did tend to have more of their land in enclosed holdings that were conveniently close to their dwellings. By Tudor times, these woodland areas had become largely the province of freeholders, whose links and obligations to their lords were quite modest in comparison to those that had prevailed in the champion lands when feudalism was at its height. The lords themselves tended to come from the lower ranks of the landowning aristocracy, while the weaker development of communal institutions meant that their tenants were less dominated by the manor court or communal decisions about the rotations applied to fields or furlongs. They were freer to make their own decisions, to get on with their own affairs, and escape the prying eyes of the reeve or neighbours who might report their activities to village or manorial officials. Their easier access to woodland/hill country products, like timber for turning or charcoal, quarries or ores, gave them more opportunities to develop secondary occupations, and thus reduce their dependence on their tenancies still further. All these factors contributed to the aura of independence and otherness associated with the woodland communities: 'The Robin Hood ballads express the romance, freedom and disregard for conventional law typical of the dwellers of woodlands'(Dyer, pp.48-9).

The people living in the ends, greens and other hamlets and the farmsteads of woodland country (as well as many hamlet and small village communities in the champion countrysides) occupied land that had been removed of woodland in the course of the centuries running from the establishment of the English ascendancy to the fourteenth century. The woodland removed was not 'wildwood' in the sense of being virgin native woodland; much of it must have colonised over-worked farmland that was in decay in both the ecological and cultural senses after the withdrawal of the Romans *c.*AD 410. Medieval assarting took many forms and operated at many levels. It could exist as a large-scale operation, co-ordinated by people of great power and influence, from the king downward. It could be the policy of a religious institution or manor, or it could involve a piecemeal and illegal occupation of communal land by a small tenant. Woodhouse is a common surname, deriving from a family living in a rather isolated woodland dwelling such as might be found in an assart.

Pressures to clear woodland for agriculture and associated settlements rose sharply during the centuries following the Norman Conquest, continuing until the onset of climatic decay in the fourteenth century; the arrival of the Black Death in the countrysides in 1349 reversed the trend. At the height of the population surplus, in 1316, records show that just one wood, Hipperholme common wood in the manor of Wakefield, with agricultural potential quite inferior to that of the best southern English lands, experienced at least 14 different episodes of clearance. Entry fines to take over cleared land were paid by 13 individuals, one a widow and by one husband and wife partnership. Of the assarters, one, John son of Thomas del Rode, had a name suggesting that his father had also assarted land, while Alexander le Waynwright may have been winning timber for his cart-making activities and Andrew Forester and his wife Maroria may have been supported by Forest employment. The father of John son of Henry le Pynder may have been employed in impounding animals found feeding illegally in the woodland pastures. The wood had also contracted in the face of earlier assarting, and in 1315 the granting of licences to operate forges in the wood will have intensified the ecological pressures (Faull and Moorhouse, p.629).

Assarting took place at every conceivable level. It could involve a major re-deployment of land and massive shifts of population under the direction of a king, bishop or powerful member of the nobility. Or it could involve an impoverished squatter who was engaged in clearing trees from the land behind his hovel. Village communities that had grown to sizes that could no longer be sustained by their traditional ploughlands and grazings could make concerted assaults upon adjacent woodland, establishing satellite hamlets to accommodate the 'overspill'. The areas affected varied immensely, ranging from small plots that were furtively enclosed from a wooded common through expanses like the area of around 1000 acres (405 hectares) systematically assarted on the Bishop of Winchester's manor of Whitney in Oxfordshire to a vast area around Drax in the south of Yorkshire. This was cleared at the instigation of Henry II, who charged an entry fine of 4d (about 1.25p) to each settler taking up land. Assarting produced additions to the pattern of settlement and normally it had the effect of increasing the prominence of the dispersed element, comprising hamlets and farmsteads.

Those who engaged in assarting were not primarily the desperate, landless poor. Freeholders were often the leading elements, and many of them would move from village-based farmsteads to new farm holdings set up apart from the community in newly-cleared lands. The settler and the assarter need not be one and the same; some land was cleared by specialists (the Sart surname revealed such people) and then sold to a farming household. A special class of isolated dwellings comprise those that originated as hermitages. Unlike the cells of anchorites,

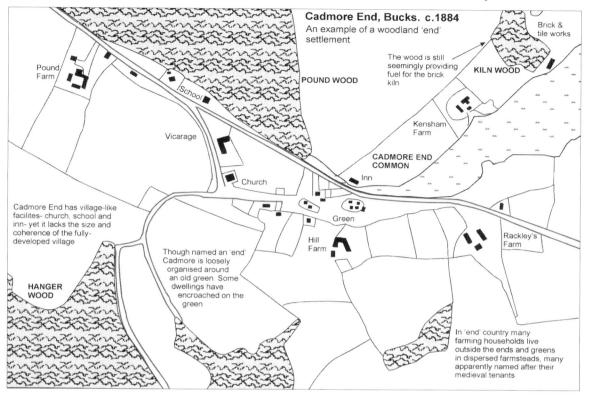

Cadmore End, Bucks. c.1884
An example of a woodland 'end' settlement

Brick & tile works

The wood is still seemingly providing fuel for the brick kiln

KILN WOOD

POUND WOOD

Pound Farm

School

Vicarage

Kensham Farm

CADMORE END COMMON

Inn

Church

Green

Cadmore End has village-like facilites- church, school and inn- yet it lacks the size and coherence of the fully-developed village

Though named an 'end' Cadmore is loosely organised around an old green. Some dwellings have encroached on the green

HANGER WOOD

Hill Farm

Rackley's Farm

In 'end' country many farming households live outside the ends and greens in dispersed farmsteads, many apparently named after their medieval tenants

hermitages were not totally removed from other settlements and could even be in towns. The place name Hermetrode, recorded in West Yorkshire in 1460, implies that hermits may have been amongst those involved in making 'royds' or clearings. After numerous rebuildings, a farmstead on assarted land may look like any of the thousands of dispersed farmsteads created by Parliamentary Enclosure, mainly in the period 1750-1850. The most obvious hint of assarting origins could be provided by place names associated with medieval land clearance – like *Brake, Royd, Ridding, Rudding, Sart, Stocks, Stubbs and Stubbings*, while *Hay* is a word for hedges and small woods that can sometimes relate to land assarted and hedged. The new hamlets and farmsteads created new demands on the infrastructure of services. Roads developed to serve them and 'To meet the needs of such folk [in the fourteenth century], St John's chapel was founded in upper Weardale beyond the limits of the bishop's park, and hamlets such as Cowshill, Daddry Shields, Irehopeburn, and others, came into being at Wearhead' (Raistrick, 1968, p.93).

If the medieval assarters generally represented a cross section of their society, with families of substance and good character being well represented, one must wonder about the origins of the deprived rural classes of cottagers and squatters who so intimidated the commentators and landowners of their day? What was the ancestry of the pauper who was evicted from one parish to the next lest he become a burden on the Poor Rate or the wastrel who infested the common and bred new generations of wastrels? Such people feature prominently in the recorded concerns of the respectable classes, but they being deprived of the means and, often, the ability to record their thoughts, the picture we have is a slanted one. There is no doubt that for around three centuries after the close of the medieval period the decaying Forests and the wooded commons supported excessive populations at the meanest levels of subsistence. Forest commons were attractive to the poor because they offered various resources to sustain the different grades of cottagers and Hoyle (1997, p.42) quotes the testimony, in 1584, of one Edward Belson:

> That some cottagers in Brill have small closes where they get in summer hay. Others are artificers able to buy and provide some winter stuff and many of them very poor people, whereby some live and always shall be able to live better than some and keep cattle on the wastes than others. … He knoweth cottagers in the forest to keep three or four kine and bullocks and as many horses, beasts and half a dozen swine and 20 or 30 sheep contrary to right and equity and divers other poor cottagers not able to keep one beast on the commons.

The conventional view of the rural poor concerns illegal squatting upon the common to the detriment of communal interests. The evidence at Brill, Buckinghamshire, however, suggests that cottage building had at first been tolerated if not encouraged by the local landowners. By allowing the construction of cottages, the freeholder gained additional income in rents. Then the cottager might subdivide his holding and allow another cottage to be built – and soon the failure of the local economy to expand produced problems of a surplus, poverty-stricken population, ever likely to damage woods and steal fuel from hedgerows.

Within the Forests certain settlements originated specifically as small villages built to accommodate specialist populations of foresters. The best examples come from the Yorkshire Dales, where Bainbridge near Wenseleydale, Buckden in Wharfedale and Healaugh in Swaledale are known to have been founded in this way. Raistrick (1968, p.88) writes:

> In 1227 a *quo warranto* calls upon Ranulph son of Robert to say by what warrant he made towns and raised houses in the earl's forest of Wensleydale. He answered that the town of Bainbridge was raised by the ancestors of Ranulph by service of keeping the forest of Wensleydale, built so that they could have twelve foresters there, each with a house and nine acres of ground.

Most feudal woodland communities had rights to timber for fuel and building ploughs, dead hedges and houses. Generally, restrictions applied and fuel was restricted to fallen branches and loppings from pollards, which also supplied browse

The woodland folk

Most of the people living in woodland countryside were tenant farmers, whose status and rights evolved thoughout the medieval period. Wherever woods and hunting activities dominated the rural setting, more specialised occupations would develop. In some cases, feudal tenants were burdened with impositions associated with hunting or were constrained by Forest Law. But hunting and forestry were also great employers of people and their occupations and settlements helped to diversify the agricultural character of the countryside. The Crown Forests had their chief foresters. These were officers of high status, whose offices were frequently semi-hereditary, but whose duties seem to have taken different positions on the scale between ceremony and function. They sometimes took a personal involvement in protecting and enhancing their Forest, and derived an income from it. When faced with what he regarded as an encroachment upon his customary right to timber by the Steward of Knaresborough in 1302, Henry de Scriven appealed to Edward I, claiming that he and his ancestors had enjoyed the office of Foresters of the Forest of Knaresborough for 6d (2½p) a day and the use of its common resources. His rights to pasture livestock and to take timber for repairing his house and hedging were confirmed providing that he did not fell any tree growing or bearing fruit (Grainge, 1871, pp 205-6). The chief forester was at the apex of the hierarchy of responsibility for woodland management and was expected to provide venison for visiting parties and largesse, as requested.

Below the chief forester, and more closely engaged in Forest affairs, were the lieutenants or stewards, as well as the keepers who had responsibilities for particular walks or divisions within the Forest. Where the walk was quite substantial, the keeper might be allowed to appoint a page to assist him with his work. The keeper would normally have a lodge within his territory and would often be given rights to pasture livestock in its surroundings. These lodges were elements in the medieval settlement pattern and would very often establish more permanent presences in the countryside by evolving into farmsteads, and these, perhaps, into hamlets. The chief forester was exposed to corruption in a variety of forms, for example he might take bribes to appoint more foresters than the work of the Forest required, thus burdening its populace with the need to maintain an excessive number of officials.

Keepers or foresters were appointed by the chief but might be paid no wages, it being considered that they could live from the fees and dues taken from the tenants occupying their keeping. They patrolled their territories in search of poachers, and also to protect the habitats of the deer. More time was likely to be spent upon the protection of woodland resources than in pursuing venison thieves. In the middle of the thirteenth century, Sherwood Forest was divided into the High Forest keeping, judged to require two mounted foresters and their servants and two foresters working on foot, while Rumewood, a less demanding keeping, was patrolled by a single, dismounted forester, and the Leen and Doverbeck keeping was judged to require a mounted forester and his servant and two foot foresters.

By virtue of their calling, medieval keepers were likely to be demonised in much the same way that gamekeepers would be in the nineteenth century. Consequently, one cannot be confident regarding the objectivity of the accusations levelled against them. Since they had a number of their own livestock grazing in the Forest they were strongly tempted to feed the browse lopped from pollards to any of their own animals that happened to be in their vicinity rather than to the deer for which it was intended. Any sapling was likely to be converted into a pollard, for as such it was of potential value to the domestic animals, while the deer faced heavy competition for grazing of any kind. Dyer records the proceedings of a commission held into these matters at Brill in Buckinghamshire in 1588. John Dynham, the chief forester, and his tenants were alleged to have undertaken felling in Bernwood on a grand scale. One

Medieval demands for structural timbers from standard or maiden trees and from curved boughs from pollards were immense, as exemplified in these buildings from Weobley (Herefordshire and Worcestershire) (*above*) and the East Anglian barn roof (*below*)

allegation was that from late 1574 to early 1577, 202 loads of deer browse had been cut. Some 20 loads of deer browse had been felled by keepers in Pauncell and carried to Charlton upon outmoor. This was not the soft fresh foliage like the 'watter boughs' or 'greenhews' mentioned in some northern documents, but woody branches '… of great boughs of oak such as two of them will load in a cart' (p.40). The keepers' cattle, meanwhile, were over-grazing and destroying the wood and the keepers were even enclosing pastures within the crown coppices. However, the evidence was presented within the context of a feud between the Dynhams and the Crokes, but though it may be slanted it does record types of abuses that must have caused concern at the time.

The terminology relating to Forest and woodland officials varies and the chief forester would sometimes be known as a sheriff, bailiff, master keeper, warden or keeper. To complicate matters further, he could have more than one Forest in his charge: the Somerset Forests of Exmoor, Neroche, Selwood, North Petherton and Mendip were once under a single warden. There were also strangely named officials of sometimes uncertain responsibilities who appear in the record from time to time. The evidence in a hearing of 1611 concerning the feud between Sir John Yorke and his friends and the Earl of Cumberland alleged that Appletreewick was part of the Clifford estates and that its inhabitants there who dwelled on the land of the Prior of Bolton had paid '… Forster [forester] Oates to the Bowbearer, or the forester, of the forest of Skipton [not a true Forest but a chase], and also pay Forster Hens and Castle Hens, and do suit of court yearly at the Forest Court at Skipton' (Whitaker, 1878, p.513). Here we discover examples of the feudal dues in the forms of oats and hens received by the Clifford's chief keeper or 'bowbearer' and these presumably supported him instead of payments of a regular income. The fact that they were paid to the bowbearer constituted evidence that the lands concerned lay within the chase. Such dues must have been resented by the tenantry at large and one of the clauses in the placatory *Charter of the Forest* of 1217 had promised that in the royal Forests:

No forester or beadle shall henceforth levy scotale or collect sheaves or oats or any grain or lambs or pigs; nor shall he take up any kind of collection. And by the view and oath of twelve regarders, when they make their regard, as many foresters shall be appointed to keep the forests as reasonably appear sufficient for keeping them. [Scotale was an exaction of ale or money of equivalent value on the pretext of using it in some manner of festival.]

Plainly, some Forest officials had been practising schemes of extortion organised around the feudal right to demand payments in ale. The destination of the ale concerned is easily imagined. It is also plain from the *Charter* that Forest people, and some dwelling outside the Forest, resented the inconvenience to their day-to-day lives caused by demands for attendance at Forest institutions. The Charter undertook that only those actually involved in some way in litigation would be summoned to come before the Justices of the Forest. It also stated that no swainmote (see below) would be held more often than three times a year and that these swainmotes, associated with the onset of agistment, the receipt of pannage and fawning time, would only require the attendance the foresters and verderers. It also removed another source of inconvenience or extortion by allowing any freeman to drive his swine through Crown woodland to reach other sources of pannage, wherever he pleased. The additional concession that allowed the freeman and his swine to rest overnight in a Forest without any swine being taken from him as a penalty suggested that this form of extortion had also been practised in the past.

Officials known as 'verderers' are sometimes encountered in documents relating to Forests, and these might be subordinate to the chief forester yet direct appointments of the monarch. Between two and 16 verderers might hold appointments within a particular Forest, though the normal complement was four. They were recruited from the aristocracy and petty gentry and those who were accused of flouting the rules of the Forest were presented to them at the Forest court, where the verderers and freeholders formed the Woodmote (see below). For example, in the late sixteenth century Sir Ralph Bouchier found himself in the gaze of royal verderers for taking bough timber from West Moor in the Forest of Galtres. His successor, Sir John Bouchier continued the offences, removing 60 loads away each year until summoned before Star Chamber and being fined and imprisoned for his encroachments (*V.C.H.* N.Yorks, vol.2 p.160). Agisters collected the proceeds derived from the agistment of animals on the Forest pastures, and their significance varied according to the extent of the pastures concerned. They might have been paid a percentage of the revenue collected or have received regular incomes from the Crown.

Regarders had duties that seem to have overlapped with those of their agisters and they were responsible for regularly scrutinising a Forest in search of illegal pasturing and illicit enclosures, the maintenance of hedges and ditches and encroachments of any kind. In the New Forest, the offices of lord warden, ranger, woodward and regarder survived until 1851, when an Act put their responsibilities into the hands of newly appointed Commissioners of Woods and Forests, though the verderers and their court at Lyndhurst survived and they became responsible for defending the rights of commoners, with the court's four agisters or marksmen supervising livestock and fees for pasturage.

The judicial apparatus that exerted ecological controls, provided employment and exacted penalities has been summarised as follows:

The Forest Law was administered in three distinct courts. The lowest of these was the *Woodmote, Court of Attachment, or Forty Day Court,* ordered … [under the Charter of the Forest of 1217 and slight revisions of 1225] … to be held once every forty days, but often kept very irregularly. It was merely a court of preliminary enquiry, from which attachments could be presented to the Swainmote, if the alleged offences seemed capable of being proved. The *Swainmote* or *Court of Freeholders*, in which the verderers were the judges and twelve 'swains' or freeholders of the forest formed the jury, tried all cases committed from the Woodmote. The Swainmote could order conviction and fine in all petty cases, but serious offences had to be committed to the next and highest court, the *Justice Seat* or *Eyre of the Forest*. The Charter of 1225 ordered the Swainmote to be held three times a year, fifteen days before Midsummer, when the agisters met to see to the observance of the fence month, fifteen days before Michaelmas, when the agistment of the woods began, and forty days after Michaelmas, when the agisters met to receive the pannage dues (Rodgers, 1942, p.23).

The elaborate apparatus for conserving royal resources was applied to Crown Forests. Outside these special areas, the various Assizes, Commissions and Quarter Sessions dealt with the more serious matters, while petty offences against the woodland and its resources would be dealt with by the manor courts. Thus, in 1337, officials of the large Manor of Wakefield launched a blitz of prosecution against those infringing the timber conservation code in Sowerby Wood:

William Couper and his two serving-men had made 'divers utensils' illegally for six years; Roger Couper, his serving-man William, his brother, William Couper and his serving-man, made *collokes*, or large pails; Adam de Coventre and his sons were accused of 'making planks for chests' with more oaks than they should have had; John Piper cut timber for planking; Thomas del Bothe cut wood for making spoons; Hugh Adamson cut alders to make pipes (*alvei*); and William Turnour cut alder to make dishes (*disci*). The list also records the uncommon use of the linden or lime tree (*lynde*) for making sadletres, the wooden frames of saddles. Of the people fined, five were coopers and one a turner, the 'serving-men' possibly being apprentices (Faull and Moorhouse, p.689).

The people who, probably much to their surprise, found themselves summoned before the manor court were not wretched serfs who had sneaked into the woods in desperation and not, apparently, itinerant craftsmen engaged in a swift raid. Rather, one has the impression of a number of permanent workshops having been set up in the woods. If so, this reflects the relative inability of manorial controls to regulate the woodland industries in some places. Something particularly appealing about this record concerns the thought that there are probably hundreds or thousands of people living today who take their names of Cooper or Turner from ancestors who found themselves in mercy of Wakefield manor court almost 700 years ago.

There were also officials who worked within or near a Forest, sometimes for other employers than the Crown. The function of the rangers who appear in later medieval documents is debatable. They may represent one of various synonyms for 'foresters' or they may have been active on the outer fringes or purlieus of

Oak woodland on Craigendarroch near Ballater. The name of the hill tells of a covering of oak, though the youthful nature of these trees suggest that the wood may have been one of many in Scotland that were exploited for tannin bark in the eighteenth and nineteenth centuries

Forests. Woodwards were normally employed by the owners of private woods that lay within Forests, but the woodward also had to swear special oaths of allegiance to the monarch and to function as reliable reporters of any breaches of Forest regulations. Parkers were responsible for deer parks, which sometimes bordered on Forests and their duties had much in common with those of the king's officials. The contract for Thomas Key, the forester or parker of Fountains Abbey home park for 1520 has survived (*Fountains Abbey Lease Book*, YAS Series vol. CXL, 1981. Doc. 23). He was paid 26s 8d in cash per annum, unlike foresters who survived on feudal dues extracted from the local populace. At meal times he was entitled to meat and drink for himself and his servant in the abbey hall, three gallons of best ale and three of the second best every week and also three loaves of the convent bread and three of the second best bread each week as well as two grey loafs for his hounds. He could pasture four cattle and their calves, one horse or mare and two pigs in the park, could gather firewood and was given a new jacket each year as well as a shoulder of meat from every deer slain. He also had the occupation of a farm holding on the monastic estate worth 20s 8d a year, though it had to lie within four or five miles of the monastery. All things considered, this was an occupation with quite considerable attractions.

It is clear that a very substantial body of officials (with a confusing array of designations) was involved in the administration and, sometimes, maladminis- tration of the medieval Forests and woodlands. Special courts or Forest eyres were held to consider the serious offences against Forest Law, though they only generally met at seven-year intervals. The lesser offences, of which there were usually many, were dealt with by courts of attachment, meeting around every six weeks. The administration and enforcement of Forest Law and woodland regulations created a considerable amount of employment at various social levels and scales of remuneration in localities that were often rather thinly populated. Officials were rewarded in various ways, often deriving their income by exacting feudal dues upon the populations of their localities, as we have seen. It has also been said that woodland communities enjoyed higher levels of independence and individualism than did those of the champion lands. Even so, they could be burdened not only with the support of foresters, who were often distrusted and exploitative, but also with various duties associated with the chase. Labour services tended to be lighter than on champion manors, yet the hunt brought demands for kennelling, beating and serving work in many forms. This was described by Raistrick in the case of Stanhope on the Bishop of Durham's estates (1968, p.90):

> Many of the services demanded of the tenants were connected with the forest and with the Bishop's annual Great Hunt, to which a great hoard of followers and visitors was brought. The men of Stanhope, in addition to the service already mentioned on the Bishop's demesne, had each year for the great hunt to prepare the kitchen, larder, and dog-kennels, provide bedding (rushes or bracken) for the hall, chambers, and chapel, and give other minor services about the temporary village which was erected for the Bishop and his visitors and for the use and entertainment of the participants during the hunt. Provision for all these folk were to be collected, levied on many tenants throughout the country, and carried to the hunt village.

The social and economic ramifications of such a hunt went far beyond what the modern mind might imagine. Three wood turners were employed each year in making 3,100 wooden trenchers for the hunt. Villagers in Binchester, Lanchester, Washington and Usworth were responsible for caring for greyhounds during the year and bringing them to the hunt – one of the Washington men was notified that any game caught on the way to the hunt belonged to the Bishop, though any caught on the way home could be kept. The tenantry of Aukland were responsible for erecting a fence around the numerous large prefabricated buildings erected for the hunt, while those of Heighington had to provide ropes for the deer enclosures or nets (*ibid.*). Quite frequently, the woodland tenants, with less onerous boonwork or feudal labour service on the demesne were burdened special obligations connected with aristocratic hunting. In addition, the woodland tenant might be required to perform 40 days' service in the forest as directed by the chief. This could well come at fawning or rutting, when there were pressing demands from the farm.

For members of woodland communities, being fined for flouting Forest regulations, being placed in the mercy of the manor court for offences against its lord's woods or being burdened with feudal obligations were all disagreeable so far as the offenders and servile tenants were concerned. However, the punishments and impositions were hardly ever as draconian as they are generally imagined to be. Under the Normans much harshness took place and the area of Forests expanded to the end of the reign of Henry II. Then the tide turned and both his sons Richard and John accepted payments for the disafforestation of tracts of land in well-populated and affluent counties like Surrey, Essex and Kent. The harsher aspects of medieval Forest Law were modified or removed after the revolt by the barons at the end of the reign of King John: 'The Charter of 1215 included certain general promises and in 1217 the young king, Henry III, was forced by his council to issue a long charter of the forests and provided remedies for the long-standing grievances which men resented most' (Stenton, 1951 p.109). To put matters in their perspective, according to Stenton, the imposition that people most resented was not some ghastly form of torture or extortion, but the requirement that their dogs should be 'lawed', that is to say, three toes or talons were removed from one front foot of the lawed dog, reducing its effectiveness as a courser of game. Under the new regulations, 'regards' of each Forest were to be conducted every three years by a body of 12 knights who would report to the Justices of the Forest. At the triennial meetings, the owner of an unlawed dog would be fined 3s (15p). As for poachers, the Charter of the Forest of 1217 stated that '... if anyone is arrested and convicted of taking our venison, let him redeem himself by heavy payment, if he has anything with which to redeem himself. And if he has nothing with which to redeem himself, let him lie in or prison for a year and a day.' However the Charter noted that nobody would be killed or mutilated for poaching. The tendency towards a greater leniency continued:

> In 1236 the king refused to allow magnates the right of putting these poachers in private prisons of their own. In 1275 king and lords agreed on the way the offender should be treated. The poacher went to prison, but the lord received part of the fine imposed on him (Stenton, p.184).

This did not prevent the more imperious lords in the more remote parts of the kingdom from adopting more threatening stances. Whitaker (1878), who had access to Skipton Castle and Clifford family manuscripts that he did not properly reference, stated that in the reign of Henry VIII (1509-47), the first Earl of Cumberland held a deer steeler in custody in the castle, the man only being released after pledging that he would '... be of good bearing' to the deer (p.397).

Sawing up Bagot Oaks, bearn Rugeley, Staffs. From *The English Woodland* by John Rodgers

Later, in 1575-6, Thomas Frankland, a gentleman, was held prisoner in the castle, remaining there at the current Earl's pleasure for killing 'tame' and wild deer in Littondale and Lagstroth (*op. cit.*, p.306).

Yet, as for the manor courts generally, it is not their tyranny so much as their inabilty always to impose conservational policies that impresses, particularly when local ecosystems were stressed in periods of population pressure. Many entries that might appear to represent the fining of individuals might more realistically be regarded as the lord's taking of a rent for incursions, like illegal assarting, that he was unable any longer to regulate.

Woodland craft and industry

Woodland was an environment and it was also a resource. In addition to the administrators and the feudal tenants whose terms of bondage involved hunting and related activities, there were also those who worked in the woods. As the profile of self-sufficiency was lowered and the complexity and technical aspects of the medieval economy increased, so the numbers of these sometimes solitary and isolated craftsmen increased. Before exploring their crafts it is interesting to note the great numbers of relatively common surnames associated with woodland life. There were the people, like the Woods, Atwoods, Woodends, Greenwoods, Lunds, Forests, Groves, Leighs, Hartleys, Shaws, Springs, Stubbs, (Ac-)Royds, Friths, Woodhouses and Woodgates whose forbears lived in or beside woodlands. Others descend from woodland officials and workers, like the Woodwards, Parkers, Turners, Carpenters, Ashburners, Sawyers, Barkers, Coopers, Forsters and Foresters and Colliers (who are more likely to descend from charcoal burners than coal miners).

Woods and wooded commons were favoured mining and quarrying sites. They were removed from settlement and ownership or tenancy issues, whose disruption might produce problems. They often lay on higher, steeper and more thinly soiled ground so that the presence of ore-bearing strata was more evident and might be recognised by the presence of diagnostic wild plants. The relatively lofty locations would also assist the sledging or carting-away of products to lower destinations. British woods are littered with the traces of abandoned workings. In places like the Forest of Dean there are 'scowles' where the loose rocks and strata were disturbed by the ore diggings of prehistoric iron miners. In the Weald and many other places, spreads of glassy slag from medieval iron furnaces lie below the leaf litter amongst the distorted trees of long-abandoned coppices. Among many old copses are the saucer-like hollows where charcoal was stacked and burned.

To begin to imagine the importance of woodland crafts, we have to imagine a world in which there were no plastics or other synthetic materials, very few

A Sussex Wheelwright. From *The English Woodland* by John Rodgers

metal or metal alloy goods in circulation, very few industrial chemicals and only a very limited and localised availability of fossil fuels. Timber was essential in many spheres of life, providing the structure of most homes, the fuel in the hearth, the spoons, ladles, bowls and platters used by those sitting around it and the logs or crude stools on which they sat. Normally, it was the property of the manor, with the manorial tenants enjoying customary rights, like housebote, ploughbote, hedgebote, which allowed them to take timbers for essential uses. Although the work was accomplished by hand tools and each item was made separately, an immense amount of skill was embodied in each piece. Woodland crafts survived in some places for a century or more after the onset of the Industrial Revolution around 1760, with the craftsmen putting down stocks of materials to fulfil not only their needs, but those of their children and even their grandchildren. The cartwright seasoned elm trunks for a year before sawing them and seasoned the boards for a further year. The wheelwright took elm stocks, preferably from tough hedgerow trees, soaked them in a stream for a few months before leaving them to dry and season before turning them into hubs. Each vehicle that left the workshop was precisely tailored to the countryside in which it would be used and its owner's specification. George Sturt, whose family had a workshop at Farnham, in Surrey, recalled:

Hurdle makers in the Forest of Dean. From *The English Woodland* by John Rodgers

… the curves we followed (almost every piece of timber was curved) were imposed upon us by the nature of the soil in this or that farm, the gradient of this or that hill, the temper of this or that customer, or his choice perhaps in horseflesh. The carters told us their needs. To satisfy the carter, we gave another half-inch curve to the waggon-bottom, altered the hooks for harness on the shafts, hung the water-barrel an inch nearer to the horse or an inch further away.(George Sturt, *The Wheelwright's Shop*, 1948, p.18)

Carpentry work for quite large projects as well as small ones tended to be undertaken at the source of the timber rather than on the building site. This had the advantage of eliminating the transport of unnecessary material and reducing the size of items for transport to a minimum. Thus, timber-framed buildings could be prefabricated on a level 'framing ground' which might be no more than a woodland clearing, with the components being identified by inscribed Roman numerals or other carpenters' marks. A trial assembly could be undertaken, using pulleys and shearlegs to erect the uprights, with the elements in the frame being connected by joints anchored by temporary pegs. Then the components could be removed by sledge, barge or wagon to the permanent site, which might be several miles away. Such techniques could equally be applied to windmills and

Most coppices, like these, had been abandoned by the end of the 1914–18 war

even to waterwheels or engines of war. The roof of Westminster Hall was pre-fabricated at a framing ground at Farnham in Surrey, whence the great timbers were moved by cart and barge to Westminster. Normally, the taking of timber would be negotiated with manorial officials, but there were some surprisingly blatant cases of timber being stolen. For example, in 1328 one John Wolmer found himself at the mercy of the manor court of Wakefield for taking his cart into the lord's park and removing wood, boards and laths; he was fined 12d (5p) (Faull and Moorhouse (eds), 1981, p.688).

Once broken and discarded, timber items tend to rot and disintegrate without apparent trace. Consequently, their perishable character compared to the virtually indestructible nature of fired pottery can cause us to underestimate the magnitude of the production of timber drinking vessels, platters or trenchers and turned storage items. The demand for 3,100 trenchers each year for the Bishop of Durham's hunt was noted above. The turning of wooden items could be accomplished with surprising efficiency by deriving energy from the springy character of a bent sapling and conveying it to the work piece via a length of twine looped around it and linked to the foot treddle that controlled the revolutions. Most of the output from these 'pole lathes' comprised platters and drinking vessels. The demand for relatively cheap turned furniture, like Windsor chairs, came later. Medieval homes were, at best, only sparsely furnished. Tables were often made of boards and of the tressle type that could be stacked away, benches or stumps served as seats and the arks, aumbries and other storage items were also built of boards. Large trunks were split by hammering rows of wedges into the timber, but most later boards were produced by pairs of sawyers, one of them, the 'bottom dog' working amongst the sticky gloom and showers of sawdust in the saw pit. As the expectations of ordinary people rose, so their homes began to be furnished with the beech woods of the Chilterns supporting a woodland industry for mass-produced turned chairs that focused on High Wycombe. Chairmaking and the production of turned goods was recorded here in 1725, and the first reference to the famous Windsor chair occurred in 1732, when one was ordered for the vestry of West Wycombe church. The industry was based on the essentially medieval technology and lifestyles of pole lathe operators, who re-employed the pole lathe from the production of table and storage wares to the turning of spindles which were chair parts. A century or so after the genesis of the Windsor chair industry, these people became known as 'bodgers'.

Their methods of operating remained medieval. They would buy stands of coppiced beech, sometimes at auctions, and then the bodger would frequently erect a thatched shanty amongst his trees and live there until the timber was exhausted. Other bodgers might occupy a workshop somewhere between their timber and their family home. Bodgers could be self employed, members of teams or else they might work with other turners and apprentices in the employment of a master turner. The coppice was felled, the timber split and roughed out into leg and back components with a draw knife, before being turned into the familiar spindle forms on the pole lathe. The products of the operation were then sold in large numbers to the Wycombe furniture factories. There was still employment for the board cutters in the stifling saw pits, for they provided seats, arms and backrests. According to the High Wycombe museum, the number of turners in the locality doubled in the period 1861-81, from 186 to 340, paralleling the increasing popularity of cheaply sold Windsor and other turned chairs. In villages like Bryants Bottom, Stoney Cross and Prestwood, turning completely dominated employment. By 1875, High Wycombe's output of chairs was 4,700 every day and, as the market expanded, the railways were able to extend the reach of the Chilterns factories. Furniture-makers are still present there, but changing technology and the diversification of ranges have transformed the old trade. Like the collier, the pole lathe turner has gone, leaving landscape traces that completely undervalue his former importance. The shanties and worksheds have decayed, the sapling that once powered the lathe may now be a tall tree, the work sites are overgrown. More evident are the deep hollows that were once saw pits.

Woods provided timber fuel for all manner of uses, the choice depending upon the processes involved and the availability of other fuels. The medieval shift from wood pasture to coppice woods must have been urged, at least in part, by the rising demand for coppice poles that were converted into charcoal and used

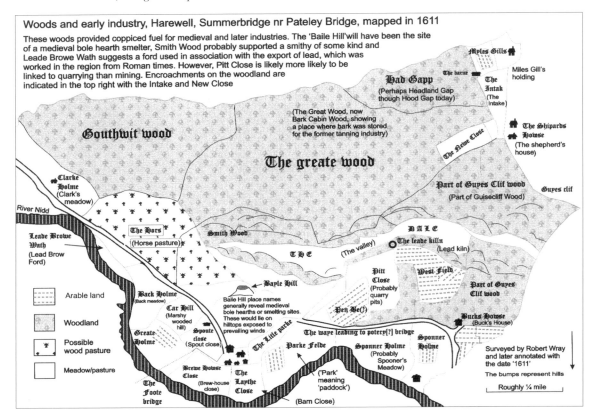

Woods and early industry, Harewell, Summerbridge nr Pateley Bridge, mapped in 1611

These woods provided coppiced fuel for medieval and later industries. The 'Baile Hill' will have been the site of a medieval bole hearth smelter, Smith Wood probably supported a smithy of some kind and Leade Browe Wath suggests a ford used in association with the export of lead, which was worked in the region from Roman times. However, Pitt Close is likely more likely to be linked to quarrying than mining. Encroachments on the woodland are indicated in the top right with the Intake and New Close

Myles Gills

The barne

The Intak
(The Intake)

Miles Gill's holding

Had Gapp
(Perhaps Headland Gap though Hood Gap today)

The Shipards Howse
(The shepherd's house)

Gouthwit wood

(The Great Wood, now Bark Cabin Wood, showing a place where bark was stored for the former tanning industry)

The greate wood

The Newe Close

Part of Gupes Clif wood
(Part of Guisecliff Wood)

Gupes clif

Clarke Holme
(Clark's meadow)

River Nidd

Leade Browe Wath
(Lead Brow Ford)

The Hors
(Horse pasture)

Smith Wood

DALE

The leade killn
(Lead kiln)

THE

(The valley)

Pitt Close
(Probably quarry pits)

West Field

Part of Gupes Clif wood

Bayle Hill

Baile Hill place names generally reveal medieval bole hearths or smelting sites. These would lie on hilltops exposed to prevailing winds

Pen Be(?)

Bucks Howse
(Buck's House)

Back Holme
(Back meadow)

Car Hill
(Marshy wooded hill)

Greate Holme

Spoute close
(Spout close)

The Litle parke

The waye leading to poterp[?] bridge

Sponner Holme
(Probably Spooner's Meadow)

Sponner Holme

Surveyed by Robert Wray and later annotated with the date '1611'

The bumps represent hills

Parke Felde

Brewe Howse Close
(Brew-house close)

The Laythe Close

('Park' meaning 'paddock')

The Foote bridge

(Barn Close)

Roughly ¼ mile

Legend:

- Arable land
- Woodland
- Possible wood pasture
- Meadow/pasture

The woods shown on the Harewell map of 1611 as seen today: the wooded area is almost intact, but the industrial uses have gone, with the local metallurgical industries

An old time charcoal burner in Sussex. From *The English Woodland* by John Rodgers

in the expanding iron industry. Seven Roman iron working bloomeries were found in the vicinity of Bardown and Holbeanwood in East Sussex and they must have been associated with an inefficient system of metal processing which required around 85 tons of timber to produce 1 ton of iron. Newly mined ore was roasted in a roasting pit to remove the damp, probably using alternating layers of ore and charcoal and burning for around a day (Cleere, 1976). In the smelting process, oxygen must be removed from the ore and in the bloomery process, where heat was applied under airtight conditions, carbon monoxide combined with ferric oxide to form carbon dioxide, leaving pure iron metal behind. Peat, coal or burnt reeds were sometimes used in the bloomery process, but charcoal made from coppiced hardwoods was much more effective. Small quantities of ore were fed into the top of the bloomery shaft, descending through increasingly hot levels where temperatures went up to 1300°C, to collect in a white hot mass in the bottom of the furnace, the only air entering the furnace coming from bellows inserted in 'tuyeres' that ran into the ore body. Two Roman ore roasting sites were recognised at Bardown and the base of a bloomery was found there, suggesting that the Roman furnaces existed as clay shafts with internal diameters of around 1ft (*c.*0.3m), walls of about the same thickness at their bases and a height of over 3ft (*c.*1m or more). The technology was relatively inefficient and this meant that its impart of the surrounding countryside must have been greater.

Modern charcoal burning kilns at East Dean, Sussex. From *The English Woodland* by John Rodgers

Perhaps 25,000 acres (roughly 10,000ha) or more of woodland might have been coppiced each year to support the Roman iron industry in the Weald.

The less complex technology of charcoal production may have evolved alongside the metal smelting technology, for charcoal could produce the temperatures needed for iron smelting that other available fuels could not provide. The methods employed by medieval colliers probably resembled those used in Roman times, and they essentially remained in use into the Industrial Age and are occasionally practised today. Without its charcoal burners, the medieval period would have been quite different – there would have been no armourers, no mail, bolts or swords, no shod warhorses, but also no iron bolts, hinges or braziers and no glass. Driven in no small part by the demands of the royal and baronial war machines, the iron industry and its insatiable appetites pushed the charcoal industry to a peak that coincided with the close of the Middle Ages and remained at about this same level until the dawning of the Industrial Age, around 1760. Charcoal is manufactured by burning hardwood timbers in conditions that virtually exclude air. Billets of hardwood around 10ft (3.04m) in length are gathered in bundles and stacked together in semi-upright positions around a thick stake or 'motty pin' to form a domed mound that sometimes stands in a shallow, saucer-shaped pit. These mounds, up to about 40ft (c.12.2m) in diameter, were then turfed-over and fired, preferably when the wind was still, with the burning sometimes lasting for over a week. Eventually, when only wisps of blue smoke were rising from the mound, the process was complete. Rather than burning away to ash, the timber processed in this way was converted to charcoal. The product was mainly employed as an industrial fuel in the iron and glass works, but when used as a component of gunpowder, juniper and alder were favoured as they produced a finer grained powder that assisted ignition. In the seventeenth century, charcoal-fuelled blast furnaces were established in relatively remote locations that were close to abundant supplies of charcoal and that could be reached by trackways that were adequate for the distribution of their products, such as cannon. In the following century, coke-burning furnaces captured their trade. In the Forest of Dean, at Gunns Mill, a charcoal furnace has been restored and at Whitecliff, near Coleford, there are the remains of an early coke-burning furnace of 1809.

Medieval records show that the methods employed were essentially the same as those used by Victorian and surviving workers, with the billets being stacked together in a shallow 'pan' around 20-30ft (6.1-9.4m) in diameter and covered in turf, loam or clay. In the Industrial Age, much of the remainder of the declining charcoal industry gravitated to steel kilns and only a tiny residue of specialist burning remains: demonstrations are given twice a year at the Dean Heritage Centre in the Forest of Dean. Charcoal was a by-product of the wood distillation process used to produce industrial gases and methylated spirit. In a few places, like Hopes Wood in the Forest of Dean, the cylindrical drums with conical tops that were employed in the process stand rusting in the rides or clearings. The tangible evidence of what was once a major and essential industry has been reduced to black flakes of carbon in the soil at the old burning sites, but in some, but by no means all, places, earthworks of the burning mounds remain as shallow depressions on level sites or step-like hearth sites on sloping terrain. Wood (1963, p.201) wrote: 'Some 20 to 30 have been traced near Flaxley, in the Forest of Dean, Gl., each circle about 8m across. Modern ones tend to be smaller (3.6 to 4.8m across) and are about 48cm deep.'

The colliers who practised this craft lived itinerant, often solitary existences, moving through the coppices as the poles matured and sometimes being joined by their families, but perhaps only for the summer. Their habitations were tent-like shelters made from materials close to hand and the home life of the collier – such as it was – seems to have changed little from medieval or earlier times to the early Industrial Age. However, there does seem to have been some variability in the lifestyles of medieval colliers, as implied by Faull and Moorhouse (pp.688-9):

> Although the medieval collier followed an itinerant craft taking him wherever a quantity of wood could be gathered to fire, the temporary structures and living shelters associated with charcoal burning may be detectable in an archaeological context. More permanent settled colliers are suggested by the documents. Part of the agreement between Walter de Calverley and William son of Elias de Bramley

made in 1377 concerning charcoal-burning rights in Calverley, Pudsey and Tong, states that William could have loppings of all the trees within specified woods 'for baking and brewing for his servants at the forge and for his supervisors there'. Such settlements would have been a major drain on woodland.

Brick kilns in Bedfordshire relied on charcoal and turf/peat, but mainly upon dried timber until the seventeenth century, when small amounts of coal, imported by barge, reached some places with access to navigable waterways. At the end of the century, wood, coal, furze or gorse, ling and even bracken were all used for firing bricks, though gradually, improvements in transport, mining technology and rising demand gave the advantage to coal. In 1840, the Duke of Bedford's steward at Crawley acknowledged that: 'The price of Fuel to the Kiln is at less price than the Sale price, on Account of the Kiln taking the whole of our Surplus produce from the Woods to bring it to a price to compete with Coals' (Cox, 1979, p.20). The old kilns were drawn to the sources of the fuel that they devoured so ravenously. In places, one may find the ruins of brick-built kilns standing remote and neglected amongst the equally neglected coppices, like the eighteenth-century tile kiln on Ebernoe Common in Sussex.

Tanbark was a valuable industrial resource of medieval and earlier times, and even in the nineteenth century farm workers would be employed in barking in slack weeks of the agricultural year (some on the eastern coast of England would fit in some barking between farming and fishing). Tannic acid can be obtained from most trees, but oak bark from young trees grown in a coppice rotation of around 25 years is the richest source. In the medieval period, oak was the only legal source of bark and it gave a better colour to the product. Oak bark was sufficiently valuable to feature in court issues, as in 1332, when three cart-loads of the commodity were stolen from the Outwood of Wakefield Wood (Faull and Moorhouse, p.689). Bark is difficult to remove, and so the stripping of bark, a labour-intensive process, was generally undertaken in the spring, when sap was rising and (after the trunks had been beaten) the bark could more easily be peeled away. The strips of bark were tied into bundles and these were stored in a shelter in the woods to dry for a fortnight or so. Then it was cut into squares and put into sacks. The tanner would soak the bark to release the tannic acid and then cure and soften hides in the resultant liquor. Important as the medieval tanning industry was, it has left few obvious marks, other than the common Barker and Tanner surnames and a mass of neglected oak coppices, particularly in central and north-east Scotland. It required no permanent structures, just flimsy shelters. Occasionally references to them may be found, like the medieval bark house at Ripley, sited close to a mill dam and, perhaps, close to the tannery. Subsequently, the industry expanded rapidly and peaked during the early decades of the Industrial Revolution, but during the eighteenth century the domestic barking industry fell into decline, with alternative tanning agents being imported from overseas.

From the information that can be gathered from the documents of the time, medieval woods contained plenty of small, workaday buildings. As well as the bark houses and the shelters of peripatetic workmen, there may have been barns where boughs from the hollins were stored and in addition to the lodges of Forest, wood and park officials there were certainly small hay barns, where supplementary winter feed for the beasts of the chase was stored. As vaccaries or cattle farms were established in numerous wooded Forest and park localities, so there were needs for fodder stores and milking sheds. These added to the needs for enclosing structures, like the oak stave palings, walls and earthworks or the deer park, the hedges that surrounded the coppice compartments and assarts, the post and rail fences sometimes associated with the vaccaries and horse studs and the lydgates that controlled the movement of the deer. The medieval wood was seldom silent and its tranquility would frequently be broken by the bustle of human activities – a far broader range of workers visited the woods far more frequently than one may expect to encounter today. And if the foresters and regarders wanted special insight into the affairs of their wood, there might even be a hermit to hand to provide it.

REFERENCES

Cleere, H., 1976, 'Ironmaking' in D. Strong and D. Brown (eds), *Roman Crafts*, Gerald Duckworth, London, pp. 127-40.

Cox, A., 1979, *Survey of Bedfordshire Brickmaking*, R.C.H.M./Bedfordshire C.C. Bedford.

Dyer, C., 1991, 'Hanbury: Settlement and Society in a Woodland Landscape', Department of English Local History *Occasional Papers*, 4.4, Leicester University Press, Leicester.

Faull, M.L. and Moorhouse, S.A. (eds), 1981, *West Yorkshire: An Archaeological Survey to 1500*, W.Y.M.C.C., Wakefield.

Grainge, W., 1871, *History and Topography of Harrogate and the Forest of Knaresborough*, John Russell Smith, London.

Homans, G.C., 1941, *English Villagers of the Thirteenth Century*, Harvard University Press, Cambridge Mass.

Horn, P., 1976, *Labouring Life in the Victorian Countryside*, Gill and Macmillan, Dublin.

Rackham, O., 1986, *The History of the Countryside*, Dent, London.

Raistrick, A., 1968, *The Pennine Dales*, Eyre Methuen, London.

Roberts, B.K. and Wrathmell, S., 1998, 'Dispersed Settlement in England: A National View' in P. Everson and T. Williamson (eds), *The Archaeology of Landscape*, Manchester University Press, Manchester.

Rodgers, J., 1942, *The English Woodland*, 2nd edn., Batsford, London.

Stenton, D.M., 1951, *English Society in the Early Middle Ages (1067-1307)*, Pelican, Harmondsworth.

Tusser, T., (1573), *Five Hundred Points of Good Husbandry*.

Whitaker, T.D., 1878, *The History of the Antiquities of the Deanery of Craven*, 3rd edn., Leeds.

Williamson, T. and Bellamy, L., 1987, *Property and Landscape*, George Philip, London.

Wood, E.S., 1963, *Collins Field Guide to Archaeology in Britain*, Collins, London.

7

Woodlands of the mind

One wood is the exact picture of another; the uniformity dreary in the extreme. There are no green vistas to be seen; no grassy glades beneath the bosky oaks, on which the deer browse, and the gigantic shadows deep in the sunbeams. A stern array of ragged trunks, a tangled maze of scrubby underbrush, carpeted winter and summer with a thick layer of withered buff leaves, form the general features of a Canadian forest (Susanna Moodie, 1852, quoted in Miller, 1994 p.82).

Everything is beautiful, the mountain changes, every, every time I look at it, it changes. The water, don't change the sound – the air is the same, flows. The spirit, when the tree is shaking then I realize that the spirit is there…. People live not even knowing, all they know is the top of their shoes today. They don't know the glory, the what we're living underneath (Jimmy Reyna, of the Taos Pueblo nation, quoted in Josephy, 1995, p.61).

Like all other features of the human setting, trees and woods have dual existences. They have an objective presence within the milieu but they also exist subjectively as features of the mindscape. In the cases of trees and woods, their mental images are very pervasive and potent. There are the perhaps intuitive connections with the parkland savannahs of our African genesis, the little understood magical associations of holy trees and sacred groves linked with pagan worship, as well as the diluted perpetuation of such beliefs in medieval superstition. Woods of different kinds acquired great symbolic importance in mental imagery, though often these images are falsely based. Some British perceptions of the wildwood are rooted in forms of woodland that never existed and some seem to be founded in myths and legends derived from quite different cultural and ecological contexts on the continental mainland.

Trees and imagery

The fact that mental images of the environment may be ill founded does not devalue their effect as instruments of behaviour and change. As long ago as 1969, Brookfield observed that decision-makers operating in a particular landscape will base their decisions upon the environment *as they perceive it to be* rather than as it actually is. Yet the decisions that they make accordingly impact upon the *real* environment rather than the perceived environment. Similarly, William Kirk, the great geographer who derived much inspiration from studying the German Gestalt school of psychology, described how we simultaneously inhabit two environments, the *phenomenal environment*, consisting of real natural and culturally derived features and the perceptual or *behavioural environment*, comprising culturally influenced ideas about the human setting.

Much that has been written on the subject of pagan religion is speculative, but enough is known for us to recognise a fundamental difference in attitudes towards the environment between prehistoric and Christian societies, whether in Europe or in North America. Pagan beliefs were characterised by the indivisibility of the natural world, the subsuming of individuality into the stream of life, a low-profile regard for property rights and the existence of meaningful relationships between humans and the trees, beasts, water bodies and landforms that constituted the context of their lives. Many native American societies believed that the Great Spirit, Wakan Tanka, had created their nations within their tribal lands and at the centre of Creation. The Creator had breathed life into them and bound their spirits to everything else in Creation. A Yakima man was recorded as saying: 'My strength, my blood is from the fish, from the roots and berries … and game … I … did not come here, I was put here by the Creator (quoted in Josephy, 1995, p.11). Christianity, however, came to be associated with control, hierarchies, and a code of values that elevated humans far above the contents of their context and saw all other creations as being subservient and provided merely for human use. In 640, St Eligius forbade Christians to place lights at temples, stones, springs or trees. In medieval Christianity a flowering tree was the attribute of a bishop. However, oaks symbolised the old pagan practices and St Boniface, who strove to convert the pagans, was represented with his foot resting on an oak just as an Edwardian big game hunter might pose to show his dominion over a slain lion (Hall, p.307).

The special potency of trees in pagan cultures is hardly surprising. Deciduous trees, which 'died' in the winter yet would revive in the spring, were associated with fertility rites concerning the rebirth of the year. Adonis was born after the gods had changed his incestuous mother into a myrrh tree. The Teutonic god, Wotan, hanged himself from an ash tree for nine days and then liberated himself to enjoy a re-invigorated existence (Schama p.84). Tacitus (*c*.AD 55–*c*.AD118)

Woods and wood pastures in the Lake District. The diverse, rapidly changing passages of scenery and the punctuation of the vistas with open areas epitomise the positive qualities of British woods as contrasted with those travellers encountered in the New World – particularly the eastern states of North America

described how the members of the Semnones, a German tribe, gathered annually in a wood that they believed to be the tribal birthplace. There they would sacrifice one of their number in a ritual which presumably signified the death and rebirth of the tribe. Nobody could enter the sacred grove unless bound by a cord which symbolised inferiority in the presence of the god: 'All this complex of superstition reflects the belief that in that grove the nation had its birth, and that there dwells the god who rules over all, while the rest of the world is subject to his sway' (Tacitus, 39).

Trees were venerated in animistic practice throughout Eurasia and even today they may be regarded as the embodiments of local deities. They were allocated roles in the more sophisticated religions that developed later and incorporated elements from animistic worship. Buddha gained enlightenment when in the shade of a bodhi tree. Bodhi and banan trees were revered by Hindus, who planted them around their temple complexes. The reasons for the cultivation of yew trees in English churchyards are uncertain; the common explanation concerns the medieval need for yew timber for the construction of longbows, though the tree, as one of very few indigenous evergreens, might have been planted to symbolise eternal life. In Hindu worship, trees were emblems for vitality and fertility, but they also provided the sites for contemplation and inspiration. The Khanty tribespeople of Siberia believe that both the cedar and the birch grow not only on earth, but also in the upper world. Personal idols are made from the wood of a cedar, and when a woman dies, her idol must be buried at the foot of the tree from which it came. As it rots, so her 'reincarnation soul' is released into society (Jordan, 2001).

Plants have proved immensely rich sources of symbolic associations. The palm, a symbol of military conquest and the victor's fame, was transferred from the secular to the religious by the Christians, who adopted it as a symbol of the resurrection. In Chinese painting the botanical symbolism is amazingly rich; the lotus, whose leaves emerge pristine from muddied waters, signifies purity. The plum, whose blossom survives the spring frost is a symbol of fortitude, while the bamboo, upright and unbending, signifies manly virtue (Lai p.21).

Taking all this into account, it becomes easy to understand the integration of paganism and environmentalism that found expression in Britain during the 1990s in a succession of non-violent civil disturbances intended to halt the destruction of countryside by road-building operations. Although some of the associated New Age beliefs were muddle-headed, the remarkable thing about these campaigns was not that they succeeded (if only temporarily) but that the conservative middle classes, traditionally the upholders of hierarchical Establishment beliefs, found much common ground with the pagan-influenced attitudes to Nature and environment. In general, however, attitudes to the environment are culturally determined. This was made clear by Wright as long ago as 1947 when he wrote to geographers:

> We are often tempted to use such expressions as 'a gloomy wood', 'bitter cold', 'majestic mountain', 'a menacing thunderhead', 'the mysterious unknown'. Budding geographers have been cautioned by their professors against employing such adjectives on the ground that they reflect the personal emotions of the writer and are not universal common denominators in the symbolism of science. A dark wood may not seem gloomy to a lumberjack, or fifty-below bitter cold to an Eskimo, or the Matterhorn majestic to all the peasants of Zermatt, or the geographically unknown mysterious to some of you (1947, p.9).

With our appraisals of the environment being guided by our culturally influenced value systems, attitudes to trees and woodland will vary from group to group. It will even vary within groups and classes, so that while the swineherd would appraise a group of trees in terms of their pannage, his neighbour in the village, a tanner, might regard them mainly as a commercial bark resource. And what the lord might regard as an idyllic venue for hunting, his land-hungry tenants might see as potential farmland. Conflicting perceptions come into the sharpest focus when different cultures collide. In North America, the indigenous people saw themselves as inseparable parts of a divine creation, while European colonists tended to treat the 'unimproved' wilderness with contempt. When they appraised

The frightening, ominous qualities of woodland are intensified by this photograph which derives its effect from infra red photography

it they did so with reference to values *current in their European homelands*: '… with many fine trees of the nature and kinds of France, such as oak, elms, ash, nut, plum trees, yews, cedars, vines, hawthorns with fruits as large as damson plums, and other trees. Beneath which there grows as good hemp as that of France, and it grows without sowing or labour' (quoted in de Vorsey, p.43).

The subjectivity was equally apparent in aesthetic terms. Travellers in the eastern states marvelled at the speed with which the loggers moved through the woods, but generally found little to admire in the wooded landscapes that had sustained native communities for many millennia. In 1861, Anthony Trollope wrote that:

> We in England, when we read and speak of the primeval forests of America, are apt to form pictures in our minds of woodland glades, with spreading oaks and green mossy turf beneath, of scenes than which nothing that God has given us is more charming. But these forests are not after that fashion, they offer no allurement to the lover, no solace to the melancholy man of thought…. Each tree, though full of the forms of life, has all the appearance of death. Even to the outward eye they seem to be laden with ague, fever, sudden chills, and pestilential malaria (quoted in Miller, 1994, p.82).

His complaints echoed those of his mother, 30 years earlier, who hated the undergrowth that characterised the woods around Cincinnati. She set off, determined to enjoy a picnic, despite having to go

... crunching knee deep through aboriginal leaves [before] reposing awhile on the trunk of a fallen tree; being all considerably exhausted, the idea of sitting down on this tempting log was conceived and executed simultaneously by the whole party, and the whole party sunk together through its uneven surface into a mass of rotten rubbish that had formed part of the pith and marrow of the eternal forest a hundred years before. [Finally, mosquitoes added to the misery and] ... we all lost patience, and started again on our feet, pretty firmly resolved never to try the al fresco joys of an American forest again (*op. cit.*, p.82-3).

Environmental mental imagery could prove to be a frighteningly potent political force. In AD 5 a Roman army, 18,000 strong, advanced to ravage villages between the Elbe and the Rhine. However, four years later at Teutoburgerwald in Saxony the Roman Ninth Legion was lured into a wood-girt defile and massacred. Ten years after that, Tacitus described the whitened bones that marked the places where men had fought or fled, the litter of weapons, the bones of horses and the skulls set on poles. Worse still, the Eagles had been lost. The great wooded expanses had allowed the Germanic tribe to maintain their identity and spared them the humiliation and 'civilising' influences that had been the fate of peoples of occupied territories. Schama has explored the association between the north/Central European woodlands and Nazi doctrine. He described the proliferation of forest themes and sylvan references in Germany after the Nazis had seized power, and provided this interpretation:

Tacitus's observation that their isolated habitat had made the Germans the least mixed of all European peoples would of course become the lethal obsession of the Nazi tyranny. *Germanentum* – the idea of a biologically pure and inviolate race, as 'natural' to its terrain as indigenous species of trees and flowers – featured in much of the archaeological and prehistorical literature both before and after the First World War (1995, p.118).

In Britain – or more particularly, England – at this time there may have been just the faintest hints of such sentiments in an emphatically middle-class culture that regarded outdoor pursuits (rambling, cycling, motoring) as wholesome and requiring a degree of refinement rather beyond the reach of the working class. Topographical interests, a curiosity regarding folk customs and organic gardening all sat very well together. However, the nationalistic association with woods was lacking, and one that was more bucolic took its place. While touring England in 1927, Morton saw the New Forest (most improbably) as a refuge where Saxons survived. These, though, where not the representatives of a master race, but rather slow, though '... well mannered, deferential people, with their wits about them and their tongues padlocked'(p.34). He added:

The place, like the people, encourages a delicious slowness. You feel that London

Under unusual circumstances, like fog which obscures landmarks and could cause disorientation, woods may become frightening

with all its fret is not quite so important in the ultimate scheme of things as Mr Smith's new litter of pigs; and it seems to you, as you lean against a fence in a portentous silence, that those things which men break their hearts upon are not worth so much in the long run as the sight of the moon tangled up in the boughs of a young birch wood (*ibid.*).

Images of landscape have been manipulated and employed in polemical manners for centuries. Such images are, for example, embedded in the foundation myths associated with several medieval religious communities. Any monastic foundation would be regarded as more favoured by God – and therefore, more worthy of endowments – if its founders had undergone various trials and tribulations before coming to rest at the (God-?) chosen spot. In 1874, Walbran (pp.90-1) published information from a source that he had discovered on the founding of Fountains Abbey:

Richard the Prior, with the sub-Prior, ten monks of St Mary's, and Robert a monk of Whitby, retired, in the depth of winter, to this secluded, and at that period, wild and uncultivated dell…. At first their only shelter was under the impending rocks; but, after a while, they thatched an enclosure under an umbrageous elm, in the middle of the valley, which was even flourishing at the time of the dissolution of the abbey.

So here there is one of many references to a foundation myth that suggested images of fortitude and devotion, while there is possibly, in the reference to the elm, a suggestion that, devout as the monks may have been, they were dwarfed by the timeless majesty of God's creation?

To the brutal yet often devout members of the Norman governing class, asceticism and deprivation were regarded as virtues that merited support. Thus, when 32 monks from Fountains settled to found a new house at Sawley in Ribblesdale in the January of 1147 they claimed to have suffered 40 years of privation in a land both rain-lashed and barren until Matilda de Percy granted them the proceeds (tithes) of three churches. The Cistercian Order was founded on the principles of hardship and endurance and became adept at capitalising upon their images. Bernard of Clairvaux, who had despatched a Cistercian mission to the starving monks of Fountains in 1133, wrote to Henry Murdac, a future abbot of Fountains:

Believe me who have had experience, you will find much more labouring amongst the woods than you ever will amongst books. Woods and stones will teach you what you can never hear from any master. Do you imagine that you cannot suck honey from the rocks and oil from the hardest stone; that the mountains do not drop sweetness … (quoted in James, 1998, p.156 and Menuge, p.32).

However, the more effective the manipulation of historical and topographical images were in the attraction of endowments, the more corrupted and diverted from its ascetic ideals the order became. When related to *actual* historical landscapes, the wildernesses and fearful desert places are seen to have been relatively harmless or even inviting. In numerous cases, Cistercian houses and granges were established in settings from which functioning lay communities had to be removed (e.g. the villages of Herleshow, Cayton, East Witton and various others in Yorkshire). When they did get control of relatively undeveloped countryside, the Cistercians treated it in a manner that would characterise the church in the New World as well as in the Old. Walter Map (1140-1210), an early critic of the order who wrote in the 1180s, at a time when the foundation myths were being fabricated, described how they invoked religion at every turn to wring a worthless plot from a rich man

… by much feigning of innocence and long importunity, putting God at every other word. The wood was cut down, stubbed up and levelled into a plain, bushes gave place to barley, willows to wheat, withies to vines, and it may be that in order to give them full time for these operations their prayers had to be somewhat shortened (Map, 1923, pp.40-1 quoted in Menuge, p.31).

The Merrie Greenwoode?

In all the popular media images of medieval England, the Merrie Greenwoode has a prominent place. Yet we must ask how a wood could be 'merry', or be seen to be so? When we delve into the evidence we encounter complexities and contradictions. There is not just one mental image of the medieval wooded countryside, and those that exist are incompatible, with each other and also with the documentary and archaeological evidence of woodland in the cultural landscape. There is one set of literary and oral traditions, represented particularly by the Robin Hood legends, that represents the greenwood as a place of joyful escape from the impositions of feudalism. But there is another, represented by old fairy stories, that portrays it as a place of danger and foreboding. Meanwhile, neither of these traditions represents the wood as it existed within the lives and contemporary landscape of woodland people.

In medieval descriptions 'fair' is probably the adjective most frequently applied to woodland; in *Robin Hood and the Monk* we find the words 'merry' and 'fair' together in the opening stanzas, both reflecting different aspects of the pleasantness of the greenwood:

> In somer, when the shawes be sheyne,
> And leves be large and long,
> Hit is full mery in the feyre foreste
> To here the foulys song:

> To se the dere draw to the dale,
> And leve the hilles hee,
> And shadow hem in the leves grene,
> Under the grene-wode tre

(quoted in Holt, 1982, p.56. S*hawes*=woods; *sheyne*=shining; *foulys*=birds; *hee*=high)

This story was recorded on a manuscript dated to about 1450, and could have been considerably older. In the seventeenth century, the stories were still popular and were sold in the streets as single printed sheets or 'broadsides', the ballads sometimes being collected together in 'garlands'. They were modified to take account of the emergence of a Protestant, partly literate society, but the old greenwood metaphor was still appreciated, despite the fact that actual Royal

Forests were being reduced by incursions, disappearing and thoroughly unpopular (see Chapter 5). In the *Ballad of Robin Hood and the Fifteen Foresters*, which was transmitted to and adapted in North America, the greenwood is still merry and still a haven for the oppressed. After his victory in an archery contest, Robin is set upon by 15 foresters and kills all but one of them. Ten foolhardy townsmen of Nottingham then join the fray, but some lost arms and some lost legs:

> Ten men came from brave Nottingham
> To take up Robin Hood
> But he's picked up his noble good bow
> And he's off to the merry greenwood

(traditional)

The greenwood, whether fair or merry, was a literary convention that transcended both the Robin Hood legends and the medieval period. Shakespeare, who lived under the threatening shadow of religious oppression, knew the potency of the myth of a greenwood where men could rally. In *As You Like It* he located the greenwood in the Forest of Arden, rather than today's preferred location, Barnsdale in South Yorkshire, and likened it to a golden world. (Barnsdale was not a Forest, though it lay between the great royal hunting reserves of Knaresborough and Sherwood.) The notion of a jocular band who lived their lawless, uninhibited lives in the verdant haven of the greenwood, feasting on the lord's venison and emerging from time to time to slaughter en masse the hated foresters must have had great appeal in all oppressed communities (whether the oppressors were foresters or religious zealots). However, a stream of quite a different kind ran against the flow of the broad river of greenwood sagas.

In the old fairy tales, the woods are dangerous places. Wolves and bears patrol the paths and glades and sinister people, of a kind quite unlike those known at home, may emerge at any time from the shadows. There are no roads and no direction signs and strangers may soon become lost in this gloomy, monotonous and horizon-less realm of trees. Perhaps the clearest domestic expression of this tradition is to be found in the story of the *Babes in the Wood*. Its oldest known published form appeared in Norwich and was published by Thomas Millington in 1595. The locale is Wayland Wood, near Griston, in Norfolk, said to have been previously known as Wailing Wood, though the attribution to Wayland, the mythical smith, might seem an older one. Two orphaned babes are placed in the care of an uncle until they inherit their estates. The uncle pays two assassins to take them into the woods to kill them. Charmed by the innocence of their intended victims, the killers abandon them alive in the woods. The babes, unable to find a way out, slowly perished. If there is a factual basis to the legend, it concerns the lack of deep parental love that may have existed in a rural society with very high infant mortality rates. This urged parents to produce many

The woods known to the contemporaries of the *Babes in the Wood* were not packed with grotesque, Rackhamesque pollards, the products of a long neglect of woodmanship, but were working woods, often airy places growing well-spaced standards over a coppiced underwood

children in the home so that one or two might inherit and live to support them in old age.

The juxtaposition of the native village as a symbol of security and the woods as a symbol of strangeness and danger is represented with even greater clarity in the *Little Red Riding Hood* stories. They may have originated in the sixteenth century; a French version was printed in the seventeenth century, while in the nineteenth century, Jakob Grimm and Wilhelm Grimm reproduced different versions of the legends. In some of the earlier forms, derived from peasant communities, the story ends when Little Red Riding Hood is eaten by the wolf, though in an Italian one she escapes without the intervention of a woodcutter. The listener is left to wonder why the grandmother is living in an isolated cottage in the woods, and why the wolf is able to kill and eat her when woodcutters are at work nearby? However, the tale achieves much of its impact when the listener shares the sense of helplessness encountered by people separated from their communities and placed in a threatening forest setting.

And so, we have two quite different perceptions of the greenwood. Firstly, one may ask whether the forest was regarded as a dangerous place? If it was, this might be because it was so vast and desolate that the stranger could become disorientated and perish, in the manner of the *Babes*. Or it might be that it harboured frightful, man-eating beasts, as suggested by the *Little Red Riding Hood* tales. Additionally or alternatively, it might be seen as threatening because it sheltered cut-throats and robbers.

In reality, no wood in Britain was so immense that one could not come out of it within a day so long as a reasonable straight line of travel could be maintained. To be benighted in a forest will always have been disconcerting, especially if clouds or foliage obscured celestial markers. At the medieval foresters' village of Bainbridge there is a tradition of blowing three blasts on a horn on the green at 10pm from Hawes Back-end Faire at the end of September to Pancake Tuesday, supposedly to guide travellers confronting a long night lost in the woods of Wensleydale. The origins of this custom seem uncertain, though there was another horn-blowing custom associated with medieval woods:

> By ancient forest law, the king could give liberty to individuals passing through the forest to take deer or other perquisites but it was demanded so that there should be no possible suspicion of poaching or secrecy that such a person should blow a horn if the forester was not with him. The custom of blowing the horn as a sign of honesty and 'open-dealing' while in the forest preserves soon became widespread and is familiar to all readers of forest romances. Passengers through the forests payed a toll, partly for privilege and partly for protection afforded by the forest officers ... (Raistrick, 1991, p.38).

On the whole, I would argue that nobody was likely to enter a wood unless they knew the way out of it. Local people will have been familiar with every tree and herb. Foresters, parkers and regarders knew their woods and their communities intimately. Traders, pilgrims and lords moving between their manors travelled the woodland roads and tracks in bodies and retinues. Monks and officials visiting outlying granges travelled familiar and well-maintained paths and friars could scarcely lose the way from one village to the next.

If the old woods were not in themselves threatening places, was there real danger from the wild animals that inhabited them? The adder, the only poisonous snake in Britain, prefers open heathland habitats where it can bask in the sun, while the shade created by a dense woodland canopy deprives it of warmth and energy. The only truly frightening mammal, the bear, appears to have been exterminated by the close of the Saxon era, if not before, though it may have survived for a little longer in Scotland and possibly in Wales. The poet Martial recorded that a bear from Caledonia was employed in the opening ceremonies for the Coliseum in Rome in AD 80. According to Lambert:

> ... the brown bear is believed to have survived in Britain until the 10th century AD, although the importation of brown bears for dancing and baiting may have confused the date of the extinction of indigenous animals (Clutton-Brock, 1991).

Radiocarbon dates for the brown bear in Scotland span from more than 7,500 years BP until about 2,700 years BP (Burleigh et al., 1976; Kitchener and Bonsall, in press), although the canine tooth found at Keiss (Ritchie, 1920) could date from as recently as 1,000 years (D.Clarke, pers. comm.). The brown bear was possibly also depicted on Pictish stones (Smout, 1993), but it is uncertain whether these carvings were based on local animals (1998, p.74).

Hunting must have played a part in the extinction of this massive, ill–tempered and unpredictable animal, but the destruction of its woodland habitat could have been decisive.

Although perceptions of the wolf today are based on nursery stories and documentaries featuring the timber wolves of Canada, the wolf was much less dependent upon a wooded habitat, with some of the last packs to survive in England being found in carr and open fell situations. There is probably no beast that inspires such dread; that this deeply rooted horror still survives is evidenced by the torrent of public opposition that led to the abandonment of a scheme to reintroduce wolves to the Scottish Highlands. In reality, instances of attacks by wolves on humans appear to have been very unusual. In England, wolves were present in the less intensively worked and settled fringes during the Middle Ages and were much more numerous in the Saxon era, when January was known as the 'wolf month', for this was when their howling was most frequent. Drawing on evidence from the Rievaulx Abbey chartulary (Surtees Soc. 304-5), the contributor to the *Victoria County History* wrote:

> With Healaugh, which became the head manor of the district, a park and free chase descended. Gilbert son of Robert de Gant granted to Rievaulx Abbey, with pasture, sheep folds and lodges, the right of keeping hounds and horns in Swaledale; the grant was confirmed by his descendants, the overlord by Henry III and Edward III. The abbey also received permission from Gilbert to catch wolves (1914, p.237).

The medieval records contain various references to bounties being offered for the slaughter of wolves, particularly by the Cistercian Abbeys. One can be quite confident that this does not reveal that the packs presented a threat to human life, but to the monastic flocks. As wildlife dwindled in the face of regular human hunting, the wolves, in desperation, may have become more dependent on preying on the flocks in the fields that had been cleared from the predators' natural habitat. These raids would have brought wolves and shepherds into close proximity and might occasionally have resulted in animal attacks. The competition between humans and wolves could have led to the demonisation of the animal and to intensified persecution. The last English wolf may have died in Yorkshire, perhaps on a remote plateau or fell in the Pennines, or maybe in the alder carr of Holderness, and wolves were gone well before the close of the medieval period. In the Scottish Borders, they seem to have gone in the 1480s. In Scotland as a whole, the more extensive fastnesses allowed the wolf to endure for centuries longer. The most widely known record names Sir Ewan Cameron of Locheil as the slayer of the last wolf, this taking place at Lochaber in 1680. Other sources identify a MacQueen as the killer, a site by the Findhorn gorge in Morayshire as the location and 1743 as the year, though the claim that this wolf had just killed two children casts some doubt on its authenticity. However, there is another, less certain, record of a wolf being killed by the Caithness–Sutherland border in 1763 – a credible location for the sole survivor (Lambert, p.75). This just leaves the lynx as a possibly intimidating forest beast, though the carnivore is too small to kill an adult human. Lynx were regarded as being amongst the prehistoric extinctions, though a skull found at Inchnadamph in Scotland has been dated to the second or third century AD.

The wild boar was a dangerous animal if hunted, for in desperation it would turn and charge its persecutors. Then, its tusks could cause ripping wounds at shin level. A few local dynasties, like the Ingilbys of Ripley, cultivated legends that their rise to greatness resulted from saving their fallen monarch from a charging boar. Such tales implied great forebears who were the chosen companions of kings, who were brave and who were granted the ability to direct the course of history – all qualities that aristocrats would like to see vested in their ancestors and dynasty. During the Middle Ages, boar were effectively hunted to extinction and the highest of nobles only persisted in hunting the animal by organising expensive exchanges to restock their parks. The last boar in England is reputed to have been killed by James I of England (James VI of Scotland) in Windsor Park in 1617. Unlike the wolf and lynx, the boar was unable to preserve a lingering presence in the Scottish wilderness, for the last boar there is thought to have been killed in the seventeenth century.

All things considered, the risk of wild animal attack while passing through woodland was too remote to be taken seriously in almost every location. Of the animals that still survive, the roe is both the smallest of the deer and the most aggressive. Anyone deterred from a woodland journey by this secretive, retriever-sized creature would be very deficient in the courage department. There were, however, more serious risks of animal attack in the woods – from domestic animals. The truly frightening aurochs, the aggressive forbear of our domestic cattle, stood 2m high at the shoulder and survived in the Polish forest until 1627. In England it was probably hunted to extinction during the Bronze Age, though it could have survived in Caithness until the end of the first millennium AD. Its smaller, domesticated descendants would often be encountered agisted and foraging freely in woods, and if anything of the temperament of their wild ancestor had survived, they might be dangerous. Also, as deer park territories diversified, so bulls associated with vaccaries and stallions associated with studs would be present, and should either break loose, travellers could be at risk. Meanwhile, the boars in the charge of the swineherd were still genetically quite similar to their wild forbears, and must have preserved some of their aggression. In these respects, the woods did still harbour potentially dangerous animals – but they were ones that could equally be encountered at the village farmstead.

Finally, there is the danger associated with ambush by humans. There were numerous localities – Barnsdale was one – where medieval travellers chose wisely to group together in parties. Whether or not a place was considered dangerous depended on much more than the presence or otherwise of trees. Distance from settlements could be crucial as could the political relationships of the leading magnates of the locality/region with the king and the prevailing state of anarchy or stability within the whole kingdom. Edward I's Statute of Winchester, which demanded (probably optimistically) that a zone be cleared of vegetation where highways passed through woodland, demonstrated an awareness that woodland and undergrowth could conceal criminals as they waited to ambush strangers. Even so, there are records of lawlessness in almost every conceivable setting. Fairs and markets with throngs of visitors were notorious as they brought conflicting interests together. Around 1440, fairs at Otley and Ripon were disrupted when men of Knaresborough arrived and claimed exemption from market tolls. In 1441, soldiers were hired by the Archbishop of York to prevent renewed violence but the Knaresborough men ambushed the mercenaries at a crossing on the river Swale as they returned to York, and two of the soldiers were killed (Jennings (ed.), p.80). Markets and fairs were anything but remote and thinly peopled, but their image was perceived as disreputable well after the close of the Middle Ages. Writing on Kent in the early 1720s, Defoe recorded:

> On the other side of the heath, north, is Charleton, a village famous, or rather infamous for the yearly collected rabble of mad-people, at Horn Fair; the rudeness of which I cannot but think, is such as ought to be suppressed, and indeed in a civilized well governed nation, it may well be said to be insufferable. The mob indeed at that time take all kinds of liberties, and the women are especially impudent for that day … (p.115).

There might have been one Robin Hood, none, or several. According to Holt, 'The most realistic early tradition of Robin is that he extorted money from travellers whom he waylaid on the Great North Road' (p.11). The two elements that are significant here are, *firstly*, the adoption of an outlaw figure and his conversion in popular mythology to a heroic, super-talented killer who redistributes wealth from the rich extortionists to the deserving poor. In this capacity, Robin Hood is an early and influential milestone in a tradition that advances through Dick Turpin to Billy the Kid, Jesse James, Butch Cassidy and Pretty Boy Floyd. *Secondly*, there is the romantic tradition and literary convention of the Merrie Greenwood, which was by no means confined to the Robin Hood ballads. The environmental context of the greenwood brought together the themes of the noble robber and the starving poacher. How better for the hero

The woodland tracks of Robin Hood's day will often have looked like this present-day track, with the flanking woods potentially providing cover for any wrong-doers

to feast than upon the king's deer – to the consternation of the hated foresters? The greenwood garnish helped to revitalise the Robin Hood legends by providing links to other mythological traditions: '... Robin was adopted into the May Games, from which his legend gained fresh characters. In its greenwood theme it mingled in one direction with Teutonic myth and the world of woodland sprites ...'(Holt, p.9). Symbols and traditions were interwoven and so stepping into a church of the Robin Hood era, one might see the old fertility symbol of the Green Man carved in the timbers of the roof, vines flowing from this mouth to symbolise the rebirth of life. The flagrant manner in which effigies of the Green Man confronted bishops on the visitations suggests that the traditions had penetrated the establishment world. The greenwood myths were just a short step removed from this.

There is no doubt that this symbolism was underpinned by reality. People did poach the king's deer and those of his high nobles. However, as shown in Chapters 4, 5 and 6, the contemporary records often reveal the poachers as professional meat dealers, gay blades off in search of thrills and rivals seeking to humiliate the park owners. In a Huntingdon incident of the reign of Henry II, a chaplain and seven clerks were said to have been found with bows and arrows in a Huntingdon Forest (Dowsett, 1942, p.174). If men in holy orders could be poachers, so too could knights and squires. (Robin of the legends also displays the courtly behaviour and deference to women that one would associate with a noble or squire rather than with a bond tenant.) Outlaws were all too common, and woods could offer concealment. Yet the outlaw would only prosper were he to be located close to routeways that would provide a supply of victims. This situation still prevailed in the eighteenth century, when Dick Turpin preyed on travellers in Epping Forest. In this respect, however, the typical, out-of-the-way manorial wood was no use at all. The feudal kingdom was full of desperate, sometimes starving victims of feudal exploitation and population surplus and many of them were outlawed. The extent to which they presented a larger or smaller threat to stability depended on the strength of centralised control, the resolve and power of local institutions and the current depths of depravity. The most desperate and dangerous situation was produced by the Tudor eviction of tens of thousands villagers to create empty sheep runs. At this time, the greatest fears of members of the establishment do not seem to have concerned the possibility that these destitute hordes would take to the woods. Rather, there was a dread that they would infest highways and byways and destabilise the whole apparatus of law and government. These people were harmless victims, but the law-breakers who were outlawed needed a place of refuge, and the larger woods did offer concealment and the possibility of poached game.

The presence of such people, particularly in the vicinity of routeways, made some zones in selected woods dangerous, but woods were by no means the only settings for ambush. There is copious evidence of the dangers faced by travellers across open heath and moor. Remoteness from settlements appears to have been a crucial factor: a map of Feckenham, Worcestershire, of 1591 marks a tree called 'Ambush Oak' in an isolated position on Ridgeway Common. As recently as 1728, three headless bodies were pulled from the peat on the moors below Great Whernside in the Yorkshire Dales and were regarded at the time as the victims of tinkers – though an unauthenticated version of the story attributed the corpses to the customers, 25 in number, said to have been murdered by a local innkeeper. Perhaps the most organised, dangerous and provocative criminals, the 'Owlers' or smugglers of the Channel ports, were indifferent to woodland and prospered because of the fear that they inspired in the population at large. Also, the place names like 'Thieves Lane' that can be found quite close to settlements, suggests that, when lawful authority was not feared then cut-throats and footpads could be encountered almost anywhere.

The typical woods – the manorial wood of the champion countrysides that was usually smaller than one of the village's open fields and the little wooded patches that heavily stippled the map of ancient countrysides – were safer places than most. As the medieval period progressed, there were fewer and fewer woods that were continuous and extensive, like the old Royal Forest of Wirral, where myth maintained that

> From Blacon Point to Hillree
> A squirrel could leap from tree to tree

There were few places where an adult could become lost in a forest while, for those who managed to, the danger posed by domestic animals was likely to be greater than that from wild beasts. Only where a highway traversed an extensively wooded area was the danger from outlaws likely to be greater than normal. The notion of the greenwood as a 'merry' place was symbolic, and little can have been more wretched than the life of the outlaw, living without a proper but conspicuous abode in woods patrolled by foresters and agisters and scanned by regarders.

For others, the local wood was a familiar and not unfriendly place. The typical woods experienced infinitely more human activity than do the woods of today. People came and went as they gathered the materials for housing, fencing, burning and fixing that were part of their customary rights. Woodsmen lopped and chopped in the coppices and among the pollards. The village swineherd watched as his charges foraged for pannage and browse, the neat saw that his cattle were not in the hags, as did the pinder, and the owners of agisted livestock came in too. Foresters, regarders or parkers moved silently by, conversing with those they met and perhaps interrogating a hermit or cooper. The tanner checked the contents of his bark house, perhaps looking forward to the season when half the village would be at work in the wood, barking branches. From one direction one might here the whirr and chatter from a pole lathe, and from another, the blue plume from a collier's clamp might be rising, while from another still, the pounding of forge hammers, perhaps the loudest noise in the medieval world, might be heard.

The real old wood was a workaday place. It provided the materials that were essential to local subsistence. It was hardly ever dangerous and was quite, quite different from the Greenwoode that figured in the tales that were told across the smouldering turf hearths in the village at night. The wood of the Merrie Greenwoode stories was a place of escape. It was also functional, because it furnished the ordinary victims of feudal impositions with an alternative and parallel milieu that their imaginations could inhabit. It was Big Rock Candy Mountain country; it was to the fourteenth-century villager what tales of Pretty Boy Floyd of the 1920s were to Oklahomans, driven from their farms by the dust storms and from their homes by the banks. And when the once great Forests were in decay, devoured by local land-grabbers like worms devour a rotten table, the public appetite for Greenwoode ballads even increased.

The myth of the Caledonian Forest

As most politicians know, once a myth has been repeated sufficiently often it becomes a 'fact'. Then other truths must be reorganised to take account of this fact, while the likelihood that the veracity of the myth/fact will be tested by research continually diminishes. There are also facts that are unpalatable and inconvenient, and if their veracity cannot be disproved then they must be sidelined. Most of what we know about global warming and related environmental problems was known in the 1970s, when there was still time to take purposeful action. One of the myths embedded in popular ideas about historical ecology concerns woodland clearance: once woods were continuous; over the millennia they were cleared, so what we have now is the residue of these ancient wildwoods. More realistic is the notion that human beings have a record of failing to learn from past mistakes of an ecological nature. This has produced a cyclical sequence of colonisation and advance – environmental degradation – population retreat and woodland expansion.

In many places and at many times, wildwood myths have been created and perpetuated. Historians assumed that at the time of the Roman Conquest England was covered in a near-continuous blanket of woodland – until pottery and other artefacts began to be discovered in places, even in the heaviest clays, that had been assumed to have been uninhabitable then. In North America, the colonists soon created a wildwood myth. It was more palatable than the reality in which culturally rich and flourishing indigenous communities had been exterminated by introduced diseases and warfare that employed the European weapons. Soon, the innumerable agricultural clearings and settlement areas were reclaimed by secondary woodland and the legends of a largely pristine and desolate North America could be forged. Some of the early colonists had sponsors to please, and like the old Cistercian monks, praise could be gained by exaggerating the danger and 'otherness' of new places. The Puritans reported that New England, that most British-like part of the continent, was a '… remote, barren wild-woody wilderness, a receptacle for Lions, Wolves, Bears, Foxes …' (quoted in Bowden, 1992, p.6).

During the nineteenth century Americans manufactured a national identity with which they could feel comfortable. It consisted of a selective stretching, diminution and falsification of the actual experiences of colonisation: 'With the Indians branded as indolent and incapable of learning the arts of civilisation, America was made by Puritan saint, yeoman, pioneer/frontiersman, sodbuster, cowboy, and latter-day saint: superhuman, overachieving, self-glorifying Americans all' (Bowden, *op. cit.,* p.20). The European settlers had come from places where woods and woodland crafts were commonplace, so perhaps the greatest call for qualities of pioneering innovation came when they encountered wood-less territory: 'For many settlers from the east, treelessness was proof of the soil's inherent infertility. Coming from a wood-based culture, settlers required vast amounts of cheap timber for fuel, building materials, fencing and farm implements' (Mills, 1997, p.20).

The assumption that on encountering the Scottish Highlands the Romans found a continuously wooded landscape became deeply rooted, with the great Caledonian Forest winning uncritical acceptance. The suggestion that this is a mythical forest was aired in a lecture by T.C. Smout in 1990 and was explored in greater detail by Breeze (2002). A forest of this name was mentioned by Pliny the elder, in AD 77 as marking the limit of the territory of Britain that was known to the Romans, though its exact location and extent were mysterious. During their invasion campaigns and occupation, the term 'Caledonian' was apparently applied to anything far-off. It could also be used in a polemical manner and commanders like Vespasian could be lauded as victors in Caledonia without having come within a week's march of the Scottish Highlands. There was also evidence from the Roman writings that the real Caledonia was not continuously wooded. Cassius Dio in his *History of Rome* recorded that the Caledonians employed chariots, vehicles of the open plain, and mentioned the presence of sheep and cattle, the former being animals of the fell and open pasture and both being destructive of tree seedlings. The location of the battle of Mons Graupius in AD 83 has been much discussed, but the account by Tacitus in his *Life of Agricola* shows that the battle took place on open ground and the defeated tribesmen were then pursued into a wood. In reality, the Caledonian Forest was a phenomenon of the Neolithic period. By Roman times it was scattered in many islands.

Subsequently the notion of a dense pine forest covering the Scottish Highlands became entrenched. Perhaps the false perception reinforced ideas about the 'otherness' of the Highlands even within the Scottish context? It was a land where people spoke Gaelic rather than Lowland Scots or English. It had its own social system based on clans or kindreds claiming common descent from a founding patriach. Its clan chieftains enjoyed quasi autonomy and claims of sovereignty over the Highlands often existed more in name than substance. So it was appropriate that this strange territory with its archaic customs should have its own ecology. In reality, the softwood forests of the Highlands had much in common with the deciduous woods of England. Both had retreated in times of population pressure and both were subjects of but partially observed conservational measures by their ruling elites. However, the ecosystems of the Highlands being more fragile, the consequences, such as waterlogging and soil erosion, resulting from their destabilisation were more severe.

During the medieval centuries the long-established pressures from the expansion of grazings intensified while, when the period closed, a trade in Scots pine timber became established. From records of customs dues charged at medieval Scottish ports we have a much clearer picture of medieval overseas trade

In this location, near Balmoral, livestock are grazing in the Scots pine forest. The trees are spreading outwards towards open grouse moors and keepers periodically cut them back

In all but the most rugged areas where the mythical Caledonian Forest stood, the essential character of the countryside is not endowed by relics of ancient woodland, but by the manicured estates of shelterbelts, plantations and tenanted farmsteads resulting from the Improvements of the eighteenth and nineteenth centuries, as here on Upper Donside

in timber than we have of internal commercial felling. Hanseatic ports of the eastern Baltic, notably Königsburg, were supplying Scotland with large quantities of oak boards, beams and barrel staves and spruce planks and spars. Norway became so valued as a supplier of softwood and some hardwood timber that the country was exempterd from a Statute of 1573 prohibiting Scottish salt exports. Around this time, one ship in three that entered Dundee was a Norwegian ship, normally carrying a cargo of timber (Smout, Macdonald and Watson, 2005, p.124-5). Perhaps many users of the timber knew the Highlands only as a place that produced pine? Some places retained a measure of stability and recently a small stand of 500-year-old trees was recognised in the Glen Moriston locality (Stewart, 2003, p.113). One was found to be 525 years old and had stood in the royal hunting Forest of Clunie. In the 1620s, pines had been cut and floated down to Inverness, but this tree must have been considered too far from the river to merit felling. It was fortunate to continue to grow, for as times passed, the demand for pine intensified, even though it was poor as a source of charcoal and would not regenerate as coppice timber. But it was useful in building, for joists, planks and spars and would be employed in Scottish ironworks when other charcoal was lacking. Exploitation reached a peak in the decades around 1800, when both the indigenous and the intrusive lairds struggled to wrest income from their estates by selling pine to the naval dockyards or for boring-out as waterpipes for London. In the eighteenth century, when estate and military maps of the Highlands became available, they depicted landscapes in which the woods were seldom more than tattered archipelagos or only took the form of young shelter belts within countrysides of rough pasture and heather moor blotched with the arable land around the *clachans* or fermtouns (hamlets).

In the nineteenth century, the Highlands and their culture became mythologised, most notably by Sir Walter Scott (1771-1832), and the romantic mythology became embedded in the Balmoralism of Victoria's reign, the sentimental paintings of Landseer (1802-73) and all the symbolism of tartan, cairngorm brooches and heathery braes. Ironically, the landscapes that the coach parties see are not really the landscapes of the proud and warlike clans. Their most obvious contents – the tumbled stones of the ruined *clachans*, the empty expanses, the shelter belts and consumption dykes packed with boulder litter – are all emblems of the defeat and humiliation of that society and the reorganisation of estates that followed Culloden.

Smout (2000, p.44) has described how:

In its modern form, the Caledonian Forest is a product of German Romanticism, mediated through the excitable and fantasy-filled minds of the Sobieski Stuarts. These two brothers of Anglo-German descent falsely claimed to be the legitimate grandchildren of Prince Charles Edward, though, reassuringly, they did not wish to press a claim on Queen Victoria's throne. They did, however, set themselves up to an admiring public as experts in the Gaelic past.... Among their publications was, in 1848, *Lays of the Deer Forest*, a compilation of poetry, passionate and breathless hunting tales, natural history, folklore and popular history, often tenuously anchored in verifiable fact.

They told of a vast forest that had survived until relatively recent times, that had teemed with wild animals and had covered the hills and plains of Scotland like a great primeval cloud. Smout noted (*ibid.*) how their treatment of the myth had most in common with the perceptions of German forest romantics, like Wilhelm Pfeil, Ernst Moritz Arndt and Wilhelm Heindrich Riehl, who were emotionally bonded to the wild woods of their homeland. It had little ecological or cultural relevance to Scotland. So why, one may wonder, did the version woven by the brothers and their followers become accepted wisdom regarding Scottish landscape history? Perhaps the reality, with its records of land-hunger and associated famines and plagues; the humiliation and the destruction of clan culture in what was effectively a Scottish civil war battle at Culloden in 1746; the clearances and evictions, the emigrations – perhaps all this was too awful to face? The myth of the vanished forest nested more comfortably with the romantic legends of Clan tartans – both of which the Sobieski Stuarts had invented.

Yet at least the Victorians had the time and the space still to mythologise their context, conceal the painful realities and make it more acceptable. Not all may be so fortunate.

REFERENCES

Bowden, M., 1992, 'The invention of American tradition', *Journal of Historical Geography*, 18, 1, pp.3-26.

Breeze, D.J., 1997, 'The great myth of Caledon' in T.C. Smout (ed.), *Scottish Woodland History*, Scottish Cultural Press, Dalkieth, pp.46-50.

Brookfield, H.C., 1969, 'On the environment as perceived', *Progress in Geography*, 1, pp.51-80.

Burleigh, R., Hewson, A. and Meeks, N., 1976, 'British Museum natural radiocarbon measurements', *Radiocarbon*, 18, pp.16-42.

Clutton-Brock, J., 1991, 'Extinct species' in Corbet, G.B. and Harris, S. (eds), *The Handbook of British Mammals*, 3rd edn., Blackwell Scientific, Oxford, pp.571-5.

Defoe, D., 1724-6, *A Tour Through the Whole Island of Great Britain*, 1971 edn. Penguin, Harmondsworth.

Hall, J., 1974, *Dictionary of Subjects and Symbols in Art*, John Murray, London.

Holt, J.C., 1982, *Robin Hood*, Thames and Hudson, London.

James, B.S., trans.1998, *The Letters of St Bernard of Clairvaux*, Sutton, Stroud.

Jennings, B.(ed.), 1983, *A History of Nidderdale*, Advertiser Press, Huddersfield.

Jordan, 2001, 'Cultural landscapes in colonial Siberia: Khanty settlements of the sacred the living and the dead', *LANDSCAPES*, 2.2, pp.83-105.

Josephy, A.M. Jr., 1995, *Five Hundred Nations*, Hutchinson, London.

Kirk, W., 1952, 'Historical geography and the concept of the behavioural environment', *Indian Geographical Journal*, **Silver Jubilee Volume**, pp.152-60.

Lai, T.C., 1992, *Chinese Painting*, Oxford University Press, Hong Kong.

Map, W., 1923, *De Nugis Curialum*, Cymmrodorion Society r.s. ix.

Menuge, N.J., 2000, 'The foundation myth: some Yorkshire monasteries and the landscape agenda', *LANDSCAPES*, 1.1, pp.22-37.

Mills, S.F., 1997, *The American Landscape*, Keele University Press, Edinburgh.

Morton, H.V., 1927, *In Search of England*, Methuen, London.

Raistrick, A., 1991, *Arthur Raistrick's Yorkshire Dales*, Dalesman, Clapham.

Schama, S., 1995, *Landscape and Memory*, HarperCollins, London.

Smout, T.C., Macdonald, A.R. and Watson, F., 2005, *A History of the Native Woodlands of Scotland, 1500-1920*, Edinburgh University Press, Edinburgh.

Smout, T.C., 1993, 'Woodland history before 1850', in *Scotland Since Prehistory*, in T.C.Smout (ed.), Scottish Cultural Press, Aberdeen, pp.40-49.

Smout, T.C., 2000, *Nature Contested*, Edinburgh University Press, Edinburgh.

Stewart, M., 2003, 'Using the woods, 1650-1850 (2) Managing for profit' in T.C. Smout (ed.), *People and Woods in Scotland*, Edinburgh University Press, Edinburgh, pp.105-127.

Tacitus, *On Britain and Germany*, translated by H. Mattingly, 1948, Penguin, Harmonsworth.

De Vorsey, L., 1987, 'The New Land: the discovery and exploration of eastern North America' in Mitchell, R.D. and Groves, P.A., *North America: the Historical Geography of a Changing Continent*, Hutchinson, London, 1987, pp.25-47.

Walbran, J.R. (1874), *A Guide to Ripon, Fountains Abbey, Harrogate etc*, A. Johnson & Co., Ripon.

Wright, J.K., 1947, '*Terra incognitae*: the place of the imagination in geography', 1946 AAAG presidential address published in *Annals of the Association of American Geographers*, 37, pp.1-15.

Index